T0400491

# THE Church History HANDBOOK

The Church History Handbook

Brentwood, Tennessee


Typesetting and design by Faceout Studio, Sisters, Oregon.

| *Style* | *ISBN* |
| --- | --- |
| Clay Cloth-over-Board | 979-8-3845-0850-2 |
| Mocha Cloth-over-Board | 979-8-3845-1809-9 |

DEWEY: 220
SUBHD: CHURCH HISTORY—HANDBOOKS, MANUALS, ETC. \ DOCTRINAL THEOLOGY

Printed in China
1 2 3 4 5 6 7 8 9 10 — 30 29 28 27 26 25 24
AP

# Contents

# Letter from the Publisher

The Bible has a lot to say about beauty and how beauty might serve as a means leading to the praise and worship of God. In fact, just looking at the Old Testament narratives involving the construction of the tabernacle and the temple, we come to realize that there is a lot of specificity and detail surrounding their craftsmanship. The detail of these designs and the level of craftsmanship involved were not merely meant to create a place that instructs God's people—those designs and the beautiful creations that resulted were also meant to point the congregation to God's glory. When the Lord told Moses, "Make holy garments for your brother Aaron," he said to make these "for glory and beauty" (Exod 28:2). In other words, these craftsmen and artisans of the Old Testament were instructed to complete their tasks for the combined effect of both glory and beauty.

Unfortunately, too often the notion of beauty is overlooked in Christian culture. However, it is good to be reminded that the medium should always be commensurate with the message. Since Christians have the most beautiful message, the one found in the pages of Scripture, it is incumbent upon us to create beautiful mediums that relay that message in hopes that they also point others to the glory of God.

The *Church History Handbook* before you seeks to do just that in a creative and informative way. Intended to be used as a stand-alone reference work and/or companion to other church history books, the *Church History Handbook* focuses on presenting important people, events, and ideas in a visually compelling way. Its presentation through intentional design and infographics helps deepen one's understanding of the historical and theological development of the Christian Church. Features include the following:

- Historical Overviews of key periods, including key events, figures, and ideas
- Essential Christian doctrines for each period
- Maps
- Timelines
- Charts and tables
- Infographics about key figures and events
- Key quotes from voices of the Church

The *Church History Handbook* is intended to enhance your reading and understanding of the history of the Christian Church and ultimately point you to "God's glory in the face of Jesus Christ" (2 Cor 4:6).

Andy McLean
Publisher

# "On Whom the Ends of the Ages Have Come": A Christian View of History

## INTRODUCTION

Why is history important? Most people rarely pause to consider this. Perhaps without realizing it, some have been conditioned to esteem the study of history as legitimate for reasons they cannot identify. Maybe it's for the sake of preserving the human legacy for posterity. Maybe it's because of a sense of patriotism and heritage for a given country or culture. Or maybe it's mainly for the sake of meeting societal standards of what it means to be an educated and well-rounded individual. Many, however, will cite the famous George Santayana quote: "Those who cannot remember the past are condemned to repeat it."

While there is some validity to these reasons, we as Christians should approach the study of the past with an even more reverent mindset. If God is the Creator and Sustainer of the world, then he is also Lord of history, the one who declares "the end from the beginning and from long ago what is not yet done" and who says, "My plan will take place, and I will do all my will" (Isa 46:10). In short, history is coherent and meaningful because of God.

## "EVERYTHING FOR HIS PURPOSE": GOD-CENTERED CHRISTIAN REALISM

If God is sovereign over the natural order and over human affairs, as the Bible indicates, then history is nothing less than *his* story. (Despite the unavoidable hokeyness of the pun, it is memorable and, most importantly, true.) Because God is the God of everything, he is the Lord of everything, not simply church history, but also world history. And though Christians should regard all of history as sacred and meaningful, we especially should appreciate *church* history, for it is the study of how God has worked through his new-covenant people since the days of Jesus's apostles and earliest disciples to bless and restore the world.

In studying church history, we cannot but help ourselves see what God has done to sustain the bride of Christ and preserve her in grace and truth. Indeed, God will always be shown to be faithful, but we must also acknowledge that his Son's bride has not always been wholeheartedly faithful. The study of church history is thus the study of sinners—albeit a body of redeemed sinners who have yet to be made perfect in Christ (1 John 3:2). So, as those who should be the least shocked when sinners behave sinfully, we must be willing to accept the church's history for all that it is, warts and all (a phrase whose origin itself intersects with church history).

Despite the church's flaws, faults, and *faux pas*, we can remain humbly committed to the truth of whatever took place in the past. There is always meaning in everything that happens—the good, the bad, and the ugly—according to a biblical worldview. "The Lord has prepared everything for his purpose—even the wicked for the day of disaster" (Prov 16:4; see also Rom 8:28; Eph 1:11). Everything doesn't just happen for a reason; it happens for God's reason.

## "IN THESE LAST DAYS": BIBLICAL ESCHATOLOGY AND CHURCH HISTORY

Not only does a Christian realism about human nature inform how we perceive the facts that the past presents us with, but a Christian theology of the future must also undergird our appreciation for this extended era we label church history. As the apostle Paul stated in the first century, the church consists of those "on whom the ends of the ages have come" (1 Cor 10:11). Relative to God's plan to redeem and restore the world through Christ, we have been living within the climax of history ever since Jesus's death, resurrection, and ascension. Hence, the New Testament (NT) came into existence to explain as much.

As a foundational and authoritative collection of supernaturally God-breathed writings alongside the Old Testament (OT), the NT is meant to govern the people of God during this extended era until the time when Jesus returns. In view of a biblical outlook on history, we can accordingly derive three definitive reasons to study church history from the NT that will frame the remainder of this treatise. (For more about the nature of the NT and the development of its canon, see the essay "Connecting and Completing the Story: The Origin and Canon of the New Testament" in *The New Testament Handbook*.)

*First, we should study church history because the last days have been here since Jesus ascended to sit at the Father's right hand.* In the taxonomy of the biblical authors, history consists of two ages: "this age" and "the age to come" (see Mark 10:29–30; Luke 20:34–35; Gal 1:4; 1 Tim 4:8). This is why the author of Hebrews followed this categorization in seeing the incarnation and ascension of Jesus as the climactic moment in the history of God's special revelation to his people:

> Long ago God spoke to our ancestors by the prophets at different times and in different ways. In these last days, he has spoken to us by his Son. God has appointed him heir of all things and made the universe through him. The Son is the radiance of God's glory and the exact expression of his nature, sustaining all things by his powerful word. After making purification for sins, he sat down at the right hand of the Majesty on high. (Heb 1:1–3)

In this passage, we should observe not only the two modes in which God has spoken (e.g., "by the prophets" and "by his Son") but also the division of history the passage presents. "These last days" refers to the period of history that coincides with Christ's ascension. While this may seem long ago from our modern standpoint, "these last days" are quite recent according to a biblical timeframe and, in fact, continue today. In short, the church has been in the "end times" since the days of the apostles because of the centrality of Jesus's first and second comings.

We live in what theologians observe to be the overlap of the ages, or better put, the "already-not yet." God's kingdom has arrived *already*, but it is *not yet* present in its fullest form. Jesus, for example, taught that on some level the kingdom had already arrived: "If I drive out demons by the finger of God, then the kingdom of God has come upon you" (Luke 11:20; see also Matt 21:31; Mark 1:15; Luke 17:21). However, he also acknowledged that the kingdom of God had a perfected form to come in teaching his disciples to pray "your kingdom come . . . on earth as it is in heaven" (Matt 6:10; see also 13:43; 26:29; Luke 13:29). We could consider this teaching even more broadly across the NT (see Rom 14:17; 1 Cor 6:9–10; Eph 1:20–21; Col 1:13; 2 Tim 4:1,18; Heb 6:4–5; Rev 11:15; 12:10), but Jesus's teaching suffices for our purposes here.

Why, then, does God's kingdom and the end of history come about in this dynamic, multifaceted manner? Apart from saying that God wanted to do it that way (which is part of the truth), the "already-not yet" correlates with how Christ achieved victory over Satan, sin, and death on our behalf. Indeed, the war was decisively won at the cross and sealed with an empty tomb, but the enemy's formal surrender has not yet arrived. Drawing from theologian Oscar Cullman, Sinclair Ferguson efficiently summarizes how World War II serves as a fitting analogy for Jesus's already-not victory:

> In that war, D-Day (the decisive intervention of the Allied Forces' invasion of Europe in 1944) took place a year before the coming of VE-Day (the end of the war in Europe in 1945). In the interim, the battles remained fierce and bloody, even although the decisive act had taken place. So it is in redemptive history. The D-Day of redemption has taken place in Christ's death, resurrection, ascension and giving of the Spirit. He has acted decisively against the powers of sin, Satan and death which tyrannized his people. Yet the skirmishes with sin (as well as with Satan and death) continue to be severe.[1]

We thus live between D-Day (Jesus's first coming) and VE-Day (Jesus's second coming), and the study of this "interim" era helps us better understand our place within God's redemptive purposes.

*Second, we should study church history because we can learn from our forebears of faith who also lived during these last days.* Looking to the wilderness experience, the apostle Paul exhorted his readers to learn from Israel's history. He went so far as to state that "these things took place as examples *for us*" (1 Cor 10:6, emphasis added). Because the coming of Jesus split history, the era in which the church exists provides God's people with unique perspective as those "on whom the ends of the ages have come" (v. 11). As already noted, the church lives during the climactic and final stage of God's plan preceding Jesus's return. Therefore, there is a lot of history that precedes this final era, a history that both offers insight concerning the human condition and attests to God's faithfulness to his people across the centuries.

In a real sense, then, the church as the new-covenant community is historically and eschatologically privileged. This is not to say that those who are born-again this side of the cross are inherently superior to the faithful who lived prior to Jesus's first coming, but it is to say that there is significant benefit to living during a time when God's kingdom has come into more vivid focus and vibrant expression. This is why Jesus said the following about John the Baptist, who served as the last prophet of the old-covenant era: "I tell you, among those born of women no one is greater than John, but the least in the kingdom of God is greater than he" (Luke 7:28).

While none of us automatically possess greater character and self-discipline than John the Baptist did simply by living as Christians in this later era, even the least among us has inherited greater eschatological privilege in the wisdom of God's plan. Thanks to the teaching of Jesus and the apostles, we possess a greater knowledge of God's kingdom purposes than John did as a prophet of a former era. Further, we also receive a richer experience of the Spirit's work by virtue of being members of the new (and better) covenant (Jer 31:31–34; Heb 8:6–13; 13:20–21; see also 2 Cor 3:6–11).

Yet, in addition to the new covenant's spiritual benefits, we also benefit from existing downstream of the church's attempts to understand and apply Scripture's teaching over the past two millennia. As you will discover throughout the pages of the *Church History Handbook*, we can find examples good, bad, and somewhere in between of what it means to live faithfully at various points in the storied history of Christianity that spans across centuries and continents.

If Israel's past could teach the first-century church about what it means to be faithful (or unfaithful), according to Paul (1 Cor 10:6,11),

1 Sinclair Ferguson, *The Holy Spirit* (Downers Grove, IL: InterVarsity Press, 1996), 150.

then twenty centuries of church history can no doubt instruct the present and future church in the same way. Israel's past happened for the church's sake, in other words, and there's no reason why the church's sundry experiences should not also serve the church's present ministry in the same manner.

*Third, we should study church history because Jesus and the apostles promised that false teaching would mark these last days.* As Jesus and the apostles taught, the last days would be marked by an escalation in false teaching.

- "For false messiahs and false prophets will arise and perform great signs and wonders to lead astray, if possible, even the elect." (Matt 24:24)
- "Now the Spirit explicitly says that in later times some will depart from the faith, paying attention to deceitful spirits and the teachings of demons, through the hypocrisy of liars whose consciences are seared." (1 Tim 4:1–2; see also 2 Tim 4:3–4)
- "Children, it is the last hour. And as you have heard that antichrist is coming, even now many antichrists have come. By this we know that it is the last hour." (1 John 2:18; see also 2 John 7)

The church lives not only at a time of both heightened kingdom power and covenant privilege, as we have observed, but also at a time where there is a continuous abundance of false teaching. With greater power, then, comes greater responsibility, and the increase in false teaching also increases our need to draw from the wisdom of those who came before us. If we may take some liberties with the famous Santayana quote, we might say that those who cannot remember past heresies are condemned to repeat them.

Indeed, the first several centuries of the church are, at least in part, the story of the church discerning what the truth is more precisely as a result of refuting error (i.e., orthodoxy coming into its own). This is perhaps most evident in the debates that surrounded the Trinity and the incarnation, the two central and distinguishing doctrines of the Christian faith. By encountering error when it came to how we should make sense of Scripture's teaching of the one God identified as three persons and of its presentation of Jesus as both truly God and truly human, the church came to articulate and preserve biblical truth with greater clarity and accuracy. Knowing the spectrum of positions that gave rise to the historic councils of Nicaea, Constantinople, Ephesus, and Chalcedon will only serve us better to understand the exegetical disputes and metaphysical deliberations that went into how their respective creeds and formulas were drafted and why the church continues to benefit from them today.

By making ourselves aware of how the church contended for the apostolic faith in the past, we better equip ourselves for contending for the same faith in the present (Jude 3). Often, the false teachings that we encounter in our own day are substantively similar to heresies of the past that are only adorned with different clothing. For example, those who deny the deity of Jesus today by arguing that he is the first and most exalted creature (e.g., Jehovah's Witnesses) follow the same line of reasoning as the fourth-century Arians who said, "There was a time when the Son was not." By looking to the faithful example of fourth-century figures like Alexander and Athanasius, we can glean effective and efficient ways to quip back, "Always God, always the Son."

Knowing the heresy, doctrinal errors, and bad practices of the past is necessary for avoiding them in the present. To ignore church history is to turn a willfully deaf ear to where God has spoken his wisdom. It is willfully to play the fool.

## CONCLUSION

The history of the church is both the history of God's faithfulness and the history of our waywardness, much like the history of Israel that we find in the OT. Though beyond the book of Acts we do not possess a supernaturally inspired record of the church's "warts and all" experiences and contributions, we nonetheless can learn from the records we have by measuring them according to Scripture. We will make mistakes like those who came before us, but the same God who preserved his people in the past will continue to preserve his people into the future.

Accordingly, the contents of the *Church History Handbook* are intended to serve as a means to the end that is the Great Commission, namely, the preservation and empowerment of God's people for their God-given mission of proclaiming the truth of the gospel to the world. By equipping the church in the present to learn from her past, we set her up to remain faithful into the future. As we study church history, may God be glorified in the church throughout all generations.

"Now to him who is able to do above and beyond all that we ask or think according to the power that works in us—to him be glory in the church and in Christ Jesus to all generations, forever and ever. Amen" (Eph 3:20–21).

# Early Church

AD 100–200

# HISTORICAL OVERVIEW

**SUMMARY**

The early church (100–200 AD) saw regular growth but also faced several challenges, most notably persecution. The saints of this era laid a solid foundation for the rise and spread of Christianity, helping to establish churches, send missionaries, and raise up church leaders who provided critical oversight and guidance through their preaching and writings.

With many lessons to learn in the centuries ahead, the church nevertheless experienced sustained growth throughout the Roman Empire during this era. Despite the persecution and internal debates, such as those mentioned above, the Christian church continued to thrive as the message of the gospel was expounded upon and spread throughout the known world.

**KEY EVENTS**

The early Christian church pursued the spreading of the gospel message within the Roman Empire despite facing persecution. Following the commandment given by the Lord Jesus Christ in Acts 1:8, these pioneering missionaries started in Jerusalem, traveled to Judea and Samaria, and eventually to the ends of the earth. But as the gospel spread, the persecution began. Nero and Domitian are two of the more notable emperors who persecuted the Christian church. But history has shown that as persecution continued, the church continued to spread, thus confirming Tertullian's statement: "The blood of the martyrs is the seed of the church."

**KEY FIGURES**

Several church leaders arose to provide oversight and guidance for the early church:

- **Polycarp of Smyrna** *(69–156)* was a disciple of the apostle John and the bishop of Smyrna. He was an opponent of Marcionism and wrote a letter to the Philippians.
- **Ignatius of Antioch** *(35–107)* wrote six letters to churches while being taken from his home in Antioch to Rome for his execution.
- **Justin Martyr** *(100–165)* was a philosopher and early Christian apologist. He defended the Christian faith against Jewish and pagan critiques.
- **Tertullian** *(ca. 155–ca. 220)* was another philosopher and early Christian apologist who defended Christianity against pagan and heretical attacks.

These leaders, along with others, wrote against the various challenges and heretical teachings that came against the church.

**KEY IDEAS**

The second century witnessed the increase of theological debates within the Christian community, which primarily focused on the person of Jesus Christ. Their desire for proper teaching and clarification against those who stood opposed to biblical teaching still endures today in the Apostles' Creed. Furthermore, various developments led to discussion and debate about issues such as monotheism, the incarnation, the resurrection of Jesus, and eternal life.

**KEY WORKS**

Early Christians developed and explained these concepts through key works, such as the following:

- ***Didache,*** or "The Teaching of the Twelve Apostles." Written around the first or second century, *Didache* provides instructions on various aspects of the Christian life.
- ***The Shepherd of Hermas.*** Written in the first half of the second century, this text recounts five visions of a former slave named Hermas.
- ***Epistles of Ignatius.*** These letters were penned by Ignatius on the way to his execution and written to church leaders. They contain advice on church unity, obedience to the bishops, and the centrality of the Lord's Supper within the Christian life.
- ***The Apologies of Justin Martyr.*** This two-volume defense of the faith provides an early glimpse into Christian beliefs and practices as they intersect with the Roman Empire.

# Timeline: The Early Church

(AD 50–200)

**69–156**
Polycarp of Smyrna

**ca. 80–110**
*The Didache* was written

**98–117**
Trajan's reign as Roman emperor

**100–200**
Growth of gnostic heretical groups

**ca. 101–165**
Felicitas of Rome

**ca. 160**
Beginning of the heretical "New Prophets" movement

**ca. 100–165**
Justin Martyr

**ca. 110**
Ignatius, bishop of Antioch, martyred

**117–138**
Hadrian's reign as Roman emperor

**ca. 130–200**
Irenaeus

**132–135**
Bar Kokhba Revolt

**138–161**
Antoninius Pius's reign as Roman emperor

**ca. 150–215**
Clement of Alexandria

**ca. 155**
Justin Martyr writes his "First Apology"

**ca. 160–225**
Tertullian

**161–180**
Marcus Aurelius's reign as Roman emperor

**ca. 180**
Irenaeus writes *Against Heresies* to refute gnosticism

**ca. 161**
Justin Martyr writes his "Second Apology"

**193–211**
Septimius Severus's reign as Roman emperor

**ca. 197**
Tertullian writes his "Apology"

# ESSENTIAL CHRISTIAN DOCTRINES

### The Goodness of Creation

*(Genesis 1:31)*

In Genesis 1, God repeatedly affirmed that all of his creation was good, even "very good" (1:31). It is good, in God's judgment, because he created it for a purpose that it fulfilled—to reflect and display the good character of the Creator. Therefore, sin and evil should not be seen as a foundational part of the creation but rather as a corruption of it. While the creation has been marred and distorted as a result of sin, it is still good in the hands of God and serves his purpose of proclaiming his glory in the world. God's people should affirm and seek to preserve the goodness of God's creation (2:15).

### God Is One

*(Deuteronomy 6:4–9)*

The Bible affirms that God is One, as seen in Deut 6:4–9, otherwise known as the Shema. In both Old and New Testament times, the advocacy of monotheism (belief in one God) was contrary to the surrounding culture. Where most cultures practiced polytheism (belief in multiple gods) or henotheism (the worship of one god with the belief in multiple gods), the people of God knew, based on God's self-revelation, that Yahweh, the Lord, was the only One, true God.

### Angels

*(Psalm 91:11)*

Besides the creation of humanity and animals, the Bible also speaks of other beings God created. Among these created beings are angels, who are also referred to in Scripture as "sons of God," "holy ones," "spirits," "principalities," and "powers." In the original languages of the Bible, the word "angel" carries the meaning of a messenger, which indicates one of their primary reasons for existence. Angels carry out a number of other functions throughout Scripture: bringing God glory, carrying out God's plans and purpose, and reminding humanity that the unseen world is real.

### Jesus's Humanity

*(Isaiah 7:14)*

In addition to being fully divine, the Bible also affirms that Jesus is fully human. Not only does the Old Testament affirm that the Promised One (Messiah) would be a man (Isa 9:6; Mic 5:3), but the New Testament also affirms that Jesus's earthly life bore all the marks of being a human. He experienced the circumstances common to living as a human being such as hunger (Matt 4), thirst (Matt 4), weariness (Matt 8:24), pain and sorrow (John 11:28–36; and the crucifixion).

### Christ's Exaltation

*(Philippians 2:9)*

Whereas the death of Christ was the ultimate example of his humiliation, the resurrection of Christ from the dead is the first and glorious example of Christ's exaltation. Christ was exalted when God raised him from the dead, and Christ was exalted when he ascended to the Father's right hand. He will be exalted by all creation when he returns. All of these aspects work together to magnify the glory and worth of Christ, resulting in the praise of the glory of his grace in rescuing sinners.

# The Spread and Persecution of Early Christianity[1]

The church's inception in Jerusalem and growth throughout the Mediterranean world gave form to God's purposes in Christ for the nations. Along with this growth came pain, as the persecuted church's willingness to suffer for the name of Jesus brought glory to God as a public testimony to the gospel's truth and power.

## TO THE END OF THE EARTH: EXPANSION DURING THE FIRST TWO CENTURIES

**Jerusalem: Ground Zero of the Gospel.** The opening of the book of Acts sets the trajectory of the gospel's spread and the church's reach, recording these commissioning words from Jesus: *"You will be my witnesses in Jerusalem, in all Judea and Samaria, and to the ends of the earth"* (Acts 1:8). **Jerusalem,** the city where Jesus was crucified, served as a base (or "ground zero") for this new movement coming out of the margins of the Jewish community that would become known as Christianity. Peter, James, and John became recognized as pillars of the early church, the former two leading primarily from Jerusalem (see Acts 15:6–21; Gal 2:9). This home base of Jewish Christianity experienced a drastic upheaval in AD 70, however, when the Roman military destroyed Jerusalem and its temple, serving as the catalyst for the Diaspora (dispersion) in which Jewish people were forced to flee to other cities across the Mediterranean, an event Jesus had prophesied about (Matt 24:1–2ff; Mark 13:1–2ff; Luke 21:5–6ff).

**Judea and Samaria: Beyond Jewish Borders.** While **Judea** was the broader territory Jews primarily occupied during the Roman Empire, **Samaria** would be considered the edges of the Jewish lands. We see the mission of the church expand to Samaria with Philip's ministry (Acts 8:4–8). Jews and Gentiles did not mix that much in terms of religious life and practice. The exception to this pattern was "God fearers" (see 10:2–4), Gentiles who were drawn to Jewish religion and even participated in synagogue services. Luke recorded Cornelius, a God fearer and centurion in the Roman army (10:1), as the first Gentile convert to Christianity.

**The End of the Earth: Taking Root in the Gentile World.** A Pharisee turned Christian missionary, the apostle Paul is the most notable human agent responsible for the early spread of Christianity across the Mediterranean world. Along with Barnabas, Paul left from **Antioch** as part of the first missionary team to the Gentiles when they set out for Cyprus (13:1–12). By the end of Paul's three missionary journeys, the gospel had spread into the far west of the Roman Empire with churches planted in **Macedonia** and **Greece**. After appearing before rulers and officials, Paul himself would take the gospel into Rome as a prisoner (Acts 21–28). Beyond Acts, church tradition holds that after his first imprisonment ended, Paul traveled to **Spain** (AD 63–67). He was eventually arrested a second time, receiving harsher treatment and being sentenced to death by Nero around AD 67.

**After Acts: The Church Finding Its Place.** By the middle of the second century, **Antioch**, **Rome**, and **Alexandria** had become the premier Christian cities in the Roman Empire. On top of geological diversity, Christianity also possessed language diversity with segments of the church speaking Latin (Italy, North Africa, western Europe), Greek (eastern Mediterranean, eastern Europe), and Syriac (Middle East, central Asia, and China). To bring unity and order in belief and practice amid this cultural diversity, the early church looked to the office of bishop: "Wherever the bishop is, there one finds the fellowship; just as wherever Jesus Christ is there is the catholic Church" (Ignatius). Though whether the office of bishop should have exercised this kind of regional authority is a matter of debate among Christian traditions, the fact that men who represented orthodox teaching held the office during the early centuries of the church is something all Christians can both acknowledge and be thankful for.

## MOMENTARY AND LIGHT AFFLICTIONS: THE NATURE AND SCOPE OF PERSECUTION IN THE EARLY CENTURIES

**"The blood of the martyrs is the seed of the church."**
**–Tertullian (ca. 160–220)**

**Jewish Persecution.** Though the Jewish community would not remain in position to persecute the budding Christian movement beyond AD 70, the book of Acts records instances where religious leaders sought to use their localized influence to stifle the church's growth (see Acts 4:1–23; 5:17–42). Stephen became the first recorded Christian martyr after being stoned to death for his bold indictment of the Jewish leaders for failing to see Jesus as the fulfillment of God's promises, making them comparable to their rebellious ancestors (6:8–15; 7:54–60). Saul, who became better known as Paul the apostle, was a prominent agent of persecution as well (8:1–3; 9:1–4) but would end up on the receiving end of persecution from the religious leaders once he became a Christian (9:20–30).

**Roman Persecution.** The persecution that came from the hand of the Roman Empire was intense at times but for the most part isolated to certain sectors of the empire. Broad-based systematic persecution of the Christian church was the exception rather than the rule, in other words. This, however, did not mean government-sanctioned persecution was not a common experience for Christians during the early centuries of the church. Among Roman emperors, these are some of the most prominent figures associated with the targeted persecution of Christians despite their efforts not being equally consistent or persistent with one another:

- Nero (AD 60s)
- Domitian (late first century)
- Trajan (early second century)
- Hadrian (second century)
- Decius (mid-third century)
- Valerian (mid-third century)
- Diocletian (early fourth century)

ADRIATIC SEA

Rome

ITALIA

Puteoli

Rhegium

SICILY

Syracuse

MALTA

# Major Base Cities for Early Christianity

BLACK SEA
MACEDONIA
THRACE
Amphipolis
Thessalonica
Neapolis
BITHYNIA AND PONTUS
Berea
Larissa
Troas
GALATIA
Pergamum
AEGEAN SEA
CAPPADOCIA
Delphi
ASIA
ACHAIA
Athens
Laodicea
Corinth
Ephesus
PHRYGIA
Lystra
CILICIA
Sparta
PAMPHYLIA
Derbe
LYCIA
Tarsus
Patara
Myra
Antioch
Salmone
CRETE
CYPRUS
SYRIA
MEDITERRANEAN SEA
Sidon
Damascus
Tyre
SAMARIA
Jerusalem
CYRENAICA
JUDEA
DEAD SEA
Alexandria
EGYPT
0 150 300 Miles
0 150 300 Kilometers

BIOGRAPHY

# Polycarp of Smyrna

Polycarp, a pupil of the apostle John, was bishop of Smyrna during the first half of the second century and faithfully taught the church the Christian truth. In a letter he wrote to the Philippians, Polycarp encouraged Christians to maintain the truth and warned them to turn away from false teachers:

Whoever does not confess, that Jesus Christ is come in the flesh, is antichrist, and

> whoever does not confess the mystery of the cross, is of the devil, and he who wrests the words of the Lord according to his own pleasure, and saith, there is no resurrection and judgment, is the first-born of Satan.

Polycarp's pastoral letter is saturated with Scripture, containing six quotes from the Old Testament and sixty-three allusions or quotes from eighteen New Testament books.

Polycarp was a younger friend of Ignatius, also a pupil of the apostle John, who was martyred in Rome in 116. Polycarp transmitted the apostolic truths he had learned to the next generation and was a teacher of Irenaeus, a theologian and bishop in Lyon at the end of the second century. As pastor of the church at Smyrna, Jesus's words in Rev 2:8–10 undoubtedly resonated with Polycarp, "Don't be afraid of what you are about to suffer. Look, the devil is about to throw some of you into prison to test you, and you will experience affliction for ten days. Be faithful to the point of death, and I will give you the crown of life."

Arrested for his Christian faith, Polycarp was brought into the stadium where the proconsul sought to persuade him to deny Christ "Have respect to your old age. . . . Swear by the fortune of Caesar," the proconsul said. When told he would be set him free if he renounced Christ, Polycarp replied, "Eighty and six years have I served Him, and He never did me any injury: how then could I blaspheme my King and my Saviour?"When the proconsul threatened Polycarp with wild beasts or fire unless he "repented" of his faith in Christ, Polycarp said he could not repent of what was good to adopt what was evil. If he were to be sent to the flames, that would last but an hour and was not to be compared with the eternal flames for the ungodly. Polycarp was then condemned to be burnt. As the funeral pyre was erected, Polycarp prayed:

> O Lord God Almighty, the Father of your beloved and blessed Son Jesus Christ, by whom we have received the knowledge of You. . . . I give You thanks that You have counted me worthy of this day and this hour, that I should have a part in the number of our martyrs, in the cup of your Christ, to the resurrection of eternal life, both of soul and body. . . . I praise You for all things, I bless You, I glorify You. Along with the everlasting and heavenly Jesus Christ, Your beloved Son, with whom, to You, and the Holy Spirit, be glory both now and to all coming ages. Amen.

BIOGRAPHY

# Ignatius of Antioch

As a young man, Ignatius had been discipled by the apostle John in Ephesus. By the beginning of the second century, Ignatius was bishop of the church at Antioch, the city where believers were first given the name of "Christian" (Acts 11:26). At a time when Christians were persecuted for not worshipping the pagan Roman gods, Ignatius confessed himself a Christian and was condemned to death. Under the guard of soldiers, he was taken from Antioch to Rome to be thrown to wild beasts. On the long journey, partly by land and partly by sea, Ignatius was able to meet with some of the Christians in communities along the way. He also wrote letters to Christians in the cities along his path (Ephesus, Magnesia, Tralles, Philadelphia, Smyrna), encouraging them in their faith. He even wrote to the Roman church, asking them not to intervene on his behalf. He especially warned Christians against the false teaching of Docetism, which held that Jesus was not truly human but only appeared to be a man. Ignatius pointed out that if Jesus was not truly human, then the crucifixion and resurrection, and his real death for our sins, were illusions as well. Following the apostle John (1 John 4:2–3; 2 John 7), Ignatius insisted that Jesus had come in the flesh and was both fully divine and fully human.

In his letters, Ignatius called himself Theophorus, which means "bearer of God." He refused to worship idols, for the church was the temple of the living God, and God said, "I will dwell and walk among them, and I will be their God, and they will be my people" (2 Cor 6:16). With an irrepressible joy, Ignatius was eager to suffer martyrdom for Christ, writing, "I endure all things for Christ . . . that I may suffer with him, while he himself inwardly strengthens me, for of myself I have no such ability." Ignatius, killed by wild beasts in the arena in Rome, was one of the earliest Christian martyrs, gladly facing death in faithfulness to Christ. He died sometime between AD 108 and AD 140.

## VOICES OF THE CHURCH

"[Christ] suffered all these things for our sakes, that we might be saved. And He suffered truly, even as also He truly raised up Himself, not, as certain unbelievers maintain, that He only seemed to suffer, as they themselves only seem to be Christians."[2]

IGNATIUS (D. 110)

BIOGRAPHY

# Felicitas

Some time in the second century (the exact date is uncertain), a noble Roman lady named Felicitas was brought before Publius, the prefect of Rome. Felicitas was a Christian who devoted herself to charitable works and was a strong witness for Christ in Rome. The pagan religious leaders brought a complaint against her before the emperor because they believed the problems Rome was facing were due to people neglecting the Roman gods, and Felicitas was drawing people to Christ away from these pagan gods. The emperor instructed her to be brought before the prefect, who tried to persuade Felicitas to worship the pagan gods. In spite of the prefect's cajoling and threats, Felicitas maintained her trust and faith in Christ and refused to honor the Roman gods. One account records that Felicitas's seven sons (Januarius, Felix, Phillippus, Sylvanus, Alexander, Vitalis, and Martial) were also arrested and brought before the prefect and told to renounce Christ. They too refused, as their mother, encouraging them in their faith, told them, "Behold heaven, my sons, and look upwards, whence you expect Christ with His saints." As each of the sons and Felicitas were condemned to death, Felicitas asked to be spared until the last of her sons died; she wanted to encourage them to be constant in their faith to the end. After witnessing the death of her seven sons, Felicitas herself was beheaded. Felicitas, along with her son Sylvanus, was buried in the catacomb of Maximus. The other brothers were buried in three different Roman cemeteries in Rome. Felicitas and her sons were faithful to the end and conquered "by the blood of the Lamb, and by the word of their testimony, for they did not love their lives to the point of death" (Rev 12:11).

BIOGRAPHY

# Biography: Justin Martyr

Justin was a truth seeker. He was born in Flavia Neapolis, in modern Palestine, around AD 100. His hometown was new, with massive marble buildings, marketplaces, and temples lining the well-engineered Roman roads. Throughout his lifetime, the Roman Empire was stable and prosperous, ruled by emperors who valued education and justice. Yet Justin's mind and soul were restless. He saw the emptiness of his culture, with its endless false striving and deceptive promises of meaning, and he knew there was more to life. This pursuit led him to Christ.

From his teenage years, Justin traveled to many cities to listen to well-known teachers of every philosophy of his day, only to find each unfulfilling. He loved wisdom, which is the true meaning of the word "philosophy," but concluded it was simply beyond reach. Finally, when he was thirty years old and participating in the diverse philosophical schools of the cosmopolitan city of Rome, conversations with an elderly Christian teacher, who guided him to the Scripture, changed his life. "A fire was suddenly kindled in my soul," he recounts. "I fell in love with the prophets [the Old Testament] and these people who had loved Christ [the New Testament]; I reflected on all their words and found that this philosophy alone was true. This is how and why I became a true lover of Wisdom." He became a student of the Scripture and active in a circle of Christians.

In the Roman society of the time, Christianity was mildly tolerated but tremendously misunderstood. Scandalous rumors about Christians and their practices were widespread. Here, Justin stepped in as one of the earliest apologists (those who explain and defend the faith), writing prolifically in a style his contemporaries could understand. Justin covered vast topics and also provided compelling, practical explanations of what Christians actually did in their Sunday gatherings, providing one of the earliest and most detailed descriptions of early Christian worship. In each writing, the theme of Col 2:6–8 is present: every "wisdom" and lifestyle offered by the world is ultimately hopeless. The only way to find roots instead of restless seeking is to receive the teachings of Christianity and follow Christ, who is Wisdom itself. Philosophical learning in itself is never "bad," Justin emphasized, but it will only lead to more questions unless it is anchored in Christ. Justin believed all truth belonged to God, wherever it was found. In fact, his expertise in philosophy helped build bridges to pagan audiences as Justin offered an intellectually respectable defense of Christian theology.

Justin continued to teach, write, and learn. He gained enough attention among civil authorities in Rome that he was brought to public trial and accused with undermining the empire in his teachings. He stood in his confession of the truth, insisting that he could never stop teaching "the true love of Wisdom," and was martyred around AD 165. For this reason, he is called Justin Martyr (meaning "Justin the witness"). His voice is a reminder that our restless culture longs for truth but cannot provide fulfillment. Ultimate truth is found only in Christ: this wisdom is worth seeking, receiving, and sharing.

## VOICES OF THE CHURCH

"[God] promises that he would deliver from the bites of the serpent . . . all those who believe in him who was to be put to death by this sign, namely, the cross."[3]

JUSTIN MARTYR (CA. 100–165)

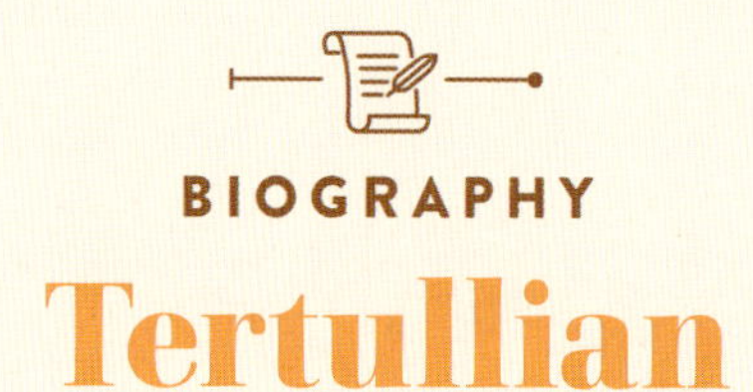

BIOGRAPHY

# Tertullian

Tertullian (ca. AD 160–225) was a second- and third-century Roman writer who lived in Carthage, a primary city in Roman-owned North Africa. He is often called "the father of Latin Christianity" primarily because of his theological and apologetic acumen and because he was the first prolific Christian to publish in Latin. Scholars debate over whether he remained a layman until his death or at some point became a priest, but no one disputes the influence he had not only on Latin theology but on Western theology as a whole.

The son of a Roman centurion, Tertullian enjoyed the privilege of Roman citizenship, including receiving an excellent education. This upbringing benefitted him later in life—he was beloved in the Christian community because of his eloquence, wit, and sheer brilliance. Even two thousand years later, one can read Tertullian and find his writing not only brilliant and humorous but also extremely quotable.

Unlike many prominent early theologians, the Western or Eastern Church has not sainted him. This is largely because he joined a heretical group called the Montanists later in life and because some of his theology was out of line with later orthodox theology. Nonetheless, Tertullian is credited with coining the terms "Trinity" and "economy," which were key concepts in the later debates over the divinity of Christ and the Holy Spirit. Though he was not formally a Nicene Trinitarian, the group that later defined the orthodox view of the Trinity was indebted to him.

Tertullian's main opponents were Modalists, most notably one named Praxeas, to whom Tertullian wrote a letter that is still available to read today. Modalists were monotheists who taught that Christ and the Holy Spirit were not divine persons but rather "modes" or "faces" of God. In his letter to Praxeas and in other writings, we see Tertullian trying to maintain monotheism, while also acknowledging that Christ and the Holy Spirit are in some sense divine and individual persons within the unified Godhead. Within these debates Tertullian began to develop the early Trinitarian language that would be used by later Nicene Christians.

Tertullian also wrote on a variety of moral issues like marriage and religious liberty. Most scholars also believe he quoted portions of 21 of the 27 books of the New Testament, making his writings a source of confidence for the authority of the books that later became the New Testament portion of the biblical canon. However, as mentioned, Tertullian's influence on Trinitarian theology is his greatest and most important contribution to Christian history.

## VOICES OF THE CHURCH

"That we are a chosen people is clear enough, but Peter said that we are a royal people because we have been called to share Christ's kingdom and we belong to Him."[4]

CLEMENT OF ALEXANDRIA (AD 150–215)

BIOGRAPHY

# Irenaeus of Lyons



Irenaeus served as bishop in Lyons (modern-day France) over a Christian community suffering from persecutions and theological disputes with various heretical groups. He was born in Smyrna between ca. AD 120 and 140 and became a disciple of Polycarp before migrating west to Lyons. Irenaeus died around AD 202, and two of his works survive: an immense five-volume refutation of Gnosticism commonly known as *Against Heresies* and a short catechetical manual entitled *The Demonstration of the Apostolic Preaching.*

The main heresy that concerned Irenaeus was Gnosticism, which boasted a complex set of beliefs that aimed to supplant the Christian worldview with a competing creation myth. In general, ancient gnostics (derived from *gnosis*, the Greek term for "knowledge") believed in a supreme God above a collection of other divine figures residing in a region called the pleroma. Through the rebellion of a lower divine being, the creator of the world (also known as the demiurge) was brought forth. The gnostics argue that the demiurge was ignorant of the superior gods above him and through evil desires created the material world. At the same time, unbeknown to the demiurge, a divine element or "divine spark," was implanted in human beings. An enduring conflict between spirit and matter ensued until a redeemer figure appeared to impart the "knowledge" of this myth and the salvation found in the ultimate separation of the divine spark from the body and material creation at death to return to the pleroma.

In *Against Heresies*, Irenaeus responded to the prevailing streams of Gnosticism by arguing that the orthodox faith of the church precedes any heretical deviation. The apostles handed down the faith of the church; the heretics rejected the faith received by choosing to believe a different myth. In order to help guide Christians' understanding of the faith, Irenaeus held up two things: the Scriptures and the rule of faith. The Scriptures, Irenaeus argued, were given by the Spirit and possess a unity, coherence, and harmony that testifies to the work of salvation the Father accomplished through the Son. Though there are a diversity of Scripture passages, "through the many voices of the passages there will be heard among us one harmonious melody that hymns praises to God who made all things." To perceive the theological unity of the Scriptures, Irenaeus also posited the need for a rule of faith, which offered some essential theological guardrails for interpreting Scripture. Irenaeus writes that the "Church, though dispersed throughout the whole world, even to the ends of the earth, has received from the apostles and their disciples this faith." He goes on to recount the points of this rule of faith (which are themselves derived from Scripture) in summary form including the conviction that God, the Father is Creator of all things, Jesus Christ the Son became incarnate for our salvation, and the Holy Spirit proclaimed the work of Christ in the Scriptures. Irenaeus argues that this rule of faith is Scripture's thesis, or what he calls its "hypothesis," that stands in sharp contrast to the peculiar theology of the gnostic myth. Ultimately, Irenaeus is remembered as a champion of Christian orthodoxy at a time when others were exploiting and distorting the Scriptures to defend their own theological system.

## VOICES OF THE CHURCH

"It is not possible that the Gospels can be either more or fewer in number than they are. For, since there are four zones of the world in which we live, and four principal winds, while the Church is scattered throughout all the world, and the 'pillar and ground' of the Church is the Gospel and the spirit of life; it is fitting that she should have four pillars, breathing out immortality on every side, and vivifying men afresh."[5]

IRENAEUS (CA 130–200)

# Heresies of the Early Centuries

(AD 1–200)

| NAME (PERIOD) | DESCRIPTION | REPRESENTATIVES | RELEVANT BIBLICAL PASSAGES |
|---|---|---|---|
| **DOCETISM** *(late first century)* | Jesus was divine but only *seemed* or *appeared* to be human because it was beneath the divine to come into contact with matter. | Valentinus (ca. 136–165) | *1 John 4:1–3; 2 John 7–11* |
| **THE JUDAIZER MOVEMENT** *(first century)* | To become Christians, Gentiles were required to follow Jewish customs such as circumcision and dietary law. | The false teachers in Galatia | *Acts 15:1–33; Galatians 1:6–9; 2:14,21; 5:4* |
| **COLOSSIAN HERESY** *(first century)* | The specifics of the teaching are unknown, but we can infer from Paul's letter the teaching contained emphases on philosophy, angels, Jewish rituals, and asceticism. | The false teachers in Colossae | *Colossians 2:8,20–23* |
| **EBIONITES** *(second century)* | Developed from the Judaizers, this group taught that Jesus was a special human being who kept the law and was uniquely adopted by God but not fully divine. | | *Matthew 3:13–17; John 1:1–14* |
| **GNOSTICISM** *(second century)* | This was an attempt to synthesize Christian teaching with Platonic dualism where the immaterial is considered good and physical matter bad; salvation comes through secret knowledge (Greek "gnosis"). | Cerinthus (ca. 100) and Saturninus (ca. 100–120) | *John 1:1–18; 1 John 1:1–4* |
| **MARCIONISM** *(second century)* | A mixture of Christianity and Gnosticism, this movement rejected the OT, seeing its God as the evil Creator of the material realm and the NT presenting the good Redeemer God. | Marcion (d. 154) | *Romans 1:1–4; 1 Corinthians 8:5–6* |
| **MONTANISM** *(second century)* | This movement emphasized the continuation of miracles, prophecy, and tongues with a notable interest in the end times and asceticism. | Montanus (mid-second century) | *Colossians 2:18–23; Hebrews 1:1–2* |

# The Apostles' Creed

*I believe in God,*
*the Father almighty,*
*Creator of heaven and earth,*
*and in Jesus Christ, his only Son, our Lord,*
*who was conceived by the Holy Spirit,*
*born of the Virgin Mary,*
*suffered under Pontius Pilate,*
*was crucified, died and was buried;*
*he descended into hell;*
*on the third day he rose again from the dead;*
*he ascended into heaven,*
*and is seated at the right hand of God the Father almighty;*
*from there he will come to judge the living and the dead.*

*I believe in the Holy Spirit,*
*the holy catholic[6] Church,*
*the communion of saints,*
*the forgiveness of sins,*
*the resurrection of the body,*
*and life everlasting.*

*Amen.*

## VOICES OF THE CHURCH

"[God] himself gave his own son, a ransom on our behalf, the holy for the lawless, the innocent for the guilty, the righteous for the unrighteous, the incorruptible for the corruptible, the immortal for the mortal. For what else than that one's righteousness could cover up our sin? In who *else* than in the Son of God alone could our lawlessness and ungodliness possibly be justified? Oh, the sweet exchange! Oh, the fathomless creation! Oh, the unexpected benefits that the lawlessness of many should be concealed in the one righteous, and righteousness of the one should justify many lawless."[7]

EPISTLE TO DIOGNETUS (WRITTEN CA. 150–180)

# The Apostolic Fathers: A Brief Description[8]

**The group of early Christian writings collectively known as the Apostolic Fathers present us with a diverse range of literature that offers us a window into the thought, practice, and concerns of the early church. Living predominantly in the second century, these authors are labeled the "apostolic fathers" because of their close historical proximity to the apostles, which makes their writings the earliest form of Christian literature outside the New Testament. The table below offers a list of these works with a brief description of each one to give the reader a basic idea about their significance and contribution to the Christian tradition.**

| TITLE (ESTIMATED) | SUMMARY AND SIGNIFICANCE |
|---|---|
| First Clement<br>*(AD 81–96)* | The author has traditionally been thought to be Clement, one of the earliest bishops of Rome (and who is a different figure than Clement of Alexandria). Writing to the church in Corinth, the letter makes an appeal that this church should reinstitute their wrongfully expelled leaders. |
| Second Clement<br>*(AD 120–140)* | Associated with Clement because copies of this work were typically found with First Clement, this writing is considered a homily (or sermon). It is based on Isa 54 and deals with Scripture, interpretation, and exhortation, making it an example of how early Christians used the Bible in practice. |
| The Ignatian Letters<br>*(AD 110–113)* | Ignatius (35–107) was the bishop of Antioch, and he wrote this group of letters while in transport from Antioch to Rome preparing to face trial for being a Christian. Six of the letters are written to churches (Ephesians, Magnesians, Trallians, Romans, Philadelphians, and Smyrnaens), and one is to Polycarp, the bishop of Smyrna. |
| Polycarp to the Philippians<br>*(AD 110–113; 135*)* | Tradition holds that Polycarp (69–156) was a personal disciple of the apostle John. Named after this respected bishop of Smyrna, this letter is thought to have been written around the time of Ignatius's death, or at least partially around that time. Further, the letter is known for its distinguished quotations of and allusions to the New Testament. |
| Martyrdom of Polycarp<br>*(AD 155–160)* | Written from the church at Philomelium to the church at Smyrna, this letter documents the death of Polycarp (which many date to February 23, 155). It is one of the earliest martyrologies, narrating Polycarp's arrest and subsequent death that took place in a stadium. |
| Didache<br>*(AD 80–120)* | Known simply by the Greek word for "teaching," the writing's formal title is "The Teaching of the Twelve Apostles." It functions as a handbook for Christians on how to live and worship, along with containing a section on eschatology. It also bears a similarity to Matthew's Gospel with its presentation of the "Two Ways," a common feature in other early Christian writings. |
| Epistle of Barnabas<br>*(AD 96–100)* | Though later tradition came to ascribe authorship to Paul's companion Barnabas, the text does not claim a specific author. Additionally, the text displays an allegorical approach to Scripture representative of its era. |
| Epistle to Diognetus<br>*(AD 117–310)* | An apologetic work with components of homily at points, the text presents early Christian arguments against Greek paganism and Hellenistic Judaism. No author is known conclusively. |
| Shepherd of Hermas<br>*(first part: AD 90–100; second part AD 100–154)* | A complex text with an apparently complex history, the content consists of three major sections: Visions, Mandates, and Parables. The work was likely popular because it speaks to common questions of its day within the church (e.g., the problem of sin after baptism). |

# Questions about Orthodoxy: How Does Truth Win?

## WHAT DOES THE TERM *ORTHODOXY* MEAN?

The Greek word *orthodoxia* derives from the terms *orthos* ("right") and *doxa* ("opinion"), and the concept has been used to refer to the standard Christian beliefs essential to the gospel message. When used as a proper noun or proper adjective (e.g., Orthodox, Eastern Orthodoxy), the term refers to specific Christian traditions typically situated in Eastern Europe. When used with a "little o," the term carries a broader meaning that refers to universally held foundational beliefs that are considered essential to Christianity (e.g., Trinity, Jesus's true divinity and humanity, substitutionary atonement, bodily resurrection, salvation by grace, final judgment, etc.).

## HOW DID ORTHODOXY DEVELOP?

The answer depends on whom you ask. Below are three typical explanations for how "truth wins," the third being the one with which historic Protestant Christianity would agree:

~~OPTION 1~~

Truth does not win because the winners write their version of the truth (e.g., mainstream, naturalist view).

~~OPTION 2~~

Truth wins because the tradition determines what is true (e.g., Roman Catholicism, Eastern Orthodoxy).

OPTION 3

Truth wins because the apostolic teaching written and preserved in the form of the New Testament is a sufficient and infallible source for truth (e.g., *sola Scriptura*).

## WHERE CAN WE FIND ORTHODOXY?

There are succinct and declarative summations of central apostolic truths throughout the New Testament, usually described with the words "gospel," "teaching," and "tradition":

### THE DEFINITIVE GOSPEL

"The gospel I preached to you, which you received" (*1 Cor 15:1–4*; see also *2 Cor 11:4*; *Gal 1:6–9*).

### THE DISTINCT TEACHING

"Hold on to the pattern of sound teaching that you have heard from me" (*2 Tim 1:13*; see also *Rom 6:17*; *1 Tim 6:3*).

### THE DISPENSED TRADITION

"Stand firm and hold to the traditions you were taught" (*2 Thess 2:15*; see also *2 Thess 3:6*; *1 John 1:1–4*; *Jude 3*).

## HOW WAS ORTHODOXY MAINTAINED DURING THE EARLY CENTURIES OF THE CHURCH?

There are four primary ways orthodoxy was promoted and preserved from the time of the apostles:

| | |
|---|---|
| **Exposure to Scripture,** namely, the Greek Old Testament, primarily in the form of the Septuagint (see *2 Tim 3:15–17*; *Rom 15:4*; *Gal 3:7–9*; cf. *John 5:39*). | **The oversight of the apostles and their associates,** along with ordained bishops and elders who succeeded them (see *Acts 15:22ff*; *Phil 2:19–24*; *Titus 1:5–9*. |
| **Teaching learned and memorized in the church's singing of hymns and spiritual songs,** a couple of which seem to be rehearsed in Paul's writings (see *Phil 2:5–11*; *Col 1:15–20*). | **Summary statements of the Christian faith** found in the New Testament (see *1 Tim 1:15*; *3:16*), what the ancient church called the Rule of Faith, and what later came to be known as the Apostles' Creed. |

# Patristic Church

AD 200–500

# HISTORICAL OVERVIEW

**SUMMARY** The Patristic Era, sometimes called the Age of the Church Fathers, spanned from the early church to medieval times. This era is characterized by the rising of influential theological figures, the further development of Christian doctrine, and the establishment of ecclesiastical structures.

**KEY EVENTS** The Patristic Era also witnessed the rise of monasticism, which emerged as a response to some who believed both the church and the world were too corrupt. Monasticism was characterized by asceticism, communal living, and devotion to prayer and contemplation. Figures like Saint Anthony the Great and Saint Benedict of Nursia played key roles in the development of monasticism, establishing monastic communities and writing rules for monastic life. Monasteries became centers of spiritual devotion, scholarship, and social welfare, exerting a significant influence on the broader Christian community.

Like Christians of every era, the Church fathers grappled with questions of theology, ethics, and spirituality. Their contributions, however, have left a uniquely enduring legacy. They sought to articulate the beliefs of the Christian faith in a way that was faithful to both Scripture and tradition while also engaging with the broader culture.

**KEY FIGURES** The Patristic Era saw the emergence of key theological figures who are known as the Church fathers. Among the most prominent are Athanasius of Alexandria (296–373), Augustine of Hippo (354–430), and Jerome (345–420). Each of these figures made unique contributions to Christian theology. Augustine explored the concept of sin and grace, whereas Athanasius defended against Arianism and penned *On the Incarnation.* Jerome completed a translation of the Bible into Latin.

**KEY IDEAS** The theological controversies and debates for the most part defined the Patristic Era. These debates focused primarily on areas that are foundational to Christian theology: the Trinity, the person and two natures of Christ, the relationship between grace and free will, and church authority in relation to baptism. The Church fathers engaged in these debates through writings, letters, and discussions in various ecumenical councils. These council meetings and their respective statements of faith played a crucial role in resolving theological disputes and establishing orthodox Christian doctrine: Nicaea (AD 325), Constantinople (AD 381), Ephesus (AD 431) and Chalcedon (AD 451)

Another important aspect of the Patristic Era was the recognition of the biblical canon. During this time, the Christian church began to more formally acknowledge certain writings as authoritative and inspired Scripture. The process of canonization was gradual and varied among different Christian communities, but by the end of the Patristic Era, the New Testament canon was largely established and virtually undisputed.

The Patristic Era represents a period of significant theological and ecclesiastical development. The contributions of the Church fathers, the theological debates, the rise of monasticism, and the formation of the biblical canon played a crucial role in shaping the trajectory of Christian history.

**KEY WORKS**

- ***Confessions***. Written by Augustine of Hippo in the fourth century, this work details Augustine's conversion to the Christian faith.
- ***City of God***. Another work by Augustine of Hippo. This volume examines the relationship between earthly politics and a Christian's citizenship of heaven.
- ***On the Incarnation***. Athanasius of Alexandria explores the Christian doctrine of the incarnation and argues this central teaching is crucial for humanity's restoration.

# Timeline: The Patristic Church

(AD 200–500)

# HISTORIC CHRISTIAN DOCTRINES

### Worship

*(Isa 6)*

While many reduce worship to an event or the singing of worship songs, worship is first and foremost something of the heart and extends to all areas of life. The aim and focus of worship is God, giving him the exact due of praise and adoration he deserves. Worship should be carried out not only at a personal level within a Christian's life but also in joining with other Christians in the corporate act of worship and stewarding our gifts for the glory of God. Corporate worship not only serves to edify and strengthen other Christians, but it also serves as a witness to nonbelievers of the greatness of God.

### God Is One in Three Persons

*(1 Cor 8:4–6)*

While the Bible affirms that God is one *(Mark 12:29)*, it also affirms that God exists as three persons—Father, Son, and Spirit. Each person of the Trinity is fully divine—the Father is God *(John 6:27)*, the Son is God *(Phil 2)*, the Spirit is God *(Acts 5:3-4)*—and each person is distinct from the others *(Matt 11:27; John 10:30; 14:16)*. This perfect unity within the three persons of the Trinity is a first-order doctrine; departing from it is to abandon orthodox Christianity.

### Deity of the Holy Spirit

*(2 Cor 13:13)*

The Holy Spirit is the Third Person of the Trinity, possessing the fullness of deity like the Father and Son. His deity can be seen in the fact that he is eternal *(Heb 9:14)*, is omnipresent *(Ps 139:7–8)*, is Creator and giver of life *(Gen 1:2; Ps 104:30; John 3:5–7)*, and is directly identified with the triune God *(Matt 12:31; 28:19)*.

### Jesus's Deity

*(Phil 2:5–11)*

Within the person of Jesus Christ, there are two natures—the divine nature and the human nature. Scripture teaches he is fully divine and fully human. His divinity is on display in passages that describe him as being equal with God *(John 1:1–18; Col 1:15–20; Heb 1:1–3)*. The New Testament also points to the deity of Christ by showing how he possesses attributes that God alone possesses *(Mic 5:2; John 1:4)*, how he performs works that only God performs *(Mark 2:5–12; John 10:28; 17:2)*, and how he himself claims to be the Son of God *(Matt 26:63–64; John 8:58; 10:30; 17:5)*.

### Enslaved to Sin

*(Rom 6:17)*

Because of the fall of Adam and Eve in the garden of Eden, all of humanity has inherited a sin nature that inclines them toward sin and rebellion. Human beings are enslaved to sin, continually living with the propensity to transgress God's commandments whenever possible. It isn't until one experiences salvation through the work of Christ that he or she is able to overcome sin's enslavement through the power of the Holy Spirit *(Rom 8:2)*.

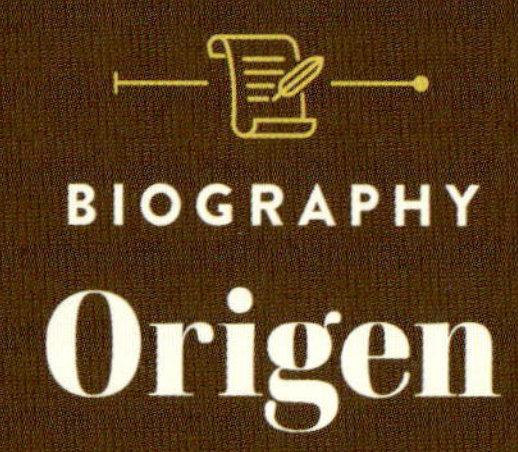

BIOGRAPHY

# Origen

The command to pray constantly *(1 Thess 5:17)* can feel overwhelming. Many have contemplated this passage over the centuries, including a third-century Egyptian Christian named Origen *(AD 186–254)*, whose life's work explored the meaning and practice of unceasing prayer.

Origen of Alexandria had Christian parents who taught him the Scriptures and provided him with an exceptional education. His hometown was a multicultural metropolis, and though the Roman Empire still considered Christianity an illegal religion, Alexandria had a large and diverse Christian population. Its churches emphasized discipleship, and Origen grew in the faith under a brilliant instructor. Then, when he was a teenager, a persecution of Christians swept the Roman world, and Origen's father Leonidas was killed. Origen could have responded in any number of ways; instead, he turned to God in prayer, the Scriptures, and the church. These would occupy the remainder of his life and work.

Over the following decades, Origen wrote prolifically, producing books of deep scholarship that speak to the reader's mind, heart, and daily life. He became well-known among Christians near and far, but when he was about 65 years old, another persecution occurred. He was arrested and severely tortured, yet he refused to renounce his faith. He was released but lived only a few more years. Origen is honored to this day as one of the fathers of the Church because of his influential writings on theology, biblical interpretation, and spirituality. His work *On Prayer* stands out as a thoughtful, practical, and passionate work for readers. He writes not as an expert, but as a lifelong student of Scripture and a Christian whose life consistently relies on his Savior.

Several of this book's insights are worth reflecting on still today. First, Origen points out that it can be tempting to use prayer as a preparation for other things like reading the Bible, listening to a sermon, or in transitioning between activities. Instead, what if we intentionally prepared our minds, hearts, and actions *before* praying? Origen's question, and his challenge to reposture even our bodies for prayer, reveals a deep respect and love for God, as well as his desire to be fully present before the God who is always present to us. If a significant aspect of prayer is being fully present, Origen hints to his reader, how does that affect the way we read 1 Thess 5:17? He comments, "The only way we can accept the command to 'pray constantly' as having real possibility is by saying that the *entire life* of the Christian, taken as a whole, is a single great prayer." That is, prayer includes but is not limited to speaking with God; prayer also involves the activity of our daily life. Then, he takes us one step further: if the unceasing heartbeat of our life in God is a consistent prayer, a communication with our Creator, then all Christians together contribute to a grand ongoing symphony of prayers before God. This means that 1 Thess 5:17 is not only feasible, but it is also happening right now!

# Ten Basic Facts about the New Testament Canon Every Christian Should Know[1]

**01** The universal church came to accept the same 27 NT books as canonical, and no ecclesiastical authority created the NT canon.

**02** The earliest codex is Codex Sinaiticus, dated to the fourth century. It was found in the nineteenth century by Constantin von Tischendorf.

**03** In the earliest four major codices (books) available (Sinaiticus, Vaticanus, Alexandrinus, Ephraemi Rescriptus), all dated between the fourth and fifth centuries, the four Gospels always appear first.

**04** The process of canonization began around the time of the early church, and the canon was declared closed by the ecclesiastical councils during the fourth and fifth centuries.

**05** Revelation was almost universally recognized as Scripture by the second century.

**06** One basic criteria for canonicity was that the book/epistle conform to the "rule of faith" (Lat. *regula fiedi*). The document must meet the criteria for orthodoxy.

**07** The early church rejected works they deemed were anonymous, though Hebrews was kept since most of the early church believed the apostle Paul was the author.

**08** Apostolicity was the most commonly mentioned criterion for canonicity by the early church fathers.

**09** A document's time of writing needed to be produced during the apostolic era. This criterion ruled out the *Didache*, *Shepherd of Hermas*, and the *Epistle of Barnabas*.

**10** A festal letter written by Athnasius and dated to AD 367 provides the exact NT canon as of today.

# Canon Formation

| DATE | EVENT |
|---|---|
| CA. 1400–BC 400 | The books of the Old Testament (Hebrew Bible) were written and divided into three sections: the Law (*Torah*), the Prophets (*Neviim*), and the Writings (*Ketuvim*). Evidence suggests this division was understood as early as the fourth century, or perhaps even earlier. |
| BC 300–BC 150S | The Septuagint (LXX), a Greek translation of the Old Testament, is produced. The earliest translation of the Pentateuch was done around the third century, and the other parts were completed by the middle part of the first century. Several books are included in the LXX that are not found in the Hebrew Old Testament, such as 1 Esdras, Judith, Tobit, the Wisdom of Solomon, Psalm 151, Ecclesiasticus, Baruch, Letter of Jeremiah, and 1–2 Maccabees. For the most part, the writers of the New Testament will cite the LXX rather than the Hebrew text when quoting a passage from the Old Testament. |
| AD 45–96 | The books and letters of the New Testament are written. |
| AD 170 | Also known as the Muratorian Fragment, the Muratorian Canon is the first official "canon" list containing several biblical books: the four Gospels, two of John's letters, Acts, the thirteen letters of Paul, Jude, and Revelation. The books are not in a particular order, but the author provides a defense of certain NT books that were identified as Scripture. |
| AD 250 | Origen's list of New Testament books provides all twenty-seven books. This evidence suggests that by the time of Origen the issue of the New Testament books was settled. |
| AD 393–419 | The Council of Hippo (AD 393) formally endorsed the canon of the New Testament as found in the festal letter written by Athnasius. In this letter, written in AD 367, Athnasius provides the exact canon of the New Testament as in Christian Bibles today. The Third Council of Carthage (397) and the Fourth Council of Carthage (419) also endorsed this same list. The canon of the New Testament has remained unchanged ever since. |

# Which Canon?

## HEBREW BIBLE

### TORAH (LAW)

- Genesis
- Exodus
- Leviticus
- Numbers
- Deuteronomy

### NEVI'IM (PROPHETS)

- Joshua
- Judges
- (1–2) Samuel
- (1–2) Kings
- Isaiah
- Jeremiah
- Ezekiel
- The Twelve (Minor Prophets)

### KETUVIM (WRITINGS)

- Psalms
- Proverbs
- Job
- Song of Songs
- Ruth
- Lamentations
- Ecclesiastes
- Esther
- Daniel
- Ezra–Nehemiah
- (1&2) Chronicles

## THE SEPTUAGINT (LXX)

### LAW

- Genesis
- Exodus
- Leviticus
- Numbers
- Deuteronomy

### HISTORY

- Joshua
- Judges
- Ruth
- 1 Samuel (Kings I)
- 2 Samuel (Kings II)
- 1 Kings (Kings III)
- 2 Kings (Kings IV)
- 1 Chronicles
- 2 Chronicles
- 1 Esdras
- Ezra–Nehemiah
- Tobit
- Judith
- Esther (with additions)
- 1 Maccabees
- 2 Maccabees
- 3 Maccabees

### WISDOM

- Psalms
- Psalm 151
- Prayer of Manasseh
- Job
- Proverbs
- Ecclesiastes
- Song of Songs
- Wisdom of Solomon
- Sirach (Ecclesiasticus)
- Psalms of Solomon

### PROPHETS

- Hosea
- Amos
- Micah
- Joel
- Obadiah
- Jonah
- Nahum
- Habakkuk
- Zephaniah
- Haggai
- Zechariah
- Malachi
- Isaiah
- Jeremiah
- Baruch
- Lamentations
- Letter of Jeremiah
- Ezekiel
- Daniel (with additions)

## THE PROTESTANT CANON

### OLD TESTAMENT (39 BOOKS)

### NEW TESTAMENT (27 BOOKS)

- Matthew
- Mark
- Luke
- John
- Acts
- Romans
- 1–2 Corinthians
- Galatians
- Ephesians
- Philippians
- Colossians
- 1–2 Thessalonians
- 1–2 Timothy
- Titus
- Philemon
- Hebrews
- James
- 1–2 Peter
- 1–3 John
- Jude
- Revelation

## ROMAN CATHOLICISM

### OLD TESTAMENT (39 BOOKS)

### NEW TESTAMENT (27 BOOKS)

### APOCRYPHA

- Tobit
- Judith
- Additions to Esther
- Wisdom
- Sirach (Ecclesiasticus)
- Baruch
- Epistle of Jeremiah
- Additions to Daniel
- Susanna
- Bel and the Dragon
- The Song of the Three Young Men
- 1–2 Maccabees

## EASTERN ORTHODOXY

### OLD TESTAMENT (39 BOOKS)

### NEW TESTAMENT (27 BOOKS)

### APOCRYPHA

### ADDITIONAL BOOKS

- 1 Esdras
- Prayer of Manasseh
- 3–4 Maccabees
- Psalm 151

BIOGRAPHY

# Athanasius

John 1:1–18 can seem like a logic-defying riddle. The Word was *with* God, and *was* God, then took on *flesh* (became human). To Athanasius, though, the Bible speaks profoundly about life and truth. God used this formidable churchman to affirm and defend fundamental truth about the full deity of the Son and Holy Spirit. He did so based on Scripture, defending the magnificent salvation it proclaims, and pointing us to a life of worshipful response.

Athanasius was born in Alexandria, Egypt, in AD 298. By the time he was 30, he had witnessed extraordinary cultural change. A government-approved persecution against Christians unleashed violence around the Roman Empire during his childhood. In his teenage years, a new emperor, Constantine, embraced Christianity, granting the church toleration and favor. Now Christian leaders had new challenges, like discipling an influx of converts, working with local politicians, and stewarding the church's increasing wealth. Athanasius saw this change firsthand. By the age of 20 he was apprenticed to Alexandria's bishop (pastor and overseer of churches in a city), and soon he became the bishop himself. This was an immense task in one of the Roman Empire's largest, wealthiest, and most diverse cities. He ministered with authority, conviction, and solicitude for the church and its doctrine. This conviction, rooted in scriptural truth, matured in the life of the church, and strengthened by his intense personality, was Athanasius's great legacy.

Before Athanasius became bishop, a priest named Arius began to teach heresy (ideas that reject fundamental, essential biblical truths about God and his salvation) about Christ. Arius proclaimed that the Father alone was God, and Jesus the Son was a great creature *made* by God. Ostensibly concerned with upholding monotheism, Arius made God's nature fit human logic: Jesus was a divine being but not deity (God). The error was recognized by many, including Athanasius, as no trivial matter. The church called together a council in AD 325 in the city of Nicaea (Iznik in modern Turkey) to address these ideas and write a unified response in the form of the Nicene Creed. This statement, composed by 318 bishops, staunchly rejected Arianism and resolutely affirmed the full deity of Jesus, the eternally begotten Son of God: "true God of true God, begotten, not created." Throughout his long ecclesiastical career, Athanasius fought Arianism's reach in churches across the empire. He wrote books, sermons, and letters with compelling arguments against Arius's views. Carefully reading passages like John 1:1–18 and 10:1–18, Matt 28:19, and Phil 2:5–11, Athanasius emphasized the biblical truth: the Son has been fully God throughout eternity, and even though he possessed equality with God (Phil 2:6; Heb 1:3) and was of the same nature as God since he was the only begotten of the Father, he nonetheless took on humanity in humility and love, accepted submission to the Father to live a blameless life, died by crucifixion but defeated death in his resurrection, and offers his victory against sin and death, welcoming us into relationship with him for eternity. Athanasius reminded the church of Christ's command to baptize in the name of the Father, Son, and Holy Spirit—those together must be the one God, or we baptize in idolatry. Athanasius also observed that no human can eternally save another human: only an action of *God* can save from death. Yet only someone fully *human* can actually die to atone for human sin; thus the beautiful scriptural truth that Jesus Christ was fully *both,* and thus was a fitting Savior. "Being the Word of the Father and above all, he alone consequently . . . was worthy to suffer on behalf of all and to intercede for all before the Father." To Athanasius, this truth was worth proclaiming, defending, and carefully preserving. He poured all his energy throughout his entire ministry career into this effort until his death in AD 373.

Mistaken understandings about Christ still exist today. Arianism is present in any view that denies Christ equality with God. Athanasius reminds us that the way we talk about Jesus has significant consequences for salvation. Yet God has not left us merely to our own speculations. He has given the Scriptures that clearly reveal Jesus's identity, and, Athanasius concludes, "We have been given this gift to live life truly," now and for eternity.

## VOICES OF THE CHURCH

"For the Word, perceiving that no otherwise could the corruption of men be undone save by death as a necessary condition, while it was impossible for the Word to suffer death, being immortal, and Son of the Father; to this end He takes to Himself a body capable of death, that it, by partaking of the Word who is above all, might be worthy to die in the stead of all, and might, because of the Word which was come to dwell in it, remain incorruptible, and that thenceforth corruption might be stayed from all by the grace of the resurrection."[2]

ATHANASIUS (295–373)

BIOGRAPHY

# Ephrem the Syrian

Our praise glorifies God but also nourishes our hearts and minds. This conviction led Ephrem to a lifetime of pastoral work in writing hymns that accomplishes this twofold.

Ephrem was born in the Roman province of Syria at the beginning of the AD 300s. His childhood saw great sorrow and many changes. After decades of economic and political chaos, a government-sanctioned oppression of Christianity in the early 300s took countless lives, left survivors with horrific scars, destroyed copies of the Scripture, and confiscated churches. Then, in 312, the new emperor Constantine ended the persecution and enforced religious toleration. He issued reparations to Christians, including new copies of the Bible, massive buildings, and money. Churches quickly grew in number, enjoying the newfound favor, but it also created a different challenge. Many of these new "Christians" did not want to be discipled and had little desire to know God. They retained ideas from paganism and learned the Bible selectively, if at all, interpreting it by their preferences. Terrible misunderstandings, especially about Christ and his work, multiplied. Ephrem understood the grave consequences. If we proclaim a God not informed by scriptural truth but a "God" who fits our own reasoning or desires, we are not in relationship with the one true God. Ephrem's concern led him to action: he knew that congregations learn about God through their songs of worship—praise that brings together spirit and understanding—and began to write hymns.

With content that is compelling and descriptive, these hymns balance biblical truths with heartfelt praise. Most of these hymns summarize biblical content, whether moving through the Gospels from the birth of Christ to his ascension, marveling at God's promises in the Old Testament, or pointing to our hope in Christ's work and return. Many hymns are made for certain seasons yet voice timeless truths. An Easter song echoes, "He saved us by His grace, for He is freely gracious and life-giving." Another combines praise and urges us to be present to the presence of God: "All these things that the Gracious One does in His mercy! May we pay attention to the things He does every day. . . . What is sufficient, compared to Him?" Ephrem was convinced that the words of the church's songs and prayers teach just like sermons; we pray and praise, after all, with the spirit and our mind.

Ephrem continued in his work, writing hundreds of hymns even as the world continued to change. When he was about sixty, his city was overtaken by Persia, and he became a refugee to Macedonia. There he continued to serve for the last decade of his life and established schools to teach the Scriptures, composition, and singing. Ephrem's lifework reminds us that the church's worship is a practical activity central to the life of its people. Individually and in our gatherings, are we praying and praising in a way that is biblically informed, involving both spirit and understanding?

## VOICES OF THE CHURCH

"In the ram that hung in the tree and had become the sacrifice in the place of Abraham's son [Gen 22:13–14], there might be depicted the day of Him who was to hang upon the wood like a ram and was to taste death for the sake of the whole world."[3]

EPHREM THE SYRIAN (CA. 306–373)

BIOGRAPHY

# The Cappadocian Fathers

Basil of Caesarea, Gregory of Nyssa, and Gregory of Nazianzus, known collectively as the Cappadocian Fathers, were instrumental in solidifying Trinitarian orthodoxy in the fourth century. Both their stories and their theological contributions are intertwined.

## A BAND OF BISHOP BROTHERS

Basil (ca. AD 330–79) and Gregory of Nyssa (ca. AD 335/340–394) were brothers. They were reared in a Christian aristocratic family in Cappadocia and were heavily influenced in their Christian faith and practice by their eldest sister, Macrina. While we do not have many details of their early life, it is evident from letters and autobiographical notes that Macrina, at least, was a devoted Christian, perhaps committed to celibacy and some ascetic practice, and she was thus also the spiritual guide for the rest of the family, parents and siblings alike. When Basil returned in 355 from receiving a classical education, first in Constantinople and then in Athens, to teach rhetoric in Caesarea, Macrina told him his studies had produced too much pride in him and he should pursue asceticism as a monk. Macrina's arguments for the ascetic life ultimately won the day when, around 356, Basil met Eusthasius of Sebaste, an ascetic and a bishop. Basil spent the next year or so traveling with Eusthasius seeing how the different versions of monasticism operated throughout the ancient world. He returned in 357, was baptized, and entered into the monastic order.

Basil was joined at that time by his friend Gregory of Nazianzus (ca. AD 330–390), whom he had met during his education and who also had become an ascetic. During the years prior to his appointment as metropolitan bishop of Caesarea in 370, both Basil and Gregory of Nazianzus were engaged in helping Eusthasius combat anti-Nicene writers such as Eunomius and Aetius. Basil's friendship with Eusthasius, his participation in the monastic life (which grew in popularity in the fourth century), and his participation in combating anti-Nicene theology led to his episcopal installation. It did not go unopposed, however, and so Basil quickly enlisted his brother, Gregory, to become bishop of Nyssa, and he also appointed his friend Gregory of Nazianzus to become bishop of Sasima. He subsequently fought for the unity of the church, both ecclesiastically and theologically. Both of these battles were waged against anti-Nicene bishops and theologians, and Basil did not see the unity that was achieved, at least in a conciliar measure, by the Council of Constantinople in 381. He died two years prior on January 1, 379.

Basil's brother, Gregory of Nyssa, did not take as quickly to a Christian vocation. When Basil returned home from his Athenian education, he tutored Gregory in the same style of learning he had just received. Gregory subsequently married, presumably continued to study Greek philosophy, and worked as a rhetorician until he reluctantly agreed to his appointment as bishop of Nyssa by his older brother. Nyssen experienced a significant amount of opposition to his bishopric, as did Basil. It is unclear how vigorously Nyssen held to his office or his theological duties before Basil's death, but after his brother passed, Nyssen came to life theologically speaking. He defended Nicene formulations about the Trinity, he wrote against anti-Nicenes as had his brother, and he defended his brother's theology and integrity. The fifteen years between Basil's death and Nyssen's in 394 thus are the context for most of his theological work.

Gregory Nazianzen also did not take kindly to Basil's appointment of him as a bishop, in his case of Sasima. Nazianzen, one of the few persons in church history to receive the honorific title, "the Theologian," was born into a well-off Christian family in Cappadocia, much like Basil and Nyssen. Unlike them, though, Nazianzen's father was a bishop, one who converted to the Nicene cause on the way to the Council of Nicaea in 325. Gregory was raised, therefore, with the expectation that, as the eldest son, he would follow in his father's ministerial footsteps. After going to Athens in 350/351 for his education (during which time he met and befriended Basil), he continued, reluctantly, to be groomed by his father for ministry until he finally fled to join Basil in the ascetic life at Pontus. He was finally strong-armed into ordination and the ecclesial life when Basil appointed him bishop of Sasima. While he remained friends with Basil until the latter died in 379, their friendship was strained in some sense by Basil's actions.

When Nazianzen arrived in Sasima, he was greeted with hostility and so left the town and his office vacant of his presence. He eventually made his way to Constantinople, where he was ordained as bishop under contentious circumstances. Gregory benefited, however, from Theodosius's position as emperor. As Lionel Wickham puts it, "If Constantine made the empire Christian, Theodosius made it Nicene" ("Introduction," *On God and Christ*). Nazianzen's geographical and theological proximity to the emperor made it easier to for him to write polemics against the anti-Nicenes, and in 381 he served as the president of the Council of Constantinople. This council solidified the Nicene position on the Trinity (one God in three persons; the Father, Son, and Holy Spirit are thus "of the same essence [*homoousios*]") and also produced the Nicene-Constantinopolitan Creed, considered the definitive summary of Trinitarian orthodoxy. Afterward, though, Gregory was ousted from his episcopate and retired to his family's home in Nazianzus.

## TRINITARIAN THEOLOGIANS

The Cappadocians are considered, along with Athanasius and Cyril of Alexandria, to be the great defenders of Trinitarian and Christological orthodoxy in the patristic period. Basil and both Gregorys are situated between Athanasius and Cyril chronologically and theologically. Chronologically speaking, all three were born after the First Council of Nicaea (325) and so entered into ecclesial life in the midst of the aftereffects of that council. Nicaea did not cease opposition to pro-Nicene Trinitarianism; on the contrary, in many ways opposition increased between Nicaea I and Constantinople I. Followers of Arius and Arius's position continued to press a subordinationist view of the Son, as did other subordinationists like Eunomius and Asterius. This opposition was not only theological; it was also ecclesiastical. Differing theological factions competed for episcopal seats and other points of ecclesiastical power, and the various emperors' theological leanings contributed to the political and ecclesial unrest. This is, in part, why all three Cappadocians experienced serious and sustained opposition to their service as bishops.

In the midst of such ecclesial and political turmoil, the Cappadocians produced the most rhetorically articulate, biblically rooted, and philosophically informed arguments for pro-Nicene understandings of the Trinity. They did so both by drawing on and expanding Athanasius's arguments for the full divinity of the Son and also by extending those same arguments to defend the full divinity of the Holy Spirit. While some anti-Nicenes continued to object to Nicaea, many who wanted to ecclesiastically fall in line with the Nicene decision and its implicit support by Constantine shifted their arguments against the full divinity of the Son to a denial of the full divinity of the Holy Spirit. It is here that the Cappadocians direct much of their attention. While Gregory of Nazianzus's most famous work, *The Five Theological Orations*, deals in large part with the full divinity of the Son, he also extends those arguments to the full divinity of the Spirit. This was unusual at the time and a significant contribution to the debate. Likewise, both Basil and Gregory of Nyssa wrote works titled *Against Eunomius*, and in both instances they argue stringently for the full divinity of the Son. But they also importantly extend those arguments to the full divinity of the Holy Spirit. Additionally, both Basil and Gregory of Nyssa produced individual works concerned primarily with the person of the Holy Spirit (*On the Holy Spirit* and *Ad Ablabium* [also called *On Not Three Gods*], respectively). Due in large part to these three theological giants, we owe what we now call Trinitarian orthodoxy—that the one God is one in essence, three in person.

## VOICES OF THE CHURCH

"It is difficult to conceive God but to define Him in words is an impossibility. . . . In my opinion it is impossible to express Him, and yet more impossible to conceive Him."[4]

GREGORY OF NAZIANZUS (329–390)

# The Nicene Creed: A Theological Drama with a Political Setting

The Council of Nicaea did not decide for the first time in the church's history that Jesus Christ, the Son of God, was equally divine with God the Father at the behest of Roman emperor Constantine. Rather, the bishops and church leaders in attendance at the council stated in clear terms what Scripture taught concerning Jesus's divine identity and relationship to the Father in view of how Arius and his followers were abusing biblical language to promote their own teaching that the Son was similar to but less than God.

## THE CAST OF CHARACTERS AT NICAEA

- Constantine, Roman emperor (ca. 280–337)
  - Defeated Maxentius at Battle of Milvian Bridge to unify Roman Empire in AD 312
  - Prior to the battle, interpreted dream of a light phenomenon in the sky resembling the Greek *chi-rho* (☧, the first two letters in the Greek word for Christ) to mean "in this sign you will conquer," leading the emperor to grant Christians and all other men religious freedom in the empire believing that the Christian God aided his conquest
  - Held a political interest more than a theological one in the debate to come that led to his calling for an ecumenical council to take place in 325 at Nicaea, which was likely attended by a little more than two hundred bishops

- Arius, presbyter in Alexandria (ca. 250–336)
  - "There was a time when the Son was not"
  - Denied the full divinity of Christ, the Son, emphasizing the exclusive transcendence and ingenerate nature of God the Father and arguing that the Son was created out of nothing as God's exalted first creature (e.g., "the firstborn over all creation")

- Alexander, bishop of Alexandria (ca. 250?–326)
  - "Always God, always the Son"
  - Refuted Arius's teaching, arguing that if Christ was not truly God, he could neither be the Creator nor the Redeemer of the world
  - Led the initial condemnation of Arius at local council of bishops in 318, a ruling that led to church leaders choosing sides between Alexander and Arius, the latter being condemned

- Athanasius (296–373)
  - Successor to Alexander, becoming bishop of Alexandria in 328, who became the chief defender of the Nicene ruling
  - *Athanasius contra mundum* (Latin "Athanasius against the world"): exiled five times between Nicaea (325) and Constantinople (381) during reigns of Constantine's sons, who were partial to Arianism
  - Among top five most important figures in Christianity
  - Significant contributions:
    - Thirty-Ninth Festal Letter (AD 367): list of 27 writings of the New Testament
    - *Life of St. Antony*
    - *On the Incarnation* (335–36)

BIOGRAPHY

# Ambrose

Ambrose of Milan is remembered as one of the greatest pastors of the early church. Yet he never sought fame: he simply valued the Scripture, his pastoral task, and accountability to the God who had given both.

Ambrose was born in the Roman province of Gaul (now Germany) to a Christian family around AD 339. He was the son of the governor, and his childhood experience included diplomatic visits from major political figures. He entered a respected career in politics and was appointed as the governor of Northern Italy, the province that held the capitol city of Milan, before he was even 30 years old. Within four years, though, Ambrose's skills were needed elsewhere. When the bishop (the leading regional pastor) of Milan died, local congregations declared that Ambrose should be given the position. A bishop's work at that time was relentless: he oversaw every church in a city and its surrounding areas, networked as a diplomat, discipled and led his own congregation, held the leaders of other congregations accountable, and gave multiple sermons weekly. Ambrose's mature spirituality, heart for prayer, and love of the Scripture, along with skills acquired in his political pursuits, made him a unique fit. He was daunted, but it was clear that this was his new vocation.

The ministry that occupied his next several decades saw both joys and challenges. Among these was a pastoral task that nearly cost Ambrose his life: he held the Roman emperor accountable for a response to a series of events that had quickly spiraled out of control. A riot in the Greek city of Thessalonica caused the death of the local governor, several citizens, and soldiers. When the emperor Theodosius received this news in Milan, he reacted severely, instructing a military legion to go kill the rioters on site. Within hours, over seven thousand people were dead, including innocent bystanders. Ambrose received the news with a heavy heart. He led the church Theodosius attended. He guided the emperor, as a member of that congregation, in song, teaching, and communion, and now Ambrose knew that this shepherding had to continue with integrity. He wrote the emperor a letter, denouncing the slaughter and reminding Theodosius that he was a Christian first, accountable to God. The letter insisted that Theodosius repent by sincerely seeking God's forgiveness as well as personal accountability, if he was to continue to be allowed to participate in the church. "I *must* admonish you," Ambrose wrote, "for it is grief to me that the death of so many innocents is no grief to you." Invoking the biblical example of Nathan and David, as well as Hebrews 13:17 and Ezekiel 33:7–11, he asked, "Am I to be silent? That would be miserable, because then my conscience would be bound. . . . My authority to speak would be abolished." Ambrose's burden is clear: he was aware that a pastor's role involves holding the congregation accountable—even when a member is the emperor. Humbled, Theodosius accepted the rebuke.

Ambrose continued in ministry until his death in 397. In this and several other instances, he stood firm in obedience to the God who had given him his leadership role. Ambrose reminds us that Christians are responsible to one another and accountable to our God. Will we bravely, wisely, and humbly live in this?

## VOICES OF THE CHURCH

"The Lord said, 'I am who I am.' You will say, 'He who is sent me.' This is the true name of God: always to exist."[5]

AMBROSE (CA. 339–397)

BIOGRAPHY

# John Chrysostom

From the time that he was young, John was a gifted speaker. He was given the title "Chrysostom" ("golden-mouthed") as an honor to his compelling sermons and ability to bring the Scriptures to life. Yet he likely would have denied that the skill of speech was actually his own. Above all else, John Chrysostom was convinced that "the earth and everything in it . . . belong to the LORD" (Ps. 24:1) truly means *everything.*

Born around AD 345, John was raised by his widowed Christian mother in Antioch, a political and commercial center in the Roman province of Syria. He received an excellent education; yet, a prosperous career never appealed to him. Even as a young man, John loved the church. He was spiritually mentored, baptized, and joined a group of Christians who lived together in service, simplicity, chastity, prayer, and accountability. He spent almost two decades this way, eventually becoming ordained as a presbyter (a teaching pastor). John's virtuous character and preaching became well-known, and he led the congregations of Antioch in active ministry, building and maintaining hostels for travelers, hospitals for the ill, and support systems for poor widows and their families. Then, at nearly fifty years old, he was called to a new challenge: he was made the archbishop of Constantinople.

As the capitol of the Eastern Roman Empire, Constantinople was a difficult city for ministry. It was a new metropolis and center for prestige, and its citizens were starkly divided between an upper class that enjoyed tremendous luxury and impoverished masses who lived in shack-like apartments, daily in danger of starvation. Many were homeless due to disability, disease, or mental illness. From cathedrals to alleyways, John ministered with conviction. He diverted his own housing money to fund hospitals and construct community shelters for lepers, labored to stop corruption in local church leadership, and preached zealous sermons with his "golden mouth." Here, his vivid portrayals of both wealth and poverty reveal his familiarity with the everyday struggles of both groups; here, too, John voiced his famous critiques of selfishness and consumerism. If we think he was simply a utopian advocate of social equality, though, we miss the point: John wanted all Christians to consider whether they took seriously God's ownership. His sermons challenged listeners: "Is not 'the earth the Lord's, and *everything* in it?' Then our possessions—and our very selves!—belong to the Lord. We are fellow-servants and stewards." This truth was applicable to the rich and the poor, and it challenged them to see one another differently. John's message motivated many to active hospitality, sharing instead of hoarding, and trust instead of fear. John's passion and high moral standards earned great trust among many but offended others, particularly the emperor and empress in Constantinople. About seven years into his ministry, he was exiled to the barren shores of the Black Sea. Within five years, the aged preacher was dead.

Centuries later, John Chrysostom's words remind us of our position as committed stewards in community, based on the ultimate conviction that all things truly do belong to the Lord. When we trust this truth, how do our own lives change?

## VOICES OF THE CHURCH

"Nothing is more characteristic of a Christian than mercy. There is nothing that unbelievers and all people are so amazed at as when we are merciful. For we ourselves are often in need of this mercy."[6]

JOHN CHRYSOSTOM (CA. 345–407)

BIOGRAPHY

# Jerome

The Bible is the most translated book in the world as well as the first book known to be translated into another language, when the Hebrew Scriptures were translated into Greek about the third century BC in Egypt. Another important translation of the Bible was made in the fourth century AD by the Latin linguist Jerome (AD 342/347–420).

Jerome was a classical scholar and ascetic who became a Christian around 366. He traveled widely through the Roman Empire and studied Latin literature and rhetoric at Rome. After 372, he traveled east to Syria where he studied Greek and Hebrew. In 381 he traveled to Turkey for the great Council of Constantinople, where the Nicene Creed was reaffirmed and finalized. In 382, Jerome became secretary to Pope Damasus in Rome, where he made the acquaintance of a community of scholarly minded Christian women who consulted him for answers to their many scriptural questions.

Latin was the official language of imperial Rome, and early translations of the Bible had been made into "Old" Latin. When Damasus asked Jerome to make a revision of the Latin translation of the Gospels, Jerome not only translated the Gospels from the Greek but went on to translate other portions of the New Testament and the Hebrew Scriptures. Jerome also wrote prologues to many of the books which served as introductions and commentary on them. He spent almost three decades working on his translation, begun in Rome and completed after he moved to Bethlehem. In addition to producing this updated Latin version of the Bible, Jerome translated several works he obtained from a library collection at Caesarea Maritima where the bishop of the city, Eusebius of Caesarea, had curated an important Christian library. Jerome translated into Latin Eusebius's *Church History* (which covered the church's first 300 years), the *Chronicon* (a massive set of overlapping time lines of various kingdoms throughout biblical history), and an atlas of places in the Holy Land called *Onomasticon*.

Several of the women he befriended were helpful in encouraging and supporting Jerome's work. Marcella, a wealthy Roman widow, was an avid student of the Scriptures who learned much from Jerome's teaching. She held Bible studies in her home and even hired scribes to copy the Scriptures. Her home became a place where people could obtain copies of the Scriptures. Paula, another wealthy Roman widow, came to faith in Christ through Marcella's ministry and became a financial supporter of Jerome, his ministry, and his translation work. She helped find biblical manuscripts for Jerome and, knowledgeable in Hebrew and Greek, edited his translation work. She and her daughter Eustochium went with Jerome to the Holy Land and established monasteries in Bethlehem where copying the Scriptures was important work.

Jerome's translation of the Bible into Latin from the Hebrew and Greek became known as the *Vulgate*, or translation "for the people." Jerome's *Vulgate* was the Bible translation used throughout Europe for a millennium. In a letter to a Christian bishop, Jerome encouragingly wrote, "Make knowledge of the Scriptures your love. . . . Live with them, meditate on them, make them the sole object of your knowledge and inquiries."

BIOGRAPHY

# Monica

Decade after decade, it could have seemed to Monica that her prayers went nowhere. She was married to an unbeliever whose temper made homelife difficult at best. Together, they had three children, at least one of whom lived his first thirty years in selfish ambition, pleasure-seeking, and restlessness. Yet Monica's continued prayers, voiced with faithful conviction that her tears were seen and that the grace of God would prevail, show a resolute patience that can inspire us still today.

Just before her death, both her husband and her wayward son came to Christ. That son would, in fact, become one of Christianity's greatest pastor-authors, contributing immensely to the way Christians speak about grace, God, faith, work, and desire—in sum, everything voiced in the prayer of 2 Thessalonians 1:11–12. His name was Augustine, and he never forgot his mother's constant prayers and example of patient faithfulness.

Monica was born in AD 332 in a prosperous Roman province on the north coast of Africa (in present-day Algeria). She was a Berber, of ancient Arabic descent, and while she was raised in a somewhat Christian family, her faith seemed to have matured more in her adult years. She knew the power of God's grace: she struggled with alcohol addiction in her younger years, experienced a difficult relationship with her mother-in-law, often had overly high ambitions for her children, and was in a marriage that created more sorrow than joy. Yet Monica was also a patient and careful listener, a faithful and generous participant in her church, and continually matured in the Lord. She was also constantly in prayer, especially for her husband and children with words that echoed Paul's words in 2 Thessalonians 1:11–12. From this prayer, we see her certainty that God has a calling for his children, that only the Savior can transform and fulfill both our desires and our work, and that by God's grace the name of Jesus is glorified in our lives. Her wayward son Augustine was especially the focus of her prayers, as well as the cause of her tears.

In the final years of her life, before an unexpected illness and early death in 387, she was able to see God's work begin to unfold: Augustine turned his heart to God. Monica did not write anything that survives, nor was she able to witness her son's long years in active ministry. Her life as a wife and mother was not public or glamorous, much less simple or "happy." Yet her patience and prayers anchored her to a God whose faithfulness does not fail. On Monica's stone epitaph, which survives to this day, we find these words by her son: "You taught the people entrusted to you with your character." May we, with Monica, have lives that echo Paul's words: expecting and inviting God's unfolding work in us and in those around us, "we always pray."

BIOGRAPHY

# Augustine

"When I turned away from You, God, and pursued a multitude of things, I fell to pieces." Those words were penned over 1,600 years ago in a book titled simply *Confessions*. The author, Augustine, wrote prolifically over his long life (AD 354–430). Yet whether in prayers or theological volumes, sermons or personal letters, a consistent theme is evident, drawn from Augustine's own experience: only the peace of God can heal our heart's restlessness.

Augustine grew up in the lush cosmopolitan Roman province of North Africa. He died in 430, which places his life precisely in the early stages of the long crumbling of the Roman Empire. Yet the most dominant aspect of his social landscape was cultural tension between Christianity and established Roman paganism. Widespread cultural friction points, frequent economic crises and financial panic, and troubles on the Roman borders unfolded in a society that still valued public self-promotion, impatient self-absorption, and relativistic pragmatism.

Augustine grew up with a Christian mother (Monica) and a non-Christian father (Patricius). Augustine made every effort to satisfy his heart's ache for fulfillment, spending the first three decades of his life chasing academic achievement in rhetoric, intellectual friendships, sex with a local girl with whom he fathered a child, adrenaline thrills with a gang of boys, adventures abroad, career success, and service in civil life. By the time he was 31, he had achieved a lucrative, well-connected career in the capital city of Milan. In the midst of success, he was further than ever from both himself and the peace he longed for, crying out to God, "Where could my heart flee to escape itself?" He styled himself a seeker of truth and grasped after a satisfying religious experience by involving himself in an esoteric cult group called Manicheeism, a religion derived from Zoroastrianism and Gnosticism.

However, over the next three years a transformation began to unfold. From the words of a child's song, to the wisdom of Milan's great bishop Ambrose, to conversations with a friend and with his own mother, a series of events moved him through nothing less than a process of conversion. In retrospect, Augustine wrote, "Lord, You turn us back to Yourself in wondrous ways." He was discipled, turned his life to Christ, baptized, and left his career, spending the second half of his life as a bishop, overseeing churches and a monastery in Hippo (Annaba, Algeria), back in his homeland of North Africa. However, this new lifestyle was not one of repose.

In addition to the *Confessions*, he wrote books confronting the erroneous doctrines of the Manichees, books on the Trinity, political theology (*City of God*), Christian formation (*Enchiridion* or *Handbook on Faith, Hope and Love*), and left a multitude of letters. Life was also not easier: from the death of his teenage son, best friend, and mother within a short span of time, to empire-wide horror at a Visigothic attack on the city of Rome in 410, to a heartbreaking division in the churches of North Africa, Augustine's life and ministry consistently experienced sorrows and challenges. Yet in relationship with God, he had found the source of true peace, and with it the hope, rest, and connection in all things. In Augustine's life and words, "You made us for Yourself, O Lord, and our hearts are restless until they find their rest in You." Augustine found that Christ's promise, "I will give you rest" (Matt 11:28), is entirely true; in him is the peace that heals, the peace that gives us rest.

## VOICES OF THE CHURCH

"Give what you command and command what you will."[7]

AUGUSTINE (354–430)

BIOGRAPHY

# Patrick of Ireland

Patrick's name might be on calendars every March, but many of the celebrations associated with St. Patrick's Day have little do to with the actual person who lived over 1,500 years ago. Patrick passionately sought God, loved the lost with deep concern for their salvation, and often spoke of the ways God had been faithful to his promise, "I will set you free." Patrick's zeal can inspire and convict us still today.

Patrick was born in England to a Christian family around AD 390. During his youth, the powerful Roman Empire was crumbling, and Roman military forces withdrew their protection and investments in his homeland. In larger cities, many Romans who flourished in England for centuries, like Patrick's family, remained. Sixteen-year-old Patrick had not yet committed his life to Christ when Irish raiders pillaged his city. Overnight, Patrick found himself on a ship to Ireland, where he was sold into slavery and lived for the next six years as a lonely shepherd on rainy, windswept hills in a country that knew nothing of Christianity.

There he turned to God in prayer. In a later reflection titled simply "Confession," he wrote: "This I know for certain, that even before I was brought low [in slavery], I was like a stone lying deep in the mud." To Patrick, life without Christ was a kind of slavery far worse than captivity in Ireland. "Then He who is powerful came, and in His mercy drew me up . . . and I will shout aloud in response to the Lord for such great good deeds of His, here and now and forever." God met Patrick in his desolation. Years later, God also provided a new path. In a miraculous rapid unfolding of events, Patrick escaped on a merchant ship to England and returned to his hometown.

Once home, Patrick recovered, was discipled, and received biblical instruction. But now he had a new burden, writing, "God said: 'Call on Me in the day of your distress, and I will set you free, and you will glorify Me' [Ps. 50:15]. . . . He guarded me before I knew Him! . . . I cannot be silent . . . when our lives change and we come to know God, we must praise and bear witness to His great wonders before every nation under heaven." This burden compelled him to take the gospel to the very people who had taken him captive. Patrick returned to Ireland and ministered there for over 20 years, until his death around 460. It was not easy. "I expect murder, fraud, or captivity daily," he wrote, yet "I fear none of these things because of the promises of God. I have cast myself into the hands of God Almighty, who rules everywhere." Patrick's writings and story, passionate gratitude, trust in God, and concern for the lost, even those who had enslaved him, inspire believers still.

BIOGRAPHY

# Cyril of Alexandria

Cyril of Alexandria (died AD 444), the noted bishop of Alexandria (412–444), played a pivotal role in the life of the early church at the time of the Nestorian controversy. Though a brilliant thinker and prolific writer, Cyril's most enduring theological contribution was in Christology, particularly expressed in his opposition to Nestorianism.

Political factors notwithstanding, deep Christological distinctions existed between Cyril and Nestorius, who was appointed bishop of Constantinople in 428. Their Alexandrian and Antiochene conceptions of Christology came to a head when Nestorius rejected the term *theotokos* (God bearer) as an appropriate term for Mary, the mother of Jesus. For Cyril and his predecessors, the term *theotokos* was used as a way of affirming the deity of Christ and the union of divine and human natures in the personal subject of the incarnation, God the Son (see, e.g., Cyril, *The Fourth Letter of Cyril to Nestorius,* in NPNF2, 14:198).

Whereas Cyril proposed a personal union of the divine and human natures in Christ, Nestorius preferred the term *Christotokos* (Christ bearer), proposing a more composite union of two personal subjects, divine and human. This left him open to the charge of affirming two persons in Christ, thus undermining the personal union of natures, and thereby Christ's capacity to save sinners (see, Cyril, *The Third Letter of Cyril to Nestorius,* in NPNF2, 14:202).

Nestorius argued that Cyril's Christology was Apollinarian, thus undermining Christ's full humanity. Whereas terminological clarity was later established at the Council of Chalcedon (451), it was Cyril's Christology—manifestly not Apollinarian—that paved the way for Chalcedon's definition. Indeed, in repudiating the specific charge of Apollinarianism, Cyril explained his terminology that anticipated Chalcedoninan clarity, including an affirmation of two natures in Christ.

Cyril was so committed to both the single subjectivity of the Word of God and the full humanity of Jesus he affirmed that Christ "suffered impassibly." Nestorius charged that Cyril's view must lead to an acceptance of the passibility of the divine nature. Whereas Nestorius's concern to avoid attributing passibility to the divine nature led him to dissolve the union of divine and human natures and attribute suffering only to Christ's human nature, Cyril more accurately grasped that the personal subject of the incarnation is God the Son, who appropriated human nature.

This conviction allowed Cyril to maintain that due to the Son's appropriation of humanity the person of the Son performed all his actions and experienced all his experiences humanly. In this sense, the Son's appropriated humanity became the instrument through which God the Son suffered and died, thus resolving Cyril's seeming paradox of Christ's impassible suffering.

Given his view of the personal union and duality of natures in the incarnation, Cyril denied the Word's experience of *divine* suffering, while fully allowing his experience of *human* suffering. Cyril maintained the urgency of upholding the vital unity of Christ before addressing the effect of his incarnate experiences upon his respective natures.

Though it was embroiled in ecclesiastical politics, Cyril secured the condemnation and exile of Nestorius at the Council of Ephesus in 431. The Formula of Union (433) began to resolve some the tensions between the two positions, ultimately laying the groundwork for the authoritative Christological creed of Chalcedon in 451.

## VOICES OF THE CHURCH

"He became like us that we might become like him. The work of the Spirit seeks to transform us by grace into a perfect copy of his humbling."[8]

CYRIL OF ALEXANDRIA (CA. 375–444)

# Reaffirming the Creed at Constantinople: A Tale of Two Emperors and Three Theologians

Following Constantine's death, the whole world "groaned and marveled to find itself Arian." As a result of subsequent emperors coming to favor the semi-Arian position, orthodox leaders in the church had to contend for the teaching affirmed at the Council of Nicaea in 325, which stated that Jesus, the Son of God, was "of one substance with the Father." Emperor Theodosius I thus called for the Council of Constantinople in 381 to help the church definitively dispel Arianism as a valid option. In addition, the council expanded the Nicene Creed to address the Holy Spirit's status and relationship to the Father and the Son along with dealing with Apollinaris's teaching that the divine Logos assumed the place of Jesus's human mind.

## THE CAST OF CHARACTERS AT CONSTANTINOPLE

**Julian the Apostate, Roman Emperor (reigned 361–363)**

- Successor to Constantius II, who was one of Constantine's three sons who had reigned over a united empire and who also favored Arianism over Nicene teaching
- Denounced Christianity, the faith of his upbringing, in favor of traditional Roman paganism through promotion of sacrifices and classical literature
- Succeeded by a series of rulers who favored Arianism as the empire became divided between East and West again

**Theodosius I, Roman Emperor (reigned 379–395)**

- Took office in 378 as ruler over the East of the empire after being a chief military officer and then became sole emperor in 384, known to be a committed Christian
- Affirmed views of Athanasius against Arianism, installing a Nicene-affirming bishop at the church of Constantinople, which had been occupied by a Homoean (semi-Arian) leadership for previous 40 years
- Called for an ecumenical council to take place at Constantinople in 381, which reaffirmed and amended the Creed of Nicaea

**Cappadocian Fathers (continued Athanasius's legacy)**

- Basil of Caesarea (329–379): known for his treatise, *On the Holy Spirit*, where he defended the deity of the Holy Spirit, pointing out that if he was not fully God, then there was no reason to baptize in the name of the Father, the Son, and the Spirit
- Gregory of Nyssa (335–395): wrote the treatises *That We Should Not Think of Saying There Are Three Gods* and *Against Eunomius*, which helped in developing the church's precise language for confessing a monotheism that affirmed three divine persons (e.g., *ousia*, "substance/essence"; *hypostasis*, "person")
- Gregory of Nazianzus (329–390): presided over the Council of Constantinople in 381, known for his *Theological Orations* and many other letters, lectures, and even poems, which contributed to the church's legacy of contemplating God's being, his triune nature, and the best practices for speaking about God

**Two other pressing theological issues addressed at Constantinople**

- Status of the Holy Spirit (in relation to the Father and Son)
- Applied language of "proceeding" to the Holy Spirit
- Affirmed the worship of the Spirit and referred to him as "the Lord and giver of life"
- Apollinarianism: ruled to be heresy, this teaching denied Christ's full humanity by teaching that the Logos functioned in place of a human mind rather than affirming both a human mind and a divine mind

# "Begotten, Not Made": The Emergence of Trinitarian Orthodoxy

The goal of doctrine is to summarize and synthesize biblical teaching so that we might know God and worship him most faithfully and truthfully. We see this principle perhaps most demonstrably in the development of the doctrine of the Trinity, the teaching that the one true God exists in three coeternal persons—Father, Son, and Holy Spirit. While the terminology used to present the Trinity may take us beyond explicit statements in Scripture, this does not make the doctrine any less biblical. Rather, the language the church developed to speak of God's oneness and threeness was a purposeful measure to explain the meaning of the Bible's wider teaching in contrast to false teaching, which often appealed to particular passages in a superficial and surface-level manner.

| | MODALISM (Sabellianism) | ARIANISM (heteroousios or homoiousios) | NICENE Orthodoxy (homoousios) | HOMOIANISM (homoiousios) |
|---|---|---|---|---|
| MONOTHEISM | Yes | Yes | Yes | Yes |
| COETERNAL AND COEQUAL PERSONS | No | No | Yes | No |
| THE SON AS SUBORDINATE IN BEING | No | Yes | No | Yes |

## DEFINITIONS AND DISTINCTIONS: CRITICAL TERMS OF NICENE ORTHODOXY

- Greek *ousia* / Latin *substantia*: the substance of something, what makes it what it is; interchangeable with the terms such as being, essence, and nature; this term refers to God's oneness
- Greek *hypostasis* and *prosopon* / Latin *persona*: translated as "person" but does not refer to the modern sense of a separate self-conscious individual but instead to a unique subsistence of the one divine nature that exists distinctly yet inseparably in relation with the other divine persons; this term refers to God's threeness

## AN IOTA AWAY FROM IDOLATRY: DIFFERENT, SIMILAR, OR THE SAME SUBSTANCE?

- **Modalism (Sabellianism):** one person in three successive modes
    - A heresy preceding the Nicene Council that taught God the Father is a single person who appeared in the historical modes of Son and Holy Spirit
    - Denial of the coeternal persons; emphasis on Father's supremacy
- **Arianism:** *heteroousios* ("different substance") or *homoiousios* ("similar substance")
    - A heresy arguing that the Son's substance is lesser by being "different" from or "similar" to the Father's, the Son being created by the Father's will, not eternally begotten by nature
    - Denial of coeternality and coequality of persons; affirmation of the Son's subordination in being
- **Nicene orthodoxy:** *homoousios*, "same substance"
    - Position that became orthodoxy, teaching that the Son's substance is equal with the Father's substance, the Son being eternally begotten from the Father and the two distinct according to their personhood
    - Affirmation of the coeternality and coequality of the persons; denial of the Son's subordination in being
- **A middle position:** Homoianism (*homoiousios*, "similar substance")
    - False teaching that emerged as a third option or middle position, seeking to find unity in doctrine by posing that the Father and Son were of "similar substance" as opposed to being either a different substance or the same substance
    - Denial of the coeternality and coequality of the persons in unwillingness to affirm the Son as being of the same substance for sake of ambiguity over the essence

# The Niceno-Constantinopolitan Creed (AD 381 version)

We believe in one God, the Father, the Almighty, maker of heaven and earth, and of all that is, seen and unseen.

We believe in one Lord, Jesus Christ, the only Son of God, eternally begotten of the Father, [God from God], Light from Light, true God from true God, begotten, not made, of one substance [Greek, *homoousion*] with the Father. Through him all things were made. For us men and for our salvation he came down from heaven: by the power of the Holy Spirit he became incarnate from the Virgin Mary, and was made man. For our sake he was crucified under Pontius Pilate; he suffered and was buried. On the third day he rose again in accordance with the Scriptures; he ascended into heaven and is seated at the right hand of the Father. He will come again in glory to judge the living and the dead, and his kingdom will have no end.

We believe in the Holy Spirit, the Lord, the giver of life, who proceeds from the Father [*and the Son*]. With the Father and the Son he is worshipped and glorified. He has spoken through the Prophets. We believe in one holy catholic and apostolic Church. We acknowledge one baptism for the forgiveness of sins. We look for the resurrection of the dead, and the life of the world to come. Amen.

# Augustine, Pelagianism, and Semi-Pelagianism

*"Give me the grace to do as you command, and command me to do what you will."*

**–AUGUSTINE (*CONFESSIONS* 10.29)**

| | PELAGIANISM | SEMI-PELAGIANISM | AUGUSTINE |
|---|---|---|---|
| THE FALL | Humanity's will unimpaired | Humanity's will partially impaired | Humanity's will radically impaired |
| GRACE | Unnecessary | Necessary but insufficient | Necessary and sufficient |

- Pelagius (British monk, ca. AD 354–418)
  - Alarmed by moral laxity among Christians in Rome
  - Believed humanity is capable of obeying God's commands apart from God's grace
  - Rejected of original sin (i.e., each person is a new Adam)
  - Believed perfection is possible

- Council of Carthage (AD 418)
  - Condemned Pelagian positions as heresy (i.e., anathema)

- Synod of Orange (AD 529)
  - Denounced Semi-Pelagianism in favor of belief in total corruption of man's being and abilities
  - Affirmed complete dependency on grace to initiate faith and good works

# Biblical Foundations for the Chalcedonian Definition[9]

## KEY PASSAGES FOR THE DEITY OF CHRIST

Mark 1:2–3; 14:61–64;
John 1:1–3,14,18; 5:18;
8:57–59; 20:28

1 Corinthians 8:6 (cf. Deut 6:4);
Colossians 1:15–20; Hebrews 1:3,8,10;
Titus 2:13; 2 Peter 1:1

## KEY PASSAGES FOR THE HUMANITY OF CHRIST

**MATTHEW 1:1–17; LUKE 3:23–38**
The Gospels' genealogies denote Jesus's human ancestry and birth.

**LUKE 2:40,52**
"The boy grew up and became strong, filled with wisdom, and God's grace was on him. . . . And Jesus increased in wisdom and stature, and in favor with God and with people."

**MATTHEW 4:2**
"After he had fasted forty days and forty nights, he was hungry."

**JOHN 19:28**
"After this, when Jesus knew that everything was now finished that the Scripture might be fulfilled, he said, 'I'm thirsty.'"

**JOHN 4:6**
"Jacob's well was there, and Jesus, worn out from his journey, sat down at the well. It was about noon."

**LUKE 23:46**
"And Jesus called out with a loud voice, 'Father, into your hands I entrust my spirit.' Saying this, he breathed his last."

**HEBREWS 2:17**
"Therefore, he had to be like his brothers and sisters in every way, so that he could become a merciful and faithful high priest in matters pertaining to God, to make atonement, for the sins of the people."

## KEY TEXTS FOR A TWO-NATURE CHRISTOLOGY

### LUKE 1:31–32

"Now listen: You will conceive and give birth to a son, and you will name him Jesus. He will be great and will be called the Son of the Most High, and the Lord God will give him the throne of his father David."

### PHILIPPIANS 2:6–7

". . . who, existing in the form of God, did not consider equality with God as something to be exploited. Instead he emptied himself by assuming the form of a servant, taking on the likeness of humanity."

### COLOSSIANS 1:19; 2:9

"For God was pleased to have all his fullness dwell in him. . . . For the entire fullness of God's nature dwells bodily in Christ."

### MARK 13:31–32

"Heaven and earth will pass away, but my words will never pass away. Now concerning that day or hour no one knows—neither the angels in heaven nor the Son—but only the Father."

### 1 CORINTHIANS 2:8

"None of the rulers of this age knew this wisdom, because if they had known it, they would not have crucified the Lord of glory."

# "Truly God and Truly Man": Defining the Mystery of the Incarnation at Chalcedon

As the church of the fourth and fifth centuries debated about the most biblically faithful ways to speak about Jesus, the Council of Chalcedon produced the statement on the doctrine of Christ that became the standard of orthodoxy for the three primary branches of Christianity: Roman Catholicism, Eastern Orthodoxy, and Protestantism.

## THE CHRISTOLOGICAL AFFIRMATIONS OF THE ECUMENICAL COUNCILS

**FIRST COUNCIL: NICEA (AD 325)**
Condemned *Arianism*.
Soteriological axion: "God alone can save us."

**THIRD COUNCIL: EPHESUS (AD 431)**
Condemned *Nestorianism*.
Specified the one person of Christ.

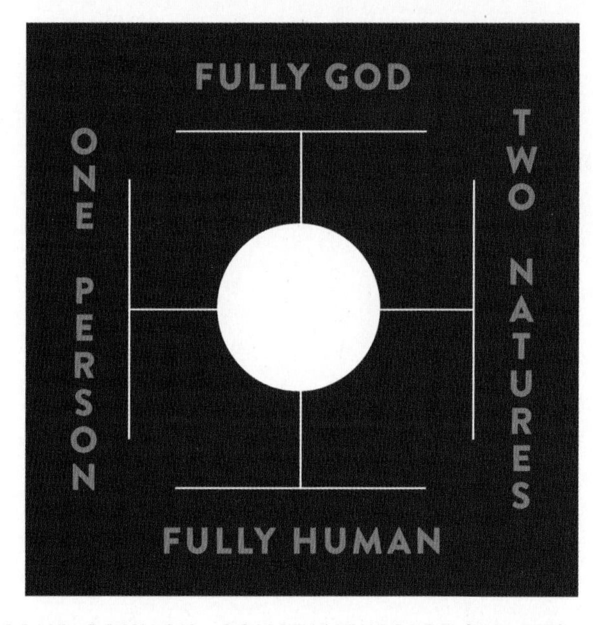


**FOURTH COUNCIL: CHALCEDON (AD 451)**
Condemned *Eutychianism*.
Maintained the two natures without confusion or change, separation or division.

**SECOND COUNCIL: CONSTANTINOLPE (AD 381)**
Reaffirmed Nicaea, condemned *Apollinarianism*.
Soteriological axiom: "That which is not assumed is not healed."

## THE CONTEXT: REHEARSING THE HERESIES

- The Council of Nicaea (AD 325)
  - Condemned Arianism, which denied the full deity of Christ
  - Axiom concerning salvation: "God alone can save us."
    - The Council of Constantinople (AD 381)
    - Condemned semi-Arianism (or homoianism), which denied the full deity of Christ
    - Condemned Apollinarianism, which denied the full humanity of Christ
- Apollinarianism: The divine *Logos* (second divine person) functions as Jesus's mind, so instead of possessing a human mind, his mind is divine.
  - Axiom concerning salvation: "That which is not assumed is not healed."

## THE CONTROVERSY: SHOULD WE REFER TO MARY AS "MOTHER OF GOD"?

- Nestorius, bishop of Constantinople (ca. 381–451)
  - Influenced by Theodore of Mopsuestia, who was from the Antioch area like Nestorius
  - Opposed the title "God bearer" (Greek *theotokos*) for Mary
  - Preferred the title "Christ bearer" (Greek *Christotokos*)
- Cyril, bishop of Alexandria (ca. 375–444)
  - The abiding differences between Antioch and Alexandria, two of the early apostolic cities, seem to have factored into Cyril's disfavor toward Nestorius, who had been appointed bishop of Constantinople, a new influential city in Christianity
  - Despite this, the primary motivation seems to have been theological more than political with Cyril taking exception to Nestorius's formulation that suggested God was united to *a* man rather than God becoming man by acquiring an additional nature that is human
- The Council of Ephesus (AD 431)
  - Eventually Nestorius lost the will to defend his position, and Cyril's position persuaded the parties involved
  - The council condemned Nestorianism for its denial of the unity of the two natures existent in one person: "Not as parted or separated into two persons, but one and the same Son and Only-begotten God the Word, Lord Jesus Christ."

## THE CONSENSUS: ONE PERSON WITH TWO NATURES

- The Council of Chalcedon (AD 451)
  - Condemned Eutychianism, which denied distinction of natures, positing that the human nature absorbed into the divine
    - Monophysitism: the concept of Eutychianism wherein a new kind of substance results from the incarnation (i.e., *tertium quid* = "a third thing")
    - The two natures combined to bring about a new nature in Christ, which would mean Christ is not "truly God and truly man" but something else
  - Promoted the concept of hypostatic union, a mysterious personal uniting of the divine nature and the human nature (e.g., one person with two natures "without confusion, without change, without division, without separation")

## THE TAKEAWAY: HOW SHOULD WE TALK ABOUT JESUS?

1. Jesus is fully God (eternally begotten Son of the Father).
2. Jesus is fully human (supernaturally conceived in and historically born of Mary).
3. Jesus is one person (e.g., Jesus *is*, not Jesus *are*).
4. Jesus possesses two distinct natures (i.e., he is the God-man).
5. Without being fully God, he could not save us.
6. Without being fully man, he could not represent us and redeem us.

# The Chalcedonian Definition

Therefore, following the holy fathers, we all with one accord teach men to acknowledge one and the same Son, our Lord Jesus Christ, at once complete in Godhead and complete in manhood, truly God and truly man, consisting also of a reasonable soul and body; of one substance with the Father as regards his Godhead, and at the same time of one substance with us as regards his manhood; like us in all respects, apart from sin; as regards his Godhead, begotten of the Father before the ages, but yet as regards his manhood begotten, for us men and for our salvation, of Mary the Virgin, the God-bearer [Greek *theotokos*]; one and the same Christ, Son, Lord, Only-begotten, recognized in two natures, without confusion, without change, without division, without separation; the distinction of natures being in no way annulled by the union, but rather the characteristics of each nature being preserved and coming together to form one person and subsistence, not as parted or separated into two persons, but one and the same Son and Only-begotten God the Word, Lord Jesus Christ; even as the prophets from earliest times spoke of him, and our Lord Jesus Christ himself taught us, and the creed of the fathers has handed down to us.

# The First Four Ecumenical Councils of the Church

BLACK SEA

Constantinople

Chalcedon

Nicaea

Ephesus

MEDITERRANEAN SEA

**FIRST COUNCIL OF NICAEA (AD 325)**
This council condemned Arianism and affirmed the full deity of Christ.

**FIRST COUNCIL OF CONSTANTINOPLE (AD 381)**
This council condemned Apollinarianism and reaffirmed the First Council of Nicaea.

**COUNCIL OF EPHESUS (AD 431)**
The council condemned Nestorianism and specified the one person of Christ.

**COUNCIL OF CHALCEDON (AD 451)**
This council condemned Eutychianism and maintained Christ has two natures without confusion or change, separation or division.

# Trinitarian Truths: Three Basic Axioms from Scripture[10]

1. **There is only one Creator God (i.e., biblical monotheism).**
   - ***Deuteronomy 6:4:*** "Listen, Israel: The LORD our God, the LORD is one."
   - ***Isaiah 43:10–11:*** "'You are my witnesses'—this is the LORD's declaration—'and my servant whom I have chosen, so that you may know and believe me and understand that I am he. No god was formed before me, and there will be none after me. I—I am the LORD. Besides me, there is no Savior.'"
   - See also *Jeremiah 10:10–12; John 17:3; 1 Timothy 2:5; James 2:19*

2. **There are three divine persons: Father, Son, and Holy Spirit.**
   - ***Matthew 3:16–17:*** "When Jesus was baptized, he went up immediately from the water. The heavens suddenly opened for him, and he saw the Spirit of God descending like a dove and coming down on him. And a voice from heaven said, 'This is my beloved Son, with whom I am well-pleased.'"
   - ***Matthew 11:27:*** "All things have been entrusted to me by my Father. No one knows the Son except the Father, and no one knows the Father except the Son and anyone to whom the Son desires to reveal him."
   - ***1 Corinthians 2:10–11:*** "Now God has revealed these things to us by the Spirit, since the Spirit searches everything, even the depths of God. For who knows a person's thoughts except his spirit within him? In the same way, no one knows the thoughts of God except the Spirit of God."
   - See also *Matthew 28:19; John 1:18; 14:13–17; 17:5,23–24; Acts 5:3–5; 1 Cor 12:11; 2 Cor 13:13* (CSB); *1 John 5:20*
   - Each of the persons is distinguished by their relation to the others:
     - The Father is "unbegotten" as the one who eternally begets the Son (*Ps 2:7; John 3:16; Acts 13:33; Heb 1:5; 5:5*).
     - The Son is "eternally begotten of the Father" (*John 1:18; 5:18–19,26; Col 1:15; Heb 1:3*).
     - The Spirit is the one who "proceeds from the Father [and the Son*]" (*John 14:26; 15:26; 16:7*).

* The phrase "and the Son," which is known as the *filioque* clause, was added to the Nicene Creed at the Third Council of Toledo in 589, a decision that created further tension between churches in the East and the West at the time and continues to exist as a source of disagreement.

3. **The three persons are coequal and coeternal.**
   - ***1 Corinthians 8:4–6 (cf. Deut 6:4):*** "'There is no God but one.' For even if there are so-called gods, whether in heaven or on earth—as there are many 'gods' and many 'lords'—yet for us there is one God, the Father. All things are from him, and we exist for him. And there is one Lord, Jesus Christ. All things are through him, and we exist through him."
   - ***Acts 28:25–27 (cf. Isa 6:8–10):*** "The Holy Spirit was right in saying to your ancestors through the prophet Isaiah when he said, Go to these people and say: You will always be listening, but never understanding; and you will always be looking, but never perceiving. For the hearts of these people have grown callous, their ears are hard of hearing, and they have shut their eyes; otherwise they might see with their eyes and hear with their ears, understand with their heart and turn, and I would heal them."

- **Romans 10:9,13 *(cf. Joel 2:32)*:** "If you confess with your mouth, 'Jesus is Lord,' and believe in your heart that God raised him from the dead, you will be saved. . . . For everyone who calls on the name of the Lord will be saved."
- See also *John 12:37–41 (cf. Isa 6:1–3); John 8:24,58; 13:19; 18:5–6; 20:28 (cf. Exod 3:14; Isa 41:4; 43:10–11; 44:6; 48:12);* Heb 1:10 *(cf. Ps 102:25–27); Col 2:9; Titus 2:13; 2 Pet 1:1*

**So-called "Arian" Passages**

- ***Colossians 1:15*:** "He is the image of the invisible God, the firstborn over all creation."
  - Explanation: Because Paul uses the word "firstborn" in this passage, the Arian movement was quick to appeal to it as evidence that the Son was the first created being through whom the Father created everything else. First, the title of firstborn does not communicate chronology but instead title and privilege. The Son had special prerogative because "all things have been created *through* him and *for* him" (v. 16). Second, verse 16 does not state that "everything *else* was created by him" but that "*everything* was created by him." If the Son created everything, then he could not be a creature himself (see *John 1:3*).
- **John 14:28:** "If you loved me, you would rejoice that I am going to the Father, because the Father is greater than I."
  - Explanation: Context and situation matter, especially given the Son's incarnation in which he acquired a human nature and also accepted a temporal and subordinate role as the messianic Servant sent to suffer for the sins of his people (see *Isa 52:13–53:12; Matt 20:28*). This voluntary position of servanthood is what theologians call Christ's state of humiliation, a condition that was necessary for the Son to experience prior to the state of exaltation that would come following his death and resurrection. While truly and eternally God, the Son also became truly human and "learned obedience from what he suffered" (*Heb 5:8*). As God, Jesus is equal with the Father, but as human, he is lesser than the Father, as particularly demonstrated at this moment just ahead of his crucifixion. That's why the disciples should rejoice that Jesus was going to the Father, the one who was positionally greater than he was at that time.

# Middle Ages

AD 500–1500

# HISTORICAL OVERVIEW

**SUMMARY** The Middle Ages was a complex period within European history. Several significant political, cultural, and social issues affected the church. During this time, several kingdoms rose in power, and while others fell, Christianity continued to spread. Both feudalism and medieval culture arose as well. Covering roughly a millennium, the Middle Ages was a period of great change. It is characterized by war, death, the spread of Christianity, and the creation of new social, political, and cultural institutions.

**KEY EVENTS** Three movements shaped and defined the Middle Ages. First, the Crusades were a series of military expeditions that began in the late eleventh century. These were organized by European Christians to reclaim the Holy Land from Islamic rule. The Crusades spanned until the late fifteenth century and began to decline rapidly on the cusp of the Protestant Reformation.

Second, the Black Death (1347–1351) was one of the deadliest pandemics in human history. This plague ravaged Europe, killing as many as 50 million people and causing economic, social, and religious distress. Many people believed God abandoned them or sent the plague as punishment, which may have incidentally contributed to the decline in confidence in both the church and its ministers.

Third, the creation of the Magna Carta (1215) limited the power of the monarchy and established the principle of rule of law. It was a response to the oppressive governing of King John of England, who was under threat of civil war. Signing this document provided the foundation for a constitutional government. It also influenced the development of democratic institutions. Despite its annulment by Pope Innocent III shortly thereafter, the Magna Carter continued to influence the development of democratic institutions in England and other governing bodies.

Furthermore, two key events also shaped this period. The Great Schism (1054) separated the entities that would eventually become known as the Eastern Orthodox Church and the Roman Catholic Church. This divide was the result of key theological, cultural, and political differences between the Eastern and Western church. Furthermore, the Hundred Years' War (1337–1453) was a lengthy conflict between England and France. Their dispute was primarily over land and dynastic claims, and the war had significant consequences for both countries.

**KEY FIGURES** Some key figures of the Middle Ages include Charlemagne (742–814), William the Conqueror (1028–1087), Joan of Arc (1412–1431), and Thomas Aquinas (1225–1274).

**KEY IDEAS** Also during the Middle Ages feudalism developed, a hierarchical system based on land ownership and loyalty to lords who provided land for them. In the realm of academics, scholasticism became a particular means to reconcile faith with reason. For example, Thomas Aquinas applied Aristotelian philosophy to theological questions as he attempted to show the combinability between faith and reason.

**KEY WORKS** As a result, scholasticism produced some notable works:

- The *Summa Theologica* by Thomas Aquinas is a comprehensive study of theology that seeks to combine Christian doctrine with Aristotelian philosophy. It addresses topics such as the existence and attributes of God, the relationship between nature and grace, the doctrine of Christ, the church, the sacraments, and Christian morality.
- *The Imitation of Christ* by Thomas à Kempis is a devotional work that emphasizes one's devotion to Christ through personal piety and humility.
- *The Divine Comedy* by Dante Alighieri takes the reader through Dante's journey of *Inferno* (hell), *Purgatorio* (purgatory), and *Paradiso* (heaven), offering theological insights along the way.

# Timeline

(AD 500–1500)

**ca. 540–604**
Gregory the Great

**675–749**
John of Damascus

**800**
Charlemagne becomes emperor of the Holy Roman Empire

**ca. 1033–1109**
Anselm of Canterbury

**1054**
The Great Schism

**1066–1071**
Norman Conquest of England

**1096–1099**
The First Crusade

**1098**
Founding of the Cistercian monastic order

**1147–1149**
The Second Crusade

**1181–1226**
Francis of Assisi

**1189–1192**
The Third Crusade

**1202–1204**
The Fourth Crusade

**ca. 1209**
Founding of the Franciscan monastic order

**1215**
Founding of the Dominican monastic order

**1215**
Fourth Lateran Council

**1217–1221**
The Fifth Crusade

**1225–1274**
Thomas Aquinas

**1228–1229**
The Sixth Crusade

**1248–1254**
The Seventh Crusade

**1270**
The Eighth Crusade

**1330–1384**
John Wycliffe

**1347–1380**
Catherine of Siena

**1347–1351**
The Black Death, which killed approximately 25 million Europeans

**ca. 1370–1415**
Jan Hus

**1380–1471**
Thomas à Kempis

**1453**
The Fall of Constantinople

# HISTORIC CHRISTIAN DOCTRINES

## God Is Infinite

*(Job 11:7–9)*

God's infinity means there are no boundaries on his qualities and existence (Job 11:7–9; Ps 147:5). For instance, God is infinite when it comes to space and time, meaning he is not confined by material space, nor is he restricted by time since he is timeless (Ps 90:1–2). God's infinity also extends to his knowledge of things (see God Is Omniscient) as well as his power to do all things according to his will (see God Is Omnipotent).

## God Is Omniscient

*(Job 37:16)*

Scripture teaches that God is all knowing. He is the One who has "perfect knowledge" (Job 37:16), and this knowledge extends to all things past, present, and future, including the future decisions of his free creatures. His knowledge is complete, and as he is outside of time, he has known from all eternity whatever will come to pass. In response to God's omniscience, we admit our finite knowledge and trust his decisions as wise and good.

## God Is Omnipotent

*(Job 42:2)*

God is all-powerful: there is nothing God cannot do so long as it does not contradict his own nature or law. God has power and authority over the universe he created, from the largest solar system to the smallest particle. Affirming that God is all-powerful does not mean God can sin—since that would go against his perfect moral nature. As Christians, we rest in the belief that the God who has all power is good, and we gain great comfort by knowing that an all-powerful God is working for our good and joy.

## Church and Kingdom

*(Mark 10:25)*

The church and the kingdom of God are closely related, though not identical. When the Bible speaks of the kingdom of God, it is referring to the reign of God in the world. The church is the people of God who live under his loving rule now, in anticipation of the full manifestation of God's kingdom in the future. The church's mission is to witness to God's kingdom, proclaiming God's message of salvation through Christ and demonstrating the power of the gospel through good works, so that others may be brought to live under God's reign.

## Satisfaction Theory of Atonement

*(Heb 8:12)*

According to this theory, the atonement of Christ satisfies every requirement for God to forgive the failures of humanity. God has not been given the proper honor he is due; in his death, Jesus compensated for the failure to give honor by willingly going to the cross as the God-man to pay the price for humanity's sins.

# The Rule of Benedict: Shaping Monastic Life in the West

Benedict of Nursia (AD 480–543) is the most influential figure of monasticism in the West. Though he came from a family of wealth, as a young man, Benedict rejected the privilege and education he received while living in Rome, mainly because of the paganism and immorality he observed in the city. Thus, he chose to leave Rome and live as a hermit in a cave thirty miles away from the city. After coming to see the wisdom and practicality of living in community years later, he eventually established thirteen monasteries and acted as the abbot (or head monk) over all of them. The most well-known monastery associated with Benedict is Monte Cassino, located about 80 miles south of Rome.

More than his service as an abbot, Benedict is famous for his vision of monastic life expressed in "The Rule of Saint Benedict" (or The Benedictine Rule). Often referred to concisely as "the Rule," this document provided a framework for the monastic community, aiming to establish a life of order, discipline, and moderation instead of promoting extreme asceticism. The Rule placed an emphasis on poverty, chastity, and agricultural work along with allowing for a minimal amount of speaking. Additionally, the permanent nature of one's residency at the monastery he originally joined—that is, unless ordered to go to another—stands among the most notable requirements of the Rule. Perhaps its most distinguishing component, however, is its insistence on complete obedience to the abbot. To give readers a sense of the Rule's expectations communicated across its 73 chapters, here is an excerpt on obedience:

> The first step of humility is to obey without delay. This is proper for those who—because they have promised holy subjection, or because of the fear of hell, or the glory of life everlasting—hold nothing more precious than Christ. The moment the Abbot commands anything they obey instantly as if commanded by God himself. As the Lord says, "As soon as they hear they obey me" [Ps 18:44]. . . . This obedience, though, will be acceptable to God and men, only if it is done without hesitation, delay, lukewarmness, grumbling or complaint, because the obedience which is given to Abbots is given to God. For [Jesus] himself says to the teachers, "Whoever listens to you listens to me" [Lk 10:16]. Disciples must obey with good will, "since God loves a cheerful giver" [2Co 9:7]. If they obey with ill will, and murmur with their lips and in their hearts, even if they fulfill the command, it is not acceptable to God, who sees the heart of the murmurer. Such action deserves punishment rather than reward.[1]

## VOICES OF THE CHURCH

"The unbelief of Thomas is more profitable to our faith than the belief of the other disciples; the touch by which he is brought to believe, confirming our minds in belief, beyond all question."[2]

GREGORY THE GREAT (CA. 540–604)

BIOGRAPHY

# Maximus the Confessor

Maximus the Confessor (ca. AD 580–662) was a seventh-century monk, theologian, and controversialist. He is often considered the father of Byzantine theology, who harvested and synthesized the best of early Eastern Christianity. Maximus is perhaps most well-known for the decisive role he played in the Monothelite controversy—the debate over the number of "wills" in the incarnate Christ—which culminated in the Sixth Ecumenical Council (the Third Council of Constantinople, 680–81) and its proclamation that Christ has two wills (Dyothelitism) that correspond to his two natures. Maximus was so convinced of this position that he was willing to endure torture and exile. As such, he has received the title "Confessor," which in Eastern Christianity refers to one who suffers (short of martyrdom) for the sake of orthodoxy.

## LIFE

Specifics about Maximus's early life are difficult to discern because the two surviving accounts offer conflicting and sometimes spurious details. The so-called "Syriac Life" of Maximus sets out to defame him and the "Greek Life" to praise him. But whatever his origins, it was Maximus's public life and ministry that proved influential. At age 30, Maximus became a secretary in the imperial court of Heraclius, but he left his position after only three years to pursue a life of prayer. He became a monk, first at Chysopolis and then at Cyzicus. War caused Maximus to flee his quiet life, and he eventually found refuge in Carthage, where he produced some of his most important theological works, including the *Ambigua to John* (which dealt with difficult passages in Gregory of Nazianzus), *Questions to Thalassius*, and *Two Hundred Chapters on Theology*.

When the monothelite debate erupted in 638, Maximus found himself at the center of the controversy. The emperor and the pope himself (Honorius I) had approved the monothelite (one-will) formula as a way of resolving theological tensions in the empire. But Maximus and his dyothelite (two-wills) compatriots believed that the monothelite position contradicted the two-natures doctrine of the Council of Chalcedon. The controversy witnessed Maximus's famous *Disputation with Pyrrhus* (645) and led to a period in Rome, where Maximus enjoyed friendly relations with the dyothelite Pope Martin I. The imperial court remained committed to monothelitism, however, and Maximus was forced to undergo a series of trials and exiles. After his final trial, Maximus was sentenced to have his tongue cut out and his right hand cut off. He died in exile on August 13, 662.

## LEGACY

Maximus's most abiding legacy is, no doubt, the pivotal role he played in defeating the monothelite heresy. The dispute concerned the relation of the will, that is, the faculty of choice, to the incarnation. Does Christ have one will or two? More generally, is the will an attribute of a *nature*, or is it a function of a *person*? If the latter, then by the logic of Chalcedon, Christ can only have one will. But if the former, then also by Chalcedonian logic, Christ must have two wills. Maximus was convinced the one-will position threatened the genuine incarnation of the Son of God and thus threatened the salvation he came to accomplish. Maximus made the same argument against the monothelites that Gregory of Nazianzus had made against the Apollinarians in the fourth century: the unassumed is unhealed. In other words, if Christ did not assume a discrete human will (in addition to the divine will he shares eternally with the Father and the Holy Spirit), then how can he heal and redeem fallen human wills? If Christ has no human will, then his incarnation would be incomplete and his adequacy as a Savior called into question. Among other places in Scripture, Maximus saw evidence for the two-wills position in the Gethsemane narrative and the deeply human prayer of Jesus found there: "Nevertheless, not my will, but yours, be done" (Luke 22:42). While to modern ears the monothelite controversy may seem like theological nitpicking, Maximus rightly discerned the monothelite error as a threat to the gospel itself. Only a two-natured and thus two-willed Christ can accomplish the world's redemption.

But Maximus's theological legacy is much richer and wider than this single doctrinal controversy. Indeed, his work is nothing less than cosmic in scope, in that he sees the whole of reality—everything from personal piety and the church's worship to the created order and the task of philosophy—as summed up in the Incarnate Logos and the Triune God that he reveals.

## VOICES OF THE CHURCH

"Love is the great divide between the children of God and the children of the devil. Those who have love are children of God, and those who do not are children of the devil. Have anything else you like, but if you lack this one thing, then all the rest is of no use to you whatsoever. On the other hand, you may lack almost anything else, but if you have this one thing, you have fulfilled the law."[3]

THE VENERABLE BEDE (673–735)

BIOGRAPHY

# John of Damascus

John of Damascus (675–749) believed God gave humans artistic creativity as a way to worship him. At a time when this idea came under attack and art was being removed from churches, John turned to the Scripture and voiced a compelling defense of artisanship in the service of God's glory.

By AD 675, Damascus (in present-day Syria) was the capital of a powerful Muslim kingdom. Here, Christianity was now on the fringes, viewed with suspicion at best. In this context John was born into a Christian family. His world was further complicated by his father's prominent status as a leading political official, and when his father died, John was placed in this role. Holding this office put him in a demanding public position in a difficult context, and his loyalty was frequently questioned. John responded prayerfully, humbly, and with persistent conviction. After many years, he retired from his post and began to serve actively in the church where his wisdom helped resolve a significant conflict that remains pertinent to this day.

Christian churches throughout the Middle East had begun to destroy their own centuries-old art, leaving only blank walls. This art depicted the biblical Christian narrative, from Genesis to Revelation, and was meant to inspire and instruct viewers in a time when it was yet not expected that people close their eyes during prayer. However, through the cultural influence of Islam, which teaches that artistic portrayal of images (humans, as well as visual depiction of their God) is blasphemous, was influencing many Christians. Joining with other leaders, John spoke against this influence, reminding Christians that the prohibition of idols and images of God in the Old Testament were against an idolatry that exists in the heart, not inherently in art. He turned to Exodus 31 and 35, where God enables and commands artisans in their creative work, work which would give honor to God and lead humans to worshipful awe in his temple. John was convinced that creative work, including the visual arts, can be made in honor to God's commands and used worshipfully. Like music, art will never represent all of God's majesty; just as no hymn captures *all* of God's character, no picture can convey God's full glory or the beauty of everything unfolding in Scripture. The artist must ask for wisdom from God, then, in stewarding his or her ability and using it in light of scriptural truth and the Great Commission. This view was the long-held position of Christians before John's time, and John's voice ensured it was upheld, reminding us that the God Christians worship is the God who says, "I have put wisdom in the heart of every skilled artisan in order to make all that I have commanded" (Exod 31:6). May we submit to God's wisdom and commands, putting our abilities to work in worshipful—and *beautiful*—ways.

## VOICES OF THE CHURCH

"He who is by nature Son of God has become firstborn among us who have by adoption and grace become sons of God and are accounted as his brothers."[4]

JOHN OF DAMASCUS (675–753)

BIOGRAPHY

# Cyril and Methodius

Brothers Constantine (827–869) and Michael (815–884) were born in Thessalonica in the ninth century to Leo, a high-ranking officer in the Byzantine army, and Maria. Constantine was the youngest and Michael the oldest of seven brothers in the family. When Constantine was 14, their father died, and the brothers came under the care of their uncle, who was an important official responsible for postal and diplomatic relations of the Byzantine Empire. Constantine and Michael attended the Imperial School of Constantinople, after which their uncle gained positions for them. Michael became abbot of a monastery in Constantinople and took the name of Methodius. Constantine also became a monk and later took the name of Cyril.

When the Khazars, east of the Black Sea, asked the Byzantine emperor Michael III, to send a Christian representative to debate with the pagans, Muslims, and Jews in the region. The emperor sent Cyril and Methodius, and they were with the Khazars for three years, demonstrating the truth of Christianity and baptizing 200 people.

In 862, Ratislav, prince of Moravia, sent a request to the emperor for someone to come and explain Christianity to his people in the Slavonic language. Cyril and Methodius were chosen for the work. Cyril was an accomplished linguist, knowing Greek, Latin, Hebrew, Aramaic, and Slavonic. Even before reaching Moravia, Cyril and Methodius developed an alphabet and began translating Christian works into Slavonic. The alphabet they developed used a combination of Greek, Hebrew, and Armenian letters, as well as some original letters. Using this alphabet, Cyril and Methodius translated large portions of the Bible into Slavonic. As Christianity spread among the Bulgarians, into Slavonia, and even as far as Kiev, the Slavonic script of Cyril and Methodius began to be used. By the end of the century, refinements were made, and what became known as the Cyrillic alphabet was established throughout the Slavic lands.

Paul's words to the Thessalonians could also be said of the ninth-century Thessalonian brothers Cyril and Methodius, "The word of the Lord rang out from you, not only in Macedonia and Achaia, but in every place that your faith in God has gone out" (1 Thess 1:8).

BIOGRAPHY

# Francis of Assisi

Francis Bernardone (1181–1226) was born to a rich merchant family in Assisi, Italy, in 1181. Francis, along with others his age, was often caught up in the frequent battles with the nobility and the neighboring state of Perugia. After one of these skirmishes, he was captured and held as a prisoner for a year. Francis returned home after his imprisonment and began to recognize the troubles in the exorbitant, decadent life of which he had participated. As a result, he began giving possessions and monies to the poor in his community.

While worshiping at the neglected church of San Damiano in Assisi, he heard Christ instructing him to restore "His Church." Francis took this instruction literally, sold his inheritance, and gave money to San Damiano. His father was furious, and Francis renounced his legacy and future living as a merchant, taking a vow to pursue poverty and care of the poor. As he traveled the countryside, walking in a long brown garment with a simple hood and a rope for a belt, other men began to join him. His writings and accounts from his contemporaries mention Francis feeling torn between preaching to larger, public groups and living a contemplative life in a monastery.

Traveling to Rome in 1209, the pope blessed Francis and his men, giving them permission to practice spiritual devotion together as a community. They then returned to Assisi where a rich young woman named Clare signaled her own desire to follow Francis's rules for poverty and physical denial in 1212. Later, she would go on to form the Poor Clares, women who would follow the Franciscan way of devotion.

Francis was known for his generosity and care of the sick, including lepers, who were greatly feared at the time. His writings and the legends surrounding his life also show a genuine care for God's creation. Francis believed that animals too were blessed by God and praised him. One Christmas in his thirties, he went to the hill town of Greccio, Italy. There he took live animals and reenacted the birth of Christ and gave out gifts to the poor, a tradition still followed in many Western countries.

Toward the end of his life, Francis had a vision where he received the stigmata, or marks symbolizing the five wounds of Christ. This image of Francis meditating while receiving the stigmata is one that has been reproduced in art for centuries as a symbol and encouragement of private devotion to God. Having lived a life ministering to the poor and the least of these, including animals, Francis died, likely from diseases he had obtained from the sick around him while preaching to all that "the kingdom of heaven has come near" (Matt 10:7).

# Scholasticism: The When, Where, How, Who, and So What?[6]

| | | SO WHAT? |
|---|---|---|
| **WHEN?** | A theological divide between monastic schools and cathedral schools developed around the 1100s, the scholastic approach stemming from the latter. From roughly 1050 to 1350, scholasticism grew into being the dominant approach to theological education. The medieval universities would emerge from these cathedral schools.<br>Accordingly, the term *scholasticism* comes from how this approach to teaching materialized in the "schools" (or among the "schoolmen"). Whereas the monastic schools from previous generations were characterized by their biblical exegesis and emphasis on the writings of the church fathers, the cathedral schools came to be identified with a more philosophical approach, seeking to navigate and exemplify the relationship between faith and reason. | Cathedral schools became the hub of theological activity in Europe during this era. The scholastic approach to theological learning and instruction became predominant rather than what had been customary in the monasteries.<br>A more philosophical approach to studying theology is not inherently bad and can be a legitimately constructive way for apprehending truth. However, reciting conventional authorities without sufficient attention to biblical exegesis and primary sources can lead to unchecked errors. This, in part, exacerbated a need to "return to the sources" (*ad fontes*) as emphasized in Renaissance humanism and the Protestant Reformation. |
| **WHERE?** | The University of Bologna (Italy)<br>The University of Paris (France)<br>Oxford University (England)<br>The University of Cambridge (England)<br>The University of Montpelier (France)<br>The School at Salerno (Italy)<br>The University of Pavia (Italy) | The growth of cities played a factor in the uprise of scholasticism because cathedral schools were connected to churches that had bishops, and these churches were usually in cities. In contrast, the monastic communities typically had remote locations away from the population. Theological activity thus moved from the monasteries to cathedral schools and eventually to the universities. As the cathedral schools grew in unison with schools teaching other subjects, the main universities of Europe came into existence. These institutions served more as hubs for scholars, both for teachers and students, than what we know today as modern universities. While "general studies" were pursued at each of these universities, some of them came to be associated with a particular field of study. |
| **HOW?** | By attempting to use sound reason, the scholastics aimed to show how the Bible, time-proven authorities (e.g., the Church fathers), and the Greek and Roman classics could be understood together in a cohesive manner. The scholastic method promoted the raising of debatable questions followed by providing cogent responses. This was done for the sake of evaluating the strengths and weakness of various theological positions and the arguments used to support them. | The standard format of scholastic theology was to begin with a debatable question, then offer opinions from several authorities that seemed to contradict one another, and finally state one's own opinion while anticipating common objections. Beyond the realm of theology and philosophy, many academics have gained from this approach the common practice of interacting carefully with other peer-reviewed sources that both support and oppose one's own thesis or conclusions. |

| WHO? | | |
|---|---|---|
| | **Anselm of Canterbury (1033–1109)** | Known for his "faith seeking understanding" approach, Anselm's works used reason to better understand the existence of God (e.g., *Monologion* and *Proslogion*) as well as the purpose of the incarnation and nature of the atonement (e.g., *Cur Deus Homo*). While not following the more developed format of later scholastic writing, Anselm's work set a precedent for navigating theological questions in an orderly, dialogical manner. |
| | **Peter Abelard (1079–1142)** | Another forerunner to the more refined scholastic format, Abelard's work *Sic et Non* (*Yes and No*) listed 158 theological inquiries and what the Bible and the Church fathers said about them, highlighting how they often contradicted. Though he seemed to intend only to stimulate further discussion, Abelard was severely criticized for his work. Later scholastics, however, would use a similar approach to Abelard by listing authorities that appeared to contradict one another but went further by providing proposed solutions for how to reconcile the varying propositions from these sources. |
| | **Peter Lombard (ca. 1100–1160)** | Lombard's *Four Books of Sentences* (commonly known as simply the *Sentences*) became the basic textbook for teaching theology in universities during this era. Theologians often produced written commentaries on the *Sentences* from using it in their classroom teaching. This custom played into the development of the standard scholastic pedagogy where students were given a theological question and then required to compile a list of differing opinions before providing their own thoughts about the question. |
| | **Albert the Great (1200–1280)** | This Dominican thinker, who was a mentor to Thomas Aquinas, insisted on a strong distinction between philosophy and theology. According to Albert, philosophy was to depend on reason alone and theology on what was only known by revelation. The latter provided more certain knowledge, but philosophers were free to pursue their own inquiries as long as they stayed within the realm of reason and did not contradict revealed truth in their conclusions. |
| | **Thomas Aquinas (1225–1274)** | Easily the most famous and influential of the medieval theologians, Thomas received his education at the monastery at Monte Cassino and at the University of Naples (Italy), and he later taught for years at the University of Paris. Thomas sought to show the utility of Aristotelian philosophy for upholding and defending Christian theology, maintaining that natural reason and special revelation complemented each other with the latter alone being sufficient for humanity's salvation. A scholastic structure for theological inquiry is modeled in his most well-known works, *Summa Contra Gentiles* and *Summa Theologica*. |
| | **John Duns Scotus (1265–1308)** | Scotus is the most famous of the Franciscan theologians and was known as the "Subtle Doctor" because of the careful distinctions he made in his system of thought (e.g., his categories of intuitive and abstractive cognition). Taking exception with some of the consensus doctrines and metaphysical beliefs of the previous generation, his contributions would carry a heavy influence on scholastic discussions that followed him. |
| | **William of Ockham (1280–1349)** | William was a student and later a professor at Oxford. He is among the most well-known nominalists (i.e., those who reject the existence of universals and see them only as mental constructs). Emphasizing God's omnipotence and "ordered power" throughout his work, Ockham asserted that natural reason could prove nothing about God and how he related to the world. For this reason, he believed faith and reason were often incompatible. His most famous argument came to be called "Ockham's Razor," which stated that simpler explanations should be preferred against complicated ones unless the latter made better sense of the data. |

Paris
Metz
Ratisbon
Vienna
CHRISTIAN LANDS
ATLANTIC OCEAN
Lyon
Venice
Genoa
Marseille
Durazzo
Lisbon
MEDITERRANEAN SEA

First Crusade, 1096-1099
Second Crusade, 1147-1149
Third Crusade, 1189-1192
Fourth Crusade, 1202-1204

# The Early Crusades

## 1096-1204

BLACK SEA

Constantinople

Edessa

Antioch

CRUSADER KINGDOMS

Candia

Limassol

Tripoli

Acre

Jerusalem

Damietta

MUSLIM LANDS

BIOGRAPHY

# Thomas Aquinas

Despite being given the least flattering of nicknames in "the Dumb Ox," Thomas (1225–1274) is widely regarded as the most brilliant and influential theologian of the Middle Ages. The nickname came about, as one might imagine, because of his reticent personality and rotund physique. However, his teacher, the famous Albert the Great (ca. 1200–1280) is credited with having said this dumb ox's "bellowing" would one day be heard throughout the world—and through his extensive writings, it was.

Born in 1225 in southern Italy near the town of Aquino (hence the family name), Thomas's family aspired for him to become an abbot. So, at age five, they sent him to Monte Cassino (the monastic community founded seven centuries earlier by Benedict of Nursia) to begin his education. At age fourteen, he went to the University of Naples, which was where he met the new Order of Friars Preachers, later more commonly known as the Dominicans.

At age nineteen, Thomas joined the Dominicans, which required taking a friar's vow to a life of simplicity and poverty. This displeased his family, who wanted him to become more politically influential and financially secure as an abbot. Consequently, his brothers kidnapped him and placed him under house arrest inside the family castle to dissuade him from this path of vocation. They even went as far as tempting him with a prostitute as well as offering to buy him the post of archbishop over Naples. Undeterred, Thomas spent that fifteen months of confinement reading the entire Bible and studying Peter Lombard's *Sentences* (the most widely used theological textbook of the day).

Once it became clear to Thomas's family that he would not be swayed, they released him, and he went to the University of Paris, where he would learn under Albert the Great. While studying under Albert, Thomas became enamored with the thought of the Greek philosopher Aristotle. There was a renewed interest in Aristotle in European intellectual life during this time with his works having been recently rediscovered. This interest was not contained to Christian theologians either, also extending to Jewish and Muslim scholars, who had taken more readily than Christians to Aristotelian thought. In view of this broader academic fascination, much of Thomas's intellectual energy throughout the rest of his life would be given to the task of vindicating the compatibility between Aristotle's philosophy and Christian theology, something that factored heavily into his larger effort of showing how reason and faith complement rather than oppose each other.

In 1252, Thomas was appointed to a position as lecturer at the University of Paris. While holding this post, he wrote a couple of his more concise works before returning to Italy in 1259. While there, Thomas wrote his *Summa Contra Gentiles*, a voluminous work that defends the claims of Christianity in view of objections from Jews, Muslims, pagans, and heretics. Around this time, he also began to work on the even larger *Summa Theologiae*, a comprehensive and systematic presentation of Christian theology that he never completed despite its heft in size and eventual breadth in influence. Around 1268, he went back to Paris for a few apparent reasons, according to biographers, one of them being to defend the utility of Aristotle's work for Christian theology.

Thomas returned one last time to Italy in 1272. During this final season of life, he resolved never to finish his *Summa Theologiae* after having repeated mystical experiences that were coupled with considerable physical fatigue. Following these episodes, Thomas famously stated that everything he had written seemed "like straw" compared to what he had seen. After sustaining a head injury while traveling to the Second Council of Lyon, Thomas died on March 7, 1274, at the Cistercian abbey of Fossanova, Italy. In 1323, he was canonized as a saint by the Roman Catholic Church, and in 1567, he was recognized as Doctor of the Church.

## VOICES OF THE CHURCH

*"Theologia Deum docet, a Deo docetur, ad Deum ducit."*[6]

(Translation: "Theology teaches of God, is taught by God, and leads to God.")

OFTEN ATTRIBUTED TO THOMAS AQUINAS (1225–1274)

# Thomas Aquinas and the Fourfold Sense of Scripture[7]

During the Middle Ages, a method for interpreting Scripture known as the Quadriga (Latin "four-horse chariot") became an established convention. Thought of as four "yokes" attached to the chariot, this approach to Scripture distinguished among four different levels of meaning within the given biblical text: literal, allegorical, tropological, and anagogical. These distinct senses of meaning were not seen to exclude or be in competition with one another, but rather the Quadriga existed to highlight the rich and layered content of Scripture and the various ways we can understand and apply its cohesive and deep meaning.

## QUADRIGA: THE FOURFOLD SENSE OF SCRIPTURE

| *Sense* | *Questions Raised about the Text* |
|---|---|
| LITERAL (HISTORICAL) | What does the passage say on the surface according to its historical context and literary genre? |
| ALLEGORICAL (SOMETIMES SYMBOLIC OR TYPOLOGICAL) | What does the passage say about the person and work of Christ (i.e., symbols, patterns, promises, and figures that point to Christ)? |
| TROPOLOGICAL (MORAL) | What does the passage say about how we should live (i.e., commands given, virtues exhibited, spiritual disciplines promoted, etc.)? |
| ANAGOGICAL | What does the passage say about our future hope in God's promises (i.e., the resurrection, final judgment, new creation)? |

Often associated with the Quadriga is Thomas Aquinas (1225–74), one of the most influential minds in the history of the church. In his most famous and voluminous work, the *Summa Theologica*, Thomas explained and defended this approach to Scripture. Early in the *Summa*, he developed the rationale for understanding how the biblical text uses material things to teach about spiritual truths. In responding to the question of whether Scripture is right to use metaphors, he wrote the following:

> It is befitting Holy Writ to put forward divine and spiritual truths by means of comparisons with material things. For God provides for everything according to the capacity of its nature. Now it is natural to man to attain to intellectual truths through sensible objects, because all our knowledge originates from sense. Hence in Holy Writ, spiritual truths are fittingly taught under the likeness of material things. . . . It is also befitting Holy Writ, which is proposed to all without distinction of persons . . . that spiritual truths be expounded by means of figures taken from corporeal things, in order that thereby even the simple who are unable by themselves to grasp intellectual things may be able to understand it. (*ST* 1.1.9)

Scripture's use of metaphor with respect to material things, then, was meant to make its teaching accessible instead of obscuring it. Further, Thomas observed what we might learn from Scripture by way of metaphor is set forth more plainly elsewhere in the canon, meaning that no point of doctrine depends on interpreting a certain metaphor in isolation. This approach reflects what many call the *analogia fidei* (Latin "analogy of faith"), a principle for "letting Scripture interpret Scripture," namely, by allowing clearer passages to inform and guide us in the conclusions we draw from more difficult passages. What we find in Thomas on this point, then, should not seem too unfamiliar to modern interpreters:

> Those things that are taught metaphorically in one part of Scripture, in other parts are taught more openly. The very hiding of truth in figures is useful for the exercise of thoughtful minds, and as a defense against the ridicule of the impious [see Mt 7:6]. (*ST* 1.1.9)

In the *Summa*, Thomas also dealt with the question of Scripture's multiple senses, arguing for the validity of the Quadriga. On this point, he prioritized God's intention as the primary author of Scripture. For this reason, our interpretation must be founded upon the literal sense of the text:

> Since the literal sense is that which the author intends, and since the author of Holy Writ is God, who by one act comprehends all things by his intellect, it is not unfitting, as Augustine says [see *Confessions* XII], if, even according to the literal sense, one word in Holy Writ should have several senses. (*ST* 1.1.10)

Accordingly, Thomas concluded that the Quadriga did not necessarily promote ambiguity and vagueness because the literal sense acted as the foundational layer of meaning: "Thus in Holy Writ no confusion results, for all the senses are founded on one—the literal—from which alone can any argument be drawn" (*ST* 1.1.10). Hence, the visual below represents the essential and primary nature of the literal sense for Thomas and others who endorsed the Quadriga.

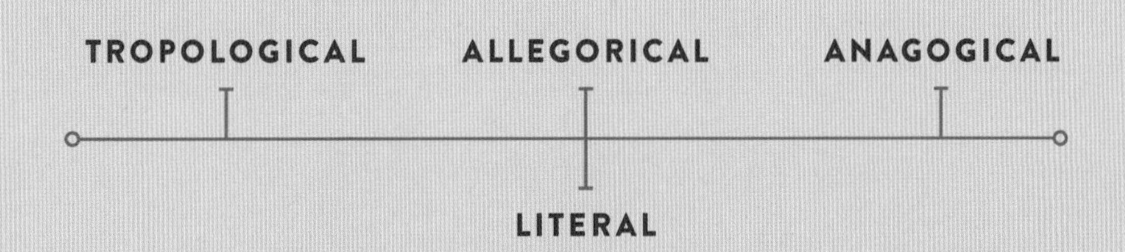

# Thomas Aquinas and the Five Ways[8]

The most well-known and influential theologian of the Middle Ages is Thomas Aquinas. Also contributing much to the realms of philosophy and apologetics, Thomas is perhaps best known for his Five Ways. The Five Ways refer to the five arguments for God's existence presented near the beginning of Thomas's *Summa Theologica*. In this section, Thomas explains why these arguments are warranted. Since God's existence is not self-evident to us, we must come to a knowledge of God by looking at the external world:

> Because we do not know the essence of God, the proposition is not self-evident to us; but needs to be demonstrated by things that are more known to us, though less known in their nature—namely, by effects. (*ST* 1.2.1)

Drawing from how Thomas formulated the arguments in his *Summa*, the table below summarizes the Five Ways.

| THE FIVE WAYS: ARGUMENTS FOR THE EXISTENCE OF GOD | | |
|---|---|---|
| **ARGUMENT** | **PREMISES** | **CONCLUSION** |
| **THE FIRST WAY: MOTION** | 1. There are some things that are moved<br>2. For anything that is moved, it must be moved by something else.<br>3. A series of movers cannot regress infinitely. | "Therefore it is necessary to arrive at a first mover, put in motion by no other; and this everyone understands to be God" (*ST* 1.2.3).<br><br>***God =***<br>***The Unmoved Mover*** |
| **SECOND WAY: EFFICIENT CAUSATION** | 1. There is an ordered series of efficient causes.<br>2. It is impossible that something be the efficient cause of itself.<br>3. A series of efficient causes cannot continue infinitely. | "Therefore it is necessary to admit a first efficient cause, to which everyone gives the name of God" (*ST* 1.2.3).<br><br>***God =***<br>***The Uncaused First Cause*** |

| | | |
|---|---|---|
| **THIRD WAY: CONTINGENCY** | 1. There are some things that are able to be and not to be.<br>2. It is impossible for things that are able to be or not to be to have always existed or always not to have existed.<br>3. Anything that exists either has necessity of itself or from something else.<br>4. Therefore, if anything has necessity of itself, it must have always existed. | "Therefore we cannot but postulate the existence of some being having of itself its own necessity, and not receiving it from another, but rather causing in others their necessity. This all men speak of as God" (*ST* 1.2.3).<br><br>***God =***<br>***The Self-Sufficient Necessary Being*** |
| **FOURTH WAY: GRADES OF PERFECTION** | 1. Among things that exist, there are some more and some less good, true, noble, and the like.<br>2. In being "more" or "less" these perfections, things resemble something that is maximally these perfections.<br>3. Therefore, something is maximally good, maximally true, and maximally noble.<br>4. Things maximal in these perfections are maximal in being.<br>5. That which has these maximal perfections has maximal being. | "Therefore there must also be something which is to all beings the cause of their being, goodness, and every other perfection; and this we call God" (*ST* 1.2.3).<br><br>***God =***<br>***The Most Perfect Being*** |
| **FIFTH WAY: GOVERNANCE** | 1. There are things that lack intelligence yet act for ends.<br>2. Anything lacking intelligence cannot move toward an end unless it is directed by something with knowledge and intelligence. | "Therefore some intelligent being exists by whom all natural things are directed to their end; and this being we call God" (*ST* 1.2.3).<br><br>***God =***<br>***The Supernatural Intelligent Designer*** |

BIOGRAPHY

# John Wycliffe

Born to a rich family near London, England, in 1330, John Wycliffe started studying at Oxford University in 1354. Later he would lecture there as well, in philosophy first and then theology. By 1372 he would earn his doctorate in theology. In 1374, King Edward III sent Wycliffe to Belgium to negotiate tribute amounts being sent to the pope and the Catholic Church. These talks were unsuccessful, and historians believe they confirmed Wycliffe's growing concerns with the Catholic Church's political power.

Back in England, Wycliffe would continue to write and argue against papal authority. Unlike the prevailing thoughts of the time, he would claim that a Christian's spiritual relationship should be based on his or her interior relationship, not participation in formal, external observances. Ecclesiastical leaders saw this not only as a challenge to their authority but as heretical teaching.

In 1377 Pope Gregory XI requested Wycliffe's arrest, but the royal family protected him. Even though Church authorities condemned his ideas, Wycliffe would continue to preach and teach, writing in English so that everyone could access his ideas. His followers known as Lollards (after the Dutch word for "mumble") would travel the country distributing his ideas. They sought to simplify church practices, arguing that sacraments and observances should be based solely on the biblical text. This would call into question the practices of confession, penance, convents, and clerical authority. Poverty was also seen as a way of following the life of Jesus.

Eventually Wycliffe's writings would go too far, pushing him out of the Oxford faculty, who were concerned that he was a heretic. In 1381 he would retire and eventually die in 1384 of a stroke. His ideas would go on to influence many, including the later Czech reformer Jan Hus and Martin Luther.

BIOGRAPHY

# Catherine of Siena

The thirteenth and fourteenth centuries ran not just metaphorical but also literal blood. The Black Death swept through Europe, and many historians now believe that close to 20 million people died between 1347 and 1352. In addition to this sweeping disease, international wars, such as the Hundred Years' War, the Crusades, and the wars between the Italian nation states, killed thousands more.

The mystic, political negotiator, and theologian Caterina di Iacopo di Benincasa (1347–1380), also known as Catherine, was born in the midst of this tumultuous time. She was the twenty-third child born into the family of an affluent tradesman in Siena, a town near Florence, Italy. Catherine began having visions when she was young; her first one was around the age of seven.

As a teenager, Catherine joined a group of widowed laywomen who were following Dominican practices by ministering to the sick and living in a loosely formed community but not in a closed convent. As they gave spiritual direction and comfort, they would wear distinctive clothing that marked them as Dominicans of the Third Way. One of the primary visions Catherine had was of the risen Christ. In this vision she saw herself being married to him, and "The Mystical Marriage of St. Catherine" would be echoed throughout Western art for centuries after her death.

From her early days as a Dominican, Catherine dedicated her life to celibacy and asceticism. For many during the medieval period, these physical acts of deprivation were seen as signs of spirituality. Throughout her life, Catherine would continue this practice by sleeping on a board, denying herself food and drink, and whipping herself. Before she was 20, she would also acquire the stigmata, a mystical mark that appeared signaling her faithfulness to God. Later, she would argue against the decadence seen in male clergy, even calling the popes to be more austere and to refrain from prostitution and gluttony. Her own lifelong practice was a witness against their own indulgences.

Catherine was also known for ministering to the sick in her community. When the Black Death once again visited her city, the women in her order cared for those who were not rich enough to flee crowded streets for the countryside.

Her influence extended across Italy and France as well. Although she could not read or write, she dictated correspondence to popes, clergymen, and rulers. She was also influential in ending the Papal Schism (1378–1417), the time when three bishops each claimed to be the true pope. Not only did this event cause confusion and strife in the Catholic Church, but the individual popes became more and more embroiled in politics, decadence, and corruption. Catherine was influential in convincing Gregory XI to return to Rome.

Her most influential work was *The Dialogue of Divine Providence*. Structured as a conversation with God, Catherine described her mystical experiences and the love of Christ. Her writings described Christ's love as being the motivator for his sacrificial death. In this text she also describes the well-known metaphor, still used by evangelists across the world, of Christ as a bridge crossing a great chasm between the sinner and God. Only by crossing the bridge of Christ can the sinner be forgiven and saved from God's wrath. Catherine's death at 33 may have ended her life on earth, but her words live on to point those who come after her to the loving Jesus she served.

# Nature-Grace Dualism and the Three Estates of Medieval Society[9]

The thought of Thomas Aquinas has contributed much good to the church and broader Western culture. Deficiencies in his theology, however, reinforced some negative aspects of medieval society. The good and the bad in Thomas is perhaps best seen in his conception of nature and grace and how the two relate, often referred to as *nature-grace dualism*.

The term *nature* refers to the original form of something, created objects as they were made and capable of reaching their potential. The term *grace*, in Thomas's thinking, refers to God's infused supernatural power coming into creation to perfect it. In drawing from Aristotle's philosophy, Thomas amended its understanding of the universe to fit with a biblical truth and thus helped recover a more Christian view of the natural order during his day and well beyond. Nancy Pearcey wrote the following about the positive elements of Thomas's thinking about nature:

> Aquinas struck a blow at the world-denying asceticism so common during the Middle Ages, and recovered a more biblical view of creation. This had an immediate effect in the arts, where it inspired a more natural and realistic style of painting in the works of artists like Cimabue and Giotto. It also encouraged the study of nature, preparing the ground for the scientific revolution.

However, the way Thomas divided reality into two realms also did a disservice to the esteemed view of creation he sought to promote. Nature seemed to function in a way that operated independently of God's higher, spiritual purposes (e.g., grace). So the aspects of the world less associated with the church and religious practice came to be seen as lesser because they did not inherently possess God's grace. In other words, they lacked the same level of supernatural goodness. This is reflected specifically in Thomas's understanding of human nature.

Whether before or after the fall, humanity needed a supplementary grace given to them. Thomas wrote as much: "In the state of perfect nature man needs a gratuitous strength superadded to natural strength for one reason . . . in order to do and wish supernatural good" (*ST* 1–2, q. 109, art. 2). This grace to be "added on" is called the *donum superadditum* (Latin "gift that is added on"). Grace was needed to elevate nature from its lower state.

**GRACE**
(supernatural add-on)

---

**NATURE**
(original form with real potential)

Thomas's nature-grace dualism thus reinforced the hierarchy of society already present in medieval Europe. Pearcey summarizes this ill effect:

> Laypeople were thought to be capable of attaining only natural, earthly ends, which were clearly inferior, while the religious elites alone were thought capable of spiritual perfection, defined primarily in terms of performing rituals and ceremonies. Thus the religious professionals took over the spiritual duties of those deemed unable to fulfill them for themselves—saying prayers, attending

mass, doing penance, going on pilgrimages, and performing acts of charity on behalf of the common folk.

This strong divide between the clergy and laity is represented in the visual below depicting the three estates of medieval society: “those who pray,” “those who fight,” and “those who work.” The second tier (“those who fight”), though still belonging to the *nature* realm, was seen as more important because those in this tier more closely served the clergy (i.e., those in the *grace* realm) by providing financial and political support along with military protection when needed. This then leaves the third tier of laborers, peasants, and other laypeople, whose work was seen as furthest removed from the *grace* realm because the end of their work was purely earthly and not tied to God’s eternal, spiritual purposes.

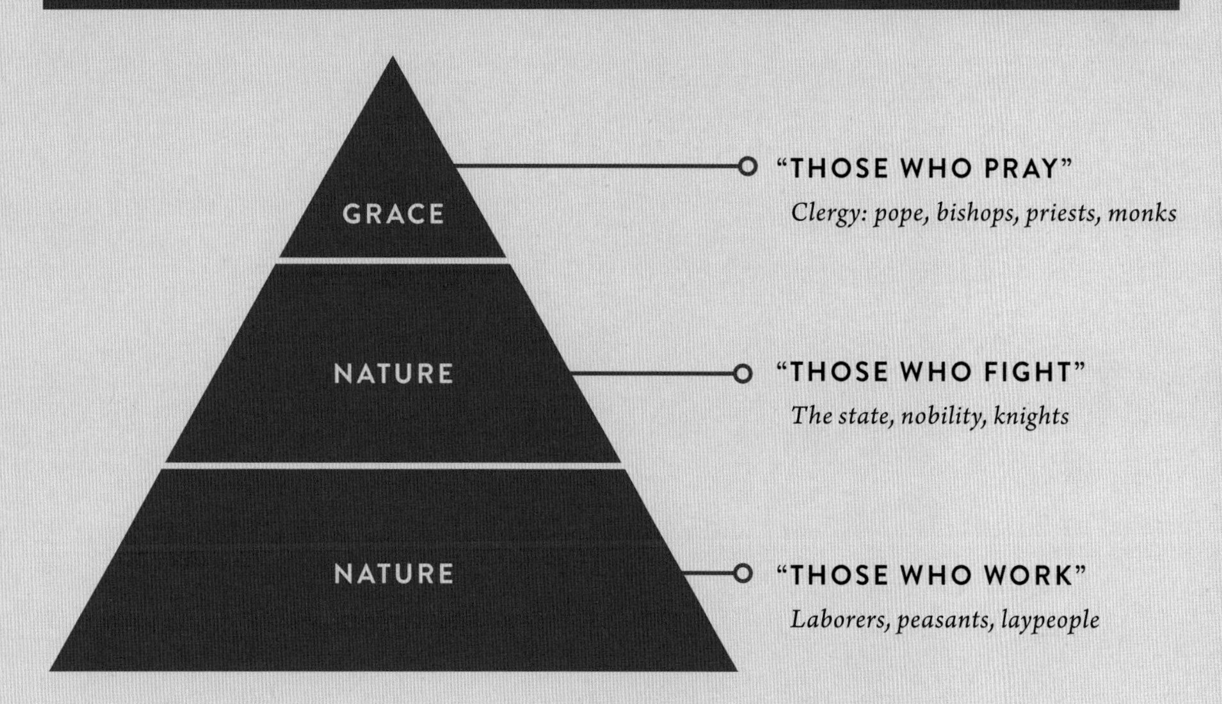


This dualistic nature-grace view contrasts with the more unified way of looking at life and work recovered in the Protestant Reformation where one’s work came to be seen as *vocation* (or calling). The Reformers sought to reclaim a vision where all legitimate work, whether overtly religious or not, was inherently tied to the goodness of God’s creation and part of the cultural mandate for humankind to “subdue the earth” (see Gen 1:28). See “The Protestant Alternative: The Grace and Goodness of Work” on page 118 for further explanation about the Reformation alternative to the nature-grace dualism of the Middle Ages.

## VOICES OF THE CHURCH

*"All pious men will suffer persecution for Christ's sake."*[10]

JAN HUS (CA. 1369–1415)

BIOGRAPHY

# Thomas à Kempis

Paul warns that spiritual gifts used without love are a "noisy gong" (1 Cor 13:1). Thomas à Kempis similarly warned in his famous book *The Imitation of Christ* that writing about theology or participating in church observances without following Christ's simple commands makes those acts worthless. Thomas was one of many in fourteenth-century Europe who began to see problems with the excess wealth and structures of the Catholic Church.

Thomas was born in the Rhineland, close to Germany, to a blacksmith father and a schoolmistress mother. When he was twelve, he joined a group called the Brethren of the Common Life, an organization seeking to reform the church by focusing on daily prayer, reading the scripture, providing care and education to the poor. Later, Martin Luther would also be educated by this order. What Thomas learned in The Brethren would go on to affect his spiritual life and writings even after he left their group to enter the monastery of St. Agnes in Zwolle, The Netherlands, where he became a monk in 1399.

While at the monastery, Thomas acted as the community's scribe, an important job in a time when all books and text had to be hand copied to be disseminated. In addition to copying texts that were already written, Thomas also wrote several books. Some of these were biographical, devotional, and historical, but the work that has had the most influence was *The Imitation of Christ*. This text is also known as one of the key proponents of the movement known as the Devotio Moderna. The Devotio Moderna was a spiritual movement that put the reforming ideas of the Brethren of the Common Life into daily life. This practice focused on the humanity of Christ, and how Christ's humanity can influence the way the Christian cares for others. *The Imitation of Christ* encourages reading and meditating on the Scripture and focusing on one's prayer life. Thomas likely knew how these practices could change a person's life as he would not only have read the Scripture in the monastery, but as a scribe, he would have copied the entire Bible multiple times. By the time Thomas died in 1471, his book about the imitation of Christ had already been translated into several other languages.

# How Did the Pope Become So Powerful?

## THE RISE OF THE BISHOP OF ROME AND THE DEVELOPMENT OF PAPAL AUTHORITY

As result of the office's proven competence, the Roman bishop came to hold widespread respect and notability throughout the Christian world. The downfall of the Roman Empire in the fifth century then left a power vacuum that the bishop of Rome was able to fill during the Middle Ages in the western portions of Europe, over time being recognized as a position of infallible and universal authority. Not always unique to one office-bearer, the title *pope* became exclusively used of the Roman bishop sometime between the sixth and ninth centuries. This claim to the office's unrivaled authority was one of the two principal issues debated during the Protestant Reformation in the sixteenth century (i.e., the source of authority and the basis salvation), and it continues to separate Protestants and Roman Catholics.

> For the Holy Spirit was promised to *the successors of Peter* not so that they might, by his revelation, make known some new doctrine, but that, by his assistance, they *might religiously guard and faithfully expound the revelation or deposit of faith transmitted by the apostles.* Indeed, their apostolic teaching was embraced by all the venerable fathers and reverenced and followed by all the holy orthodox doctors, for they knew very well that this see of St. Peter *always remains unblemished by any error,* in accordance with the divine promise of our Lord and Saviour to the prince of his disciples [Luke 22:32] . . . we teach and define as a divinely revealed dogma that when the Roman pontiff speaks **EX CATHEDRA** . . . he possesses, by the divine assistance promised to him in blessed Peter, *that infallibility which the divine Redeemer willed his church to enjoy in defining doctrine concerning faith or morals.* . . . So then, should anyone . . . reject this definition of ours: *let him be anathema.*[11]

## KEY POINTS ON THE ROAD TO PAPAL SUPREMACY

### POPE STEPHEN VS. CYPRIAN OF CARTHAGE: NOVATION CONTROVERSY (254–256)

- Stephen makes one of the first appeals to Matthew 16:15–19 ("On this rock I will build my church") as a basis for the authority of his office as the bishop of Rome.
- The argument claims that Peter (Greek *Petros*) as the "rock" (*petra*) to whom Jesus referred in verse 18 received a unique authority.

### DAMASCUS (366–384)

According to Damascus, creeds are recognized as authoritative because of the Roman bishop's endorsement.

### LEO THE GREAT (440–461)

Leo is among the earliest figures to claim that Peter's authority is mediated through the bishop of Rome.

### GELASIUS (492–496)

Gelasius states explicitly that the Roman bishop is "preeminent over all bishops" and delineates between two powers, that of sacred (papacy) and royal (emperor).

### GREGORY THE GREAT (590–604)

The extent to papal supremacy expands conceptually as evidenced in Gregory's arguments for the papacy as the supreme authority throughout the world.

### INNOCENT II (1198–1216)

Not only does papal authority stand alongside imperial authority, but papal authority is also superior, according to Innocent II.

### BONIFACE VIII (1294–1303)

Boniface threatened to excommunicate any government official who received taxes from the church and as a result was captured by Philip IV of France.

- *Unam Sanctam* (1302): This official statement of the Roman Catholic Church declared that there are two swords of authority, one spiritual and the other temporal. The temporal sword was subordinate to the spiritual because the latter dealt with eternal matters.

### PIUS IX (1846–1878)

The official dogma of *papal infallibility* was decreed at First Vatican Council in 1869–70, which claimed that the pope was incapable of error when speaking in an official capacity (see excerpt above).

# Of Popes, Penance, and Purgatory: Medieval Roman Catholic Distinctives

The Church father Cyprian famously stated, "There is no salvation outside of the Church." During the Middle Ages, the term *church* came to be identified with the institution of the Roman Catholic Church, namely, the tradition that traces its lineage back to the apostle Peter, whom it claims was the first bishop of Rome (pope). Since salvation is found exclusively through this church, the structure and theology of Roman Catholicism is built around the following key concept: the mediation of grace to the world through the church under the authority of Christ who is represented by the papacy. The tables below (labeled Part 1 and Part 2) provide further explanation about the distinctive doctrines and practices of Roman Catholicism, particularly in their form during the High Middle Ages. Each of the tables also features a column providing the Protestant alternative to each doctrine and practice during the Reformation era (1500s).

# Part 1

| DISTINCTIVES OF MEDIEVAL ROMAN CATHOLICISM | | |
|---|---|---|
| **DOCTRINE/ PRACTICE** | **WHAT IT IS** | **THE PROTESTANT ALTERNATIVE** |
| **THE PAPACY** | Claiming to have originated with the apostle Peter (Matt 16:18), Roman Catholic teaching recognizes the office of the pope (the bishop of Rome) as the leader of the universal church. The papacy is part of the larger Magisterium, the official teaching administration of the church made up of the pope and other bishops that is necessary to provide the proper interpretation of the Bible and official church doctrine along with giving continued guidance to the church in each generation.<br><br>While the office was revered during the early centuries, it was during the High Middle Ages that the office came to function on par with that of European monarchs. Though Roman Catholicism sees organic continuity in the office's authority throughout the church's history, the dogma of *papal infallibility* was not officially declared until the nineteenth century. Further, the pope's infallibility applies only when he speaks in an official capacity (i.e., *ex cathedra*). | Rather than seeing Christ as appointing a singular office to act as head of the church, Protestant churches came to emphasize Christ himself as the head of the church.<br><br>Although the various streams of Protestantism would differ over the most biblical and effective form of church government, they agreed that church leadership was to exist in the form of plurality: pastors/elders/bishops. No church office should possess universal authority like the pope, and no church leader ever speaks infallibly. Instead, Christ ruled over his church by his people submitting to his Word (see John 10:27). While there is no promise that the church will always preach and teach God's Word infallibly, Christ's promise ensures the church will endure in the truth (see Matt 16:18b; John 16:12–13; cf. 1 Tim 3:15).<br><br>Furthermore, apostolic teaching does not continue through the perpetuation of a singular office. Instead, apostolic teaching was committed to writing in the NT for the sake of the universal church and carries a higher authority than any church office or institution (see Gal 1:6–9; Jude 3). Churches should therefore be considered apostolic to the degree that they are faithful to apostolic teaching, not by whether their institutional genealogy can be traced back to the apostles. |
| **REVELATION AND SACRED TRADITION** | Not only does special revelation exist in the form of Scripture, but also any teaching officially received by the Roman Catholic church constitutes as revelation from God. This is called Sacred Tradition. Scripture thus stands as part of the larger category of Sacred Tradition, though like historic Protestantism, Roman Catholicism regards the Bible as uniquely "God breathed." However, the Magisterium, consisting of the pope and the church's bishops, is required to interpret both the Bible and Tradition correctly. | Because of its unique "God-breathed" status (2 Tim 3:16–17), the Reformers championed Scripture as the "norming norm that cannot be normed." This prioritization of the Bible came to be known as *sola Scriptura* ("Scripture alone"). This concept did not mean, however, that Protestant churches completely ignored church tradition but instead saw church tradition as a fallible guide that could be corrected by Scripture (i.e., a "normed norm"). In short, Scripture alone is an infallible authority because it is God's Word. Accordingly, with the completion of the canon having taken place during the apostolic era, standard Protestant teaching came to recognize the Bible as the exclusive source of special revelation. |

# Of Popes, Penance, and Purgatory: Medieval Roman Catholic Distinctives

## Part 2

| DISTINCTIVES OF MEDIEVAL ROMAN CATHOLICISM | | |
|---|---|---|
| **DOCTRINE/ PRACTICE** | **WHAT IT IS** | **THE PROTESTANT ALTERNATIVE** |
| **SACRAMENTS AND SALVATION** | As a renewing substance, God's grace is mediated to a sinful world through the church, specifically through the seven sacraments: baptism, confirmation, the Mass (Holy Communion), penance, marriage, ordination, and last rites.<br><br>Ideally, someone first experiences cleansing from original sin through baptism as an infant, and then by submitting to the church and continually receiving the other sacraments (mainly Holy Communion and penance), he seeks to keep himself in good standing with the church and minimize his time in purgatory. Thus, for Roman Catholicism, justification is a process where sinners "do their best" and count on God's sacramental grace to make them more righteous. Only what are considered mortal sins can cause someone to fall out of a state of justification, becoming susceptible to eternal condemnation. Venial sins, however, can be forgiven through ordinary and proportionate acts of penance. | Protestantism took exception to Rome's understanding of grace, the sacraments, and salvation. Rather than a renewing substance mediated exclusively through the ordained clergy, grace came to be seen as the condition of being in God's favor. Saving grace, for the Reformers, was received by faith alone in Christ alone, and sinners were consequently declared perfectly righteous instantly by a judicial act of God rather than made righteous over time through an extended process. Once united to Christ by faith, a person can then lead a godly life, becoming more like Jesus through the Spirit's empowering work of sanctification. However, a person's growth in godliness is not the basis of their justification before God. Protestant teaching thus made a distinction between the act of justification and the work of sanctification that Roman Catholic teaching did not.<br><br>Appealing to NT teaching, Protestants came to recognize only two sacraments (or ordinances): baptism and the Lord's Supper (communion). As rituals, neither of these communicate grace automatically apart from faith but were signs and seals that pointed to God's promises in Christ offered in the gospel and as such are seen as means of grace appropriated by faith. |

| DISTINCTIVES OF MEDIEVAL ROMAN CATHOLICISM | | |
|---|---|---|
| **DOCTRINE/ PRACTICE** | **WHAT IT IS** | **THE PROTESTANT ALTERNATIVE** |
| **THE MASS** | Jesus's death made satisfaction for sins, and sinners experience the benefits of his death anew through the repeated "unbloody" re-presentation of his sacrifice offered by an ordained priest in the Mass. While Jesus's original sacrifice took away the eternal punishment due to sinners with its benefits being applied at baptism (i.e., original sin), the Mass functioned to take care of the day-to-day sins in its reoffering of Jesus's sacrifice (i.e., venial sins). During the ritual, when the priest spoke the words of institution (*Hoc est corpus meum*, "This my body"), the bread and wine are understood to be transformed into the actual body and blood of Jesus while retaining the appearance of bread and wine (e.g., transubstantiation). For this reason, the Mass itself was of central concern for Roman Catholic life and worship.<br><br>During the Middle Ages, parishioners were only allowed to eat the bread once a year but never the wine to ensure that it was not spilled. Nevertheless, parishioners were taught that they received grace in attending the Mass merely by looking at the consecrated bread when it was raised by the priest during the ritual. | Whereas the Mass was the centerpiece of Roman Catholic worship, the preached word became central for Protestant churches. Being the unique authority containing the gospel message, Scripture was given priority as an infallible revelation of Christ and his work for sinners and the primary means through which God cultivated and strengthened faith in people.<br><br>In contrast to Rome's understanding of the Communion, Protestants came to see the Lord's Supper as a means of grace that pointed to the finality and surety of Christ's sacrifice for sinners. Instead of procuring forgiveness for venial sins as in Roman Catholicism, the consuming of the bread and wine is seen as a way of reflecting upon one's union with the crucified and resurrected Christ and strengthening one's communion with him.<br><br>The various traditions that came out of the Protestant Reformation (e.g., Lutheran, Reformed/Presbyterian, Anglican, Anabaptists, etc.) came to hold differing views about how Christ is present in the sacrament/ordinance. |
| **PENANCE AND PURGATORY** | Penance was not seen as obtaining salvation by works but rather the right response of contrition and sorrow that should come with confessing one's sin. While Jesus's death took away the eternal punishment required for mortal sin, for which sinners received forgiveness at baptism, Jesus's death did not take away the temporal punishments for venial sins. Thus, penance, in the form of doing good works, is done to remove temporal punishment at least partly.<br><br>Relatedly, since no one could make themselves righteous enough to merit salvation, purgatory was a place in the afterlife where the further "purging" of sins took place so that all who entered heaven were perfectly holy and just. This process in the afterlife was thought to take thousands of years, with the length being relative to how righteous someone was at the time of his death. Only those with excessive merit, such as the apostles, Mary, and other saints, would avoid purgatory, and their surplus of merit was stored in the Treasury of Merit for the church to dispense through indulgences. | Protestantism abandoned the teaching of purgatory not only because of its lack of biblical support but also because their understanding of Christ's atoning death and the nature of justification made it unnecessary and illogical. If Christ died for all the sins of all his people, then no punishment remained for them, eternal or temporal. If God counts sinners as perfectly righteous in Christ solely by faith in him, then there is no need for them to be made more righteous in the afterlife. Thus, one of Protestantism's most profound contributions was its offering true grounds for assurance of salvation to those who placed their faith in Christ.<br><br>While historic Protestantism did not continue the practice of penance, it did insist on the necessity of repentance for salvation, seeing it as the inevitable expression of true saving faith. The Christian's good works are not done to avoid time in purgatory or to merit salvation but rather come about because of God's transformative grace working within them. In other words, good works do not affect one's justification, but genuine saving faith will produce good works. |

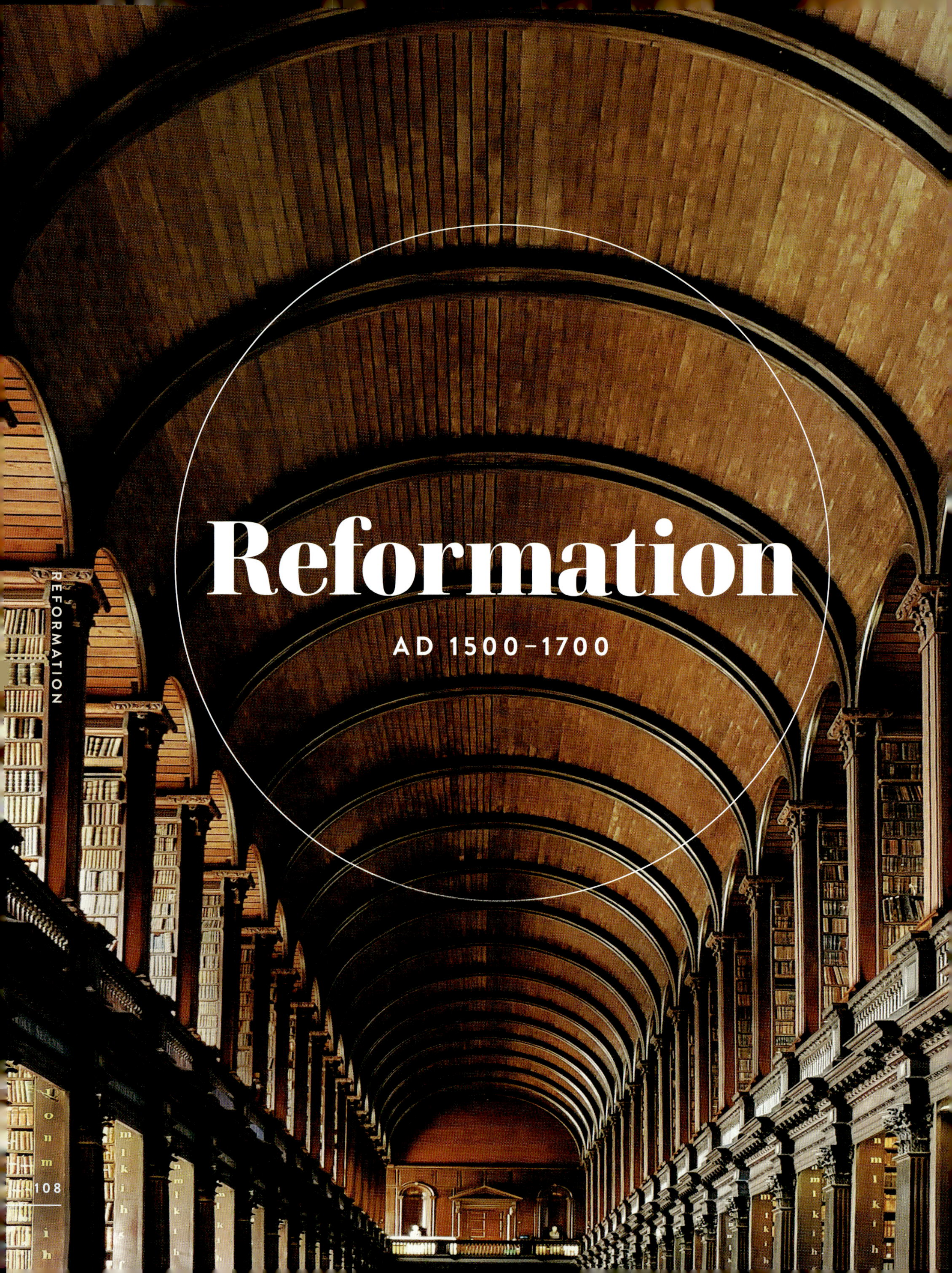

# Reformation

AD 1500–1700

# HISTORICAL OVERVIEW

**SUMMARY**

The result of multiple cultural forces coming together by the late Middle Ages, the Reformation was a decisive movement in church history. Throughout Europe in the sixteenth century, the Reformation changed the Western world's political, religious, and social landscape. This period, like those that preceded it, was marked by intense theological debate and religious divisions that continue to hold influence on the Christian Church today.

**KEY EVENTS**

Central to the Reformation was the reaction against the apparent corruption within the Roman Catholic Church. During the sixteenth century, the church grew powerful and wealthy, and the church sought to impose further means to acquire ample funds from the people to build St. Peter's Basilica. This act included but was not limited to the sale of indulgences, whereby giving alms to the church parishioners could obtain increased time out of purgatory on behalf of their deceased loved ones. In response to these sorts of practices and teaching, among other reasons, some key figures emerged throughout the century to challenge the Roman Catholic Church.

**KEY FIGURES**

Martin Luther (1483–1546), a German monk and theologian, ignited the flames of the Protestant Reformation when he posted his Ninety-Five Theses to the Wittenberg church door in 1517. Luther's teachings would continue to develop in opposition to the standard teachings of his day as he clarified that salvation was obtained by grace through faith alone.

The French theologian John Calvin (1509–1564) led the charge in Geneva. Calvin elaborated further on Luther's teachings while emphasizing proper worship, union with Christ as the center of salvation, the authority of Scripture, and the sovereignty of God. His primer, *The Institutes of the Christian Religion*, shaped and further defined Protestant theology as the Reformation continued to spread throughout Europe.

When King Henry VIII sought an annulment of his marriage to Catherine of Aragon, it led to a break with the Roman Catholic Church in his country, and the Church of England was established as a separate entity. This break, though initially started for political and social reasons, allowed the Protestant Reformation to take roots within England. Not only was Anglicanism established in Britain because of the Reformation, but also Separatism and Puritanism would emerge later in the century and into the next.

**KEY IDEAS**

As the Reformation continued to spread both on and off the Continent, more key individuals and groups began to create more changes within Christianity. Groups such as the Anabaptists in Western Europe, who like the Baptists in England, rejected infant baptism and sought a full separation between the church and state. The Anabaptists would experience persecution as they came into conflict with Roman Catholic and other Protestant groups wielding civil authority.

**KEY WORKS**

Some key works of the Protestant Reformation are:

- *The Complete Writings of Menno Simons*. Menno Simons, a founding figure among the Anabaptists, wrote extensively on defending believer's baptism and nonresistance against opposing forces.
- *The Bondage of the Will* by Martin Luther. In this work, the Reformer Martin Luther argued against the role of free will in salvation, emphasizing the necessity and sufficiency of God's sovereign grace because of man's enslaved condition to sin.
- *Book of Common Prayer* by Thomas Cranmer. This work was commissioned by King Edward VI of England. Going through several minor revisions from 1549 through 1662, Thomas Cranmer's liturgical text did much to develop and shape Anglicanism's religious identity and continues to be used across multiple Christian traditions for private devotion and public worship.

# Timeline:
(AD 1500–1700)

**1483–1546**
Martin Luther

**1484–1531**
Huldrych Zwingli

**1489–1556**
Thomas Cranmer

**ca. 1490–1536**
William Tyndale

**1496–1561**
Menno Simons

**1499–1552**
Katherina von Bora Luther

**1509–1564**
John Calvin

**ca. 1514–1572**
John Knox

**1515–1582**
Teresa of Avila

**1516–1587**
John Foxe

**1517**
Luther wrote the *Ninety-Five Theses*

**1519–1556**
Charles V reign as emperor of the Holy Roman Empire

**1524–1525**
Peasants' War in Germany

**1534**
King Henry VIII establishes the Church of England

**1536**
Calvin's *Institutes of the Christian Religion* released

**1545–63**
Council of Trent

**1547**
Beginning of Protestantism in Scotland

**1555**
The Peace of Augsburg

**1556–1598**
Philip II reigns as king of Spain

**1558–1603**
Elizabeth I reigns as queen of England

**1572**
St. Bartholomew's Day Massacre

**1612–1672**
Anne Bradstreet

**1616–1683**
John Owen

**1618–1648**
Thirty Years' War

**1623–1662**
Blaise Pascal

**1628–1688**
John Bunyan

**1674–1748**
Isaac Watts

# HISTORIC CHRISTIAN DOCTRINES

| | |
|---|---|
| **Union with Christ**<br><br>*(2 Cor 11:2)* | At the heart of our salvation is our union with Christ. The Bible describes salvation as entering into a covenant relationship with God (Eph 5:23–32), and also describes the church (which is made up of believers) as the bride of Christ. Christians believe that Christ dwells in our hearts through faith (Christ in us), and that we are simultaneously dwelling in him (Eph 3:17; Col 1:27). This union is indissoluble; it will last for all eternity. |
| **Justification by Faith**<br><br>*(Eph 2:8–9)* | Justification refers to the moment when a person is objectively declared righteous before God based on the righteousness of Christ's atoning death (Rom 8:33–34). This act of declaration takes place through faith in Christ and not as a result of human works or effort. Through justification, a person is made to be in right standing before God, resulting in what was once an estranged and hostile relationship to one of adoption into the family of God. |
| **Justification and Works**<br><br>*(Jas 2:17)* | Justification is not the result of human effort or good works but through faith in the righteousness of Christ. Although good works do not lead to justification, justification leads to good works in the life of a believer (Eph 2:10). Faith without works is dead. While good works do not establish justification, they do verify a genuine faith and make our justification evident to others. |
| **Authority of Scripture**<br><br>*(Heb 4:12)* | Since the Bible is the inspired Word from God, containing God's special revelation to humanity, the Bible is the ultimate standard of authority for the Christian. Because it is truthful in everything it teaches, Scripture is humanity's source for wisdom, instructing us on how to live life well to the glory of God. Submitting to the authority of Scripture means we are to believe and obey God by believing and obeying his Word. |
| **God's Plan and Human Action**<br><br>*(Prov 19:21)* | God's sovereignty over all of life encompasses the free actions of human beings. Proverbs 19:21 says, "Many plans are in a person's heart, but the LORD's decree will prevail." In ways we are unable to fully comprehend, the Lord's plan goes forward in a way that extends to the choices of human beings as moral agents. Even freely chosen sinful actions are factored into God's overarching plan, as is the case with the crucifixion of Jesus—an event both purposed by God through foreknowledge and yet also carried out by the wicked decisions of human beings (Acts 2:23). Knowing that God is working all things for the good of those who love him (Rom 8:28), we trust in his promise to fulfill his plan, even when we do not understand our present circumstances. |

# Key Locations of the Reformation

BIOGRAPHY

# Martin Luther

Traveling on foot from the university in Erfurt, Germany, to his home in Eisleben, young Martin Luther got caught in a terrific thunderstorm. Afraid for his life, he began to pray, promising God that he would enter the priesthood if only he could make it to his parents' house safely. He later joined an Augustinian order in 1507, where he was ordained as a priest in the Catholic Church.

Martin Luther was born in 1483 into a mining family. His father would later go on to purchase the same mine he had worked in, and wanting to continue the upward mobility of his family, his father sent Luther to Erfurt to study law. After becoming a priest, however, Martin Luther would leave to study theology at the University of Wittenberg, eventually becoming a professor of Bible. From 1513 to 1518 he delivered lectures, many of which were transcribed, on the Psalms, Galatians, Romans, and Hebrews.

Along the way, Luther began to question both papal authority and the traditional understanding of justification, the way sinners are made right before God. These questions took shape in his lectures, but also in his famous Ninety-five Theses, arguments against the sale of indulgences. Indulgences were documents that could be bought from the Roman Catholic church in order to lessen a soul's stay in purgatory. Luther's document was directed to Pope Leo X and included questions like: Why did the Pope not free all souls from purgatory? Or could not the money used to purchase indulgences be used for better things, including helping the poor? The popular story of Martin Luther nailing his Ninety-five Theses on the church door in Wittenberg on October 31, 1517, is likely a myth. However, 1517 was the year his theses would be published and distributed as pamphlets, infiltrating Europe with questions about the status quo.

By 1521, Luther had been declared a heretic by the Pope and an outlaw by the Holy Roman Emperor, putting his life in danger. He sought safety in Wittenberg. His message of freedom from the systems of the traditional Catholic Church would begin to change almost every aspect of life in Wittenberg and beyond. This is evident even in his personal life when he married a former nun, Katherina von Bora in 1525. Not only had Martin and Katherina formerly dedicated themselves to celibacy and the church, but Martin had continued to be a clergyman. A married clergyman was a new phenomenon; some of his enemies even speculated whether the Luthers' offspring would not even be human. They eventually had six children. Luther's letters to his wife and mentions of her to other people are full of affection and respect, evidencing a marriage that, by all accounts, was a happy one.

One of Luther's biggest concerns was that laypeople have access to the Bible. Formerly, only clergy would have access, and the Bible was rarely published in the people's language. In 1522 Luther began his translation of the complete Bible into German. During his life he would also write liturgies, hymns meant for communal singing, sermons, commentaries, correspondence with many other people, and university lectures. Luther's key points of theological contention would focus on the relationship between God and the sinner. Instead of God's judgment resulting in a sinner who was constantly unsure of forgiveness, God's mercy could lead to a confident saint. The Bible was a joint tool, which could be used both for conviction and for hope, both found in Jesus Christ.

VOICES OF THE CHURCH

*"Works or love are not the ornament or perfection of faith; but faith itself is a gift of God, a work of God in our hearts, which justifies us because it takes hold of Christ as the Savior. Human reason has the law as its object. It says to itself: 'This I have done; this I have not done.' But faith in its proper function has no other object but Christ."*[1]

MARTIN LUTHER (1483–1546)

BIOGRAPHY

# Katherina von Bora Luther

Very few women can claim to have been a nun, wife to one of the most famous preachers of their time, and mother, but Katherina von Bora Luther has just that claim. Born to a noble family outside of Leipzig, Germany, she joined a convent at the age of nine for her education. After her mother died, her father and stepmother seem to have influenced her to join the Cisterian convent at the age of 16. In her order, Katherina and her sisters would have spent from three in the morning to eight at night singing, studying theology and the Scriptures, praying, and attending services. Many of these women came from rich or noble families and, unlike other convents, did not perform manual labor, instead they hired others to do these tasks.

Historians believe that her time in the convent allowed Katherina to learn Latin, a skill that would be important to the second half of her life, as the partner and wife of one of the most controversial figures of the time. At some point in the 1520s, Martin Luther's writings arrived at the convent where Katherina and her sisters read them. Later, in April 1523, Luther himself arranged for a merchant to smuggle Katherina and several other nuns out of the convent in a fish wagon. Even though "kidnapping" nuns could have earned him a death sentence, the merchant safely delivered the women to Wittenberg. Katherina had lived in the convent for almost 20 years, and she now exited penniless and without a trade to provide for herself. Several of the former nuns ended up teaching in girls' schools or marrying leaders in the Protestant movement, marriages which Luther himself often encouraged or arranged. Phillip Melancthon, Luther's co-Reformer, and Lucas Cranach, the famous painter, both befriended Katherina, housing her in their respective homes. Here she learned the many household management skills she had missed during her convent years.

Luther attempted to arrange several different marriages for Katherina. Finally, he began to take an interest in her himself. By the summer of 1525, they were married in a former Augustinian monastery which would be their home. Martin and Katherina by all accounts had an affectionate and fairly equal marriage. His letters and references to her were often playful, calling her "Mrs. Doctor" and the "Morningstar of Wittenberg." They would go on to have six children, although two would never reach adulthood.

Katherina would spend the two decades married to Luther managing the "Black Cloister," which functioned almost as a revolving door. It was not uncommon for her to oversee and make meals for 30 to 40 people, which included visitors, refugees, family members, or students of her husband's. When Martin encouraged her to take the time to read the Scripture and her catechism, she reminded him that she had spent years building up her faith; now she needed to live it out. None of Katherina's letters to Luther survive, although it is evident that she would often participate in theological discussions with him. After the death of her husband, Katherina wrote of her grief and struggled with the political and legal factions of the day to retain care of her children and lands. Eventually, she died at the age of 53, having led a busy and likely fulfilled life of not only cloistered contemplation but also the busy whirlwind that would accompany being the partner to one of Christianity's most well-known theologians.

# Martin Luther: Distinctives of His Theology[2]

## Theologian of Glory vs. Theologian of the Cross

Martin Luther's contrast between a "theology of glory" with a "theology of the cross" is emphasized in his Heidelberg Disputation (April 1518). In some ways more significant than his famous Ninety-five Theses, Luther delivered this disputation to his own monastic order, the Augustinian Order. In it, he took exception to the common approach to theology of late medieval Roman Catholicism. He set a concrete theology of what God has done for sinners in Christ rooted in revelation over against the speculative theology about what God might do rooted in reason. Luther's delivering of the Heidelberg Disputation led to his debate with Johann Eck, a German scholastic-theologian, in June-July 1519.

"That person does not deserve to be called a theologian who looks upon the invisible things of God as though they were clearly perceptible in those things which have actually happened (Rom 1:20; cf. 1 Cor 1:21–25)." (*Heidelberg Disputation* 19)

"He deserves to be called a theologian, however, who comprehends the visible and manifest things of God seen through suffering and the cross." (*Heidelberg Disputation* 20)

"He is not righteous who does much, but he who, without work, believes much in Christ." (*Heidelberg Disputation* 25)

"The love of God does not find, but creates, that which is pleasing to it. The love of man comes into being through that which is pleasing to it." (*Heidelberg Disputation* 28)

## The Heart of the Divide: God's Sovereignty, Man's Sin, and Scripture's Clarity

The difference between Luther's theology and that of his contemporaries was further highlighted in his written debates with the Renaissance humanist scholar Desiderius Erasmus (1469–1536). This discussion is captured in their respective works, Erasmus's *On the Freedom of the Will* (1524) and Luther's *The Bondage of the Will* (1525). Two primary issues that undergirded the entirety of the Reformation emerged from their discourse: (1) the nature of man after the fall and his role in salvation; and (2) the perspicuity (or clarity) of Scripture.

"A man cannot be thoroughly humbled till he realizes that his salvation is utterly beyond his own powers, counsels, efforts, will and works, and depends absolutely on the will, counsel, pleasure, and work of Another—God alone. As long as he is persuaded that he can make even the smallest contribution to his salvation, he remains self-confident and does not utterly despair of himself, and so is not humbled before God." (*Bondage of the Will*, 100)

"We hold that all spirits should be proved in the sight of the church by the judgment of Scripture. For it should be settled as fundamental, and most firmly fixed in the minds of Christians, that the Holy Scriptures are a spiritual light far brighter even than the sun, especially in what relates to salvation and all essential matters." (*Bondage of the Will*, 125)

## The Marks of the Church: Word and Sacrament

In addition to his emphasis on justification by faith alone, Luther promoted two characteristics as being fundamental to the church's ministry: Word (the preaching and teaching of the Bible) and sacrament (the administration of baptism and the Lord's Supper. Luther esteemed the preaching of the Word because that is where sinners found the gospel of Christ, the Word made flesh, and he arranged the church's liturgy accordingly. Retaining some similarities to Roman Catholicism on these two sacraments, Luther also developed his own distinct nuances on their nature and efficacy (e.g., consubstantiation). As evidenced by these excerpts, Lutheranism, the tradition named after the boisterous Reformer, would continue to insist on Luther's nuances in these areas in its church confessions and practice.

"It is not necessary for the human nature to be transubstantiated and the divine nature contained under the accidents of the human nature. Both natures are simply there in their entirety, and it is truly said: 'This man is God; this God is man.' . . . In like manner, it is not necessary in the sacrament that the bread and wine be transubstantiated and that Christ be contained under their accidents in order that the real body and real blood remain present. But both remain there at the same time, and it is truly said: 'This bread is my body; this wine is my blood' and vice versa."(Luther's Works, vol. XXXVI, 36)

"It is not the water indeed that does them, but the Word of God, which is in and with the water, and faith, which trusts this Word of God in the water. For without the Word of God the water is simple water and no Baptism. But with the Word of God it is a Baptism, that is, a gracious water of life and washing of regeneration in the Holy Spirit." (The Small Catechism, Part IV)

# The Protestant Alternative: The Grace and Goodness of Work

In contrast to the nature-grace dualism maintained by the Roman Catholic Church during the Middle Ages (and still to this day), the Protestant Reformation brought with it an alternative understanding of the relationship between nature and grace. Instead of seeing creation as inherently belonging to a lesser state of existence and in need of spiritual consecration, the Reformers contended for a more unified view of human life and knowledge, especially with a view toward work. Evangelical author Nancy Pearcey summarizes the Reformers' opposing perspective to Roman Catholicism:

> Rejecting monasticism, they preached that the Christian life is not a summons to a state of life *separate from* our participation in the created order of family and work, but is embedded within the creation order. Whereas in the Middle Ages the word vocation was used strictly of religious callings (priest, monk, or nun), Martin Luther deliberately chose the same term for the *vocation* of being a merchant, farmer, weaver, or homemaker. Running a business or a household was not the least bit inferior to being a priest or a nun, he argued, because all were ways of obeying the Cultural Mandate [Gen 1:28]—of participating in God's work in maintaining and caring for His creation.[3]

The initial wave of the Reformation thus emphasized continuity over discontinuity between creation and God's greater purposes for humanity. They promoted unity instead of dualism between nature and grace, historical progression rather than ontological elevation. Contrary to Rome's understanding, creation did not need to be elevated but was already good—"very good indeed" (Gen 1:31)—and it was to operate under the sustaining grace of God's loving rule and steadfast care with human beings serving as God's image-bearing vice-regents. (For more on the Roman Catholic model of nature-grace dualism, see "Nature-Grace Dualism and the Three Estates of Medieval Society" on pages 98–99.)

Rather than presenting grace as a supernatural substance added on to nature (i.e., *donum superadditum*), the Reformation brought an outlook on grace as the condition of being under God's favor. Pearcey explains further the Reformers' alternative definition of grace:

> This was backed up theologically by rejecting the definition of grace as something added to nature (*donum superadditum*). That definition assumed that human nature on its own, as God created it, was not fit for relationship with Him but required infusion of an additional power—which seemed to suggest that human nature was defective in some way. The Reformers were eager to banish any form of dualism that denigrated God's creation, and so they argued that God created human nature as good in itself. Grace was not a substance added onto human nature, but was God's merciful acceptance of sinners, whereby He redeems and restores them to their original perfect state.[4]

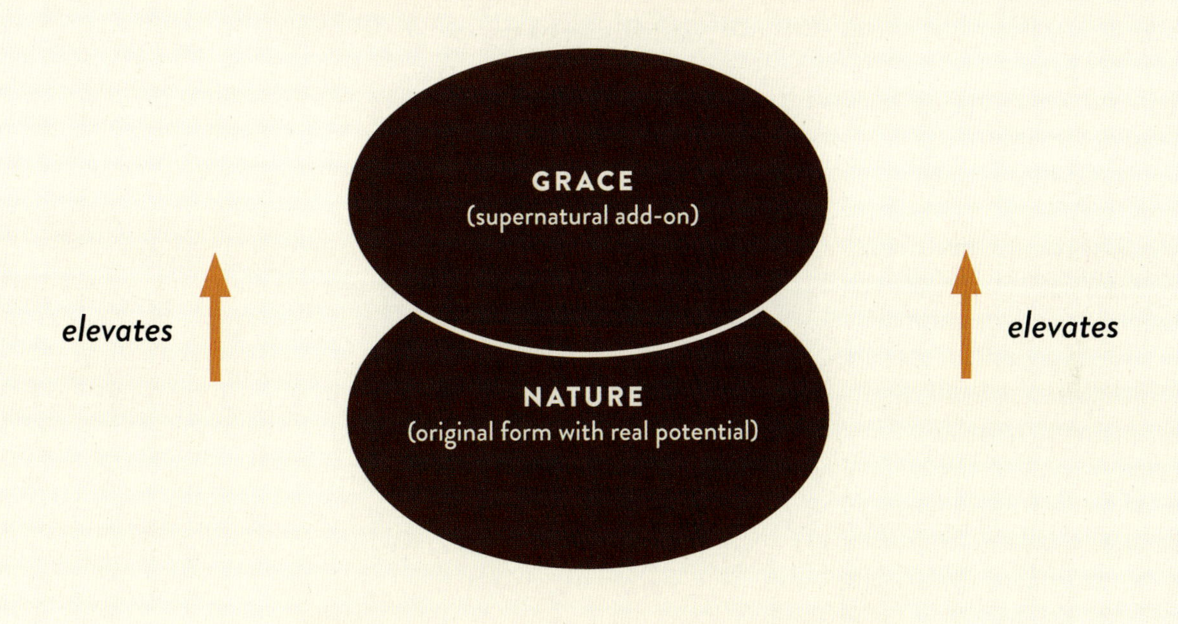
ROMAN CATHOLIC MODEL
GRACE
(supernatural add-on)
elevates
elevates
NATURE
(original form with real potential)

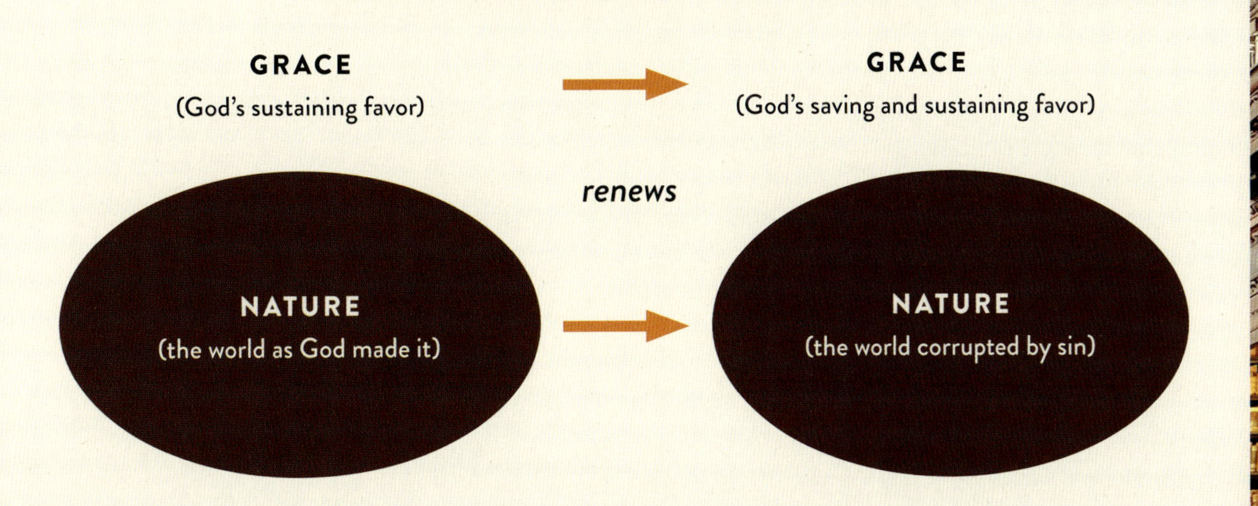
THE REFORMERS' MODEL
GRACE
(God's sustaining favor)
GRACE
(God's saving and sustaining favor)
renews
NATURE
(the world as God made it)
NATURE
(the world corrupted by sin)

# The Protestant Alternative: The Grace and Goodness of Work

CONTINUED

As others have put it, while Rome taught that grace *perfects* nature, the Reformers taught that grace *renews* nature—namely, human nature as affected by sin. Prior to the fall, all of creation was good, and humankind lived under God's blessed rule (Gen 1:31–2:3). In a sense, this is what grace looked like before there was sin. While entirely good, creation was not yet glorified, and the fall tragically took place before creation could reach its God-intended stage of immutable bliss: "For all have sinned and fall short of the *glory* of God" (Rom 3:23; emphasis added). However, this was not because creation was intrinsically deficient in any way or belonged to a lower state of being. Humanity was created good but mutable (able to change), and in our mutability, we mysteriously and regrettably made a change for the worse, going from happily abiding under God's good rule to the badness of self-rule (i.e., autonomy) and the misery that came with it.

According to the Reformers' understanding, God equipped humanity with the conditions and capacity to bring about the consummation of the "world to come" under his sovereign rulership (Heb 2:5; see Ps 8:4–6; 1 Cor 15:44b–46). In other words, if not for the fall, Adam and Eve (and their hypothetical offspring) would have been able to obey God's commission and commands to be fruitful and multiply, and at some point, they would have brought about the glorified state, partaking in the eternal life conditionally offered to them in the tree of life (Gen 1:28; 2:15–17; 3:22–24). As we know, this is not how the story went. However, grace changed the story. Though humanity rejected God's gracious offer of eternal life in the garden and instead chose to rule on our own terms, God nevertheless extended more grace to humanity with his promise to restore creation (Gen 3:15). "Where sin multiplied, grace multiplied even more" (Rom 5:20).

Grace, then, is not a supplement to creation, but as reflected in the diagram on the previous page, it is the condition of God's favor that has always been present with creation in some form. Finding itself corrupted and subjected to futility thanks to humanity's disobedience, nature needed to be rescued (see Rom 8:20–22). It needed more than sustaining grace; it needed saving grace. More particularly, human nature needed to be saved. It needed to be rescued and transformed because of the corruption and condemnation that came with sin. Thankfully, God's grace remained persistent and pervasive as it ever was, and in Christ, the last Adam, God has graciously undone what the first Adam did and has redone what he left undone. Thus, not only has Christ succeeded where Adam failed, but he overcame the effects of sin to bring creation to its appointed glory: "For just as in Adam all die, so also in Christ all will be made alive" (1 Cor 15:22). In short, Jesus came not only to do humanity's job on our behalf; through his life, death, and resurrection, he also cleaned up our mess.

What difference then does seeing Jesus as the last Adam make for how we mere humans lead our lives? This means that Christ was the Redeemer of all areas of life and culture: family, work, recreation, etc. Christian faith thus applies to every person and their everyday jobs regardless of their occupation, not only those serving as clergy. All of life was to be lived under God's gracious rule—as he intended from the beginning.

BIOGRAPHY

# John Calvin

John Calvin (Jehan Cauvin) was born on July 10, 1509, in Noyon, France. Calvin was one of four boys raised primarily by his father since his mother died during his childhood. Gérard Cauvin, Calvin's father, was able to secure him a position with a bishop, which enabled him to study at the University of Paris. He learned Latin from Mathurin Cordier, one of the premier Latin teachers who would teach alongside Calvin in Geneva in 1536–1537. Calvin would dedicate his commentaries on the Epistle to the Thessalonians to Cordier.

After completing his studies in Paris, Calvin enrolled in the Collège de Montaigu, but his father withdrew him from his studies and enrolled him at the University of Orléans to study law. Gérard believed Calvin would make more money as a lawyer than as a priest. At Orléans, Calvin would learn Greek and humanist ideas, notably the idea that one should return to the original sources (Lat. *ad fontes*). His father died during this time. While studying at the University of Bourges, Calvin also learned Koine Greek, the language of the New Testament.

During the early 1530s Calvin returned to Paris in order to study theology, and in 1532 he published his commentary on the Roman philosopher Seneca, entitled *De Clementia*. Here, Calvin's loyalty to the Roman Catholic Church and its theology began to wane as he began to study the Scriptures in their original languages. He fled to Basel, Switzerland, where he joined the Reformation movement and began his writing career. Later, he moved to Geneva where he was forced to leave.

Calvin was a notable author, penning a commentary on almost every book of the Bible as well as his most famous work, *The Institutes of the Christian Religion*. What began as a six-chapter book for the basics of the Christian faith was expanded throughout Calvin's life to 80 chapters. Although Calvin wanted to pursue a life of quiet and writing, Guillaume Farel, a Genevan reformed, persuaded Calvin to return to Germany and assist in the Reformation by a threat to pray imprecations upon Calvin! Calvin stayed, married the Anabaptist widow Idelette de Bure, and continued his work of ministry and reformation.

In Geneva, Calvin preached over two thousand sermons, preaching twice on Sunday and three times during the week. He was a prolific scholar and writer, daily pushing the limits of his body through study, writing, and prayer. Eventually this schedule took a toll on his body through various illnesses, and Calvin died on May 27, 1564.

# Calvin's Theology: A Few of Many of His Contributions[5]

Disdaining speculation that lacked grounding in Scripture and instead wishing not to go "beyond what is written" (1 Cor 4:6), John Calvin was a theologian who revered the triune God's revelation to us in Christ, promoting the purpose and goal of life as knowing God truthfully and worshiping him rightly. The table below presents Calvin's distinct contributions in three areas of theology: the doctrine of revelation and Scripture, the Trinity, and salvation and union with Christ.

| DOCTRINE | EXPLANATION OF CONTRIBUTION | EXCERPTS FROM *THE INSTITUTES* |
|---|---|---|
| REVELATION AND SCRIPTURE | Regarding God's revelation of himself, Calvin was perhaps best known for his discussion about the interdependence of humanity's knowledge of God and knowledge of self. Separating the two is not possible, and so it is difficult to discern which one precedes the other. The implanted awareness of God that all people possess is what Calvin referred to as the *sensus divinitatis* (Latin for "sense of divinity"). Thus, everyone has the capacity to apprehend God's revelation in nature and Scripture because God has already equipped them with knowledge of himself on a basic level.<br><br>Moving beyond humanity's base knowledge of God, Calvin maintained a high view of God's transcendence in view of his condescension to make himself known to creatures in Scripture. Without changing his infinite being, God accommodates the revelation of himself to our level of understanding—like a nurse "lisping" to an infant.<br><br>Calvin also offered insight on the self-authenticating nature of Scripture as our highest authority. Rather than depending on church councils or human reasoning to establish its claims of inspiration, the Bible's own distinguishing qualities commend God as its ultimate author. Calvin compared Scripture's self-witness to how colors and tastes are self-apparent. | "The knowledge of ourselves not only arouses us to seek God, but also, as it were, leads us by the hand to find him. . . . Again, it is certain that man never achieves a clear knowledge of himself unless he has first looked upon God's face, and then descends from contemplating him to scrutinize himself. For we always seem to ourselves righteous and upright and wise and holy—this pride is innate in all of us—unless by clear proofs we stand convinced of our own unrighteousness, foulness, folly, and impurity." (*Instit.* 1.1.1–2)<br><br>"Surely, his infinity ought to make us afraid to try to measure him by our own senses. Indeed, his spiritual nature forbids our imagining anything earthly or carnal of him. For the same reason, he quite often assigns to himself a dwelling place in heaven. And yet as he is incomprehensible he also fills the earth itself. But because he sees that our slow minds sink down upon the earth, and rightly, in order to shake off our sluggishness and inertia he raises us above the world. . . . For who even of slight intelligence does not understand that, as nurses commonly do with infants, God is wont in a measure to 'lisp' in speaking to us? Thus such forms of speaking do not so much express clearly what God is like as accommodate the knowledge of him to our slight capacity. To do this he must descend far beneath his loftiness." (*Instit.* 1.13.1)<br><br>"As to their question—How can we be assured that this has sprung from God unless we have recourse to the decree of the church?—it is as if someone asked: Whence will we learn to distinguish light from darkness, white from black, sweet from bitter? Indeed, Scripture exhibits fully as clear evidence of its own truth as white and black things do of their color, or sweet and bitter things do of their taste." (*Instit.* 1.7. 3) |

| DOCTRINE | EXPLANATION OF CONTRIBUTION | EXCERPTS FROM *THE INSTITUTES* |
|---|---|---|
| THE TRINITY | While Calvin is known for avoiding speculation in his approach to theology, he did not avoid engaging in the areas of density and controversy like the doctrine of the Trinity. Seeking to uphold the orthodox standards of the Nicene Creed, Calvin also sought to refine how best to understand the relations between the persons and their coequality within the Godhead.<br><br>Accordingly, Calvin posited the term *autotheos* (Greek for "self-God") with reference to the Son and the Holy Spirit along with the Father. Prior to Calvin, some formulations understood the Father as the "source" of divinity for the Son and the Spirit, meaning while all three persons were eternal, uncreated, and equally divine, the Son and Spirit derived or received their divinity from the Father. Disagreeing with this conception, Calvin argued that for each person to be truly divine, divine aseity (self-sufficiency) must therefore belong to each person. The Father alone should not be regarded as "God in himself" and functioning as the "deifier" of the other two persons. Instead, the Father is the first with respect to the logical relations among the persons, meaning that the Son's personhood is derived from the Father and the Spirit from the Father and the Son.<br><br>Rather than disregarding the teachings of the Nicene Creed, Calvin saw his contention for the *autotheos* of all three persons as a more a consistent application of the church's historic contention from Scripture that the Father, Son, and Holy Spirit are each truly and fully God. | "We teach from the Scriptures that God is one in essence, and hence that the essence both of the Son and of the Spirit is unbegotten; but inasmuch as the Father is first in order, and from himself begot his wisdom, . . . he is rightly deemed the beginning and fountainhead of the whole of divinity. Thus God without particularization is unbegotten; and the Father also in respect to his person is unbegotten. . . . We do not separate the persons from the essence, but we distinguish among them while they remain within it. If the persons had been separate from the essence, the reasoning of these men might have been probable; but in this way there would have been a trinity of gods, not of persons whom the one God contains in himself." (*Instit.* 1.13.25)<br><br>"For although the essence does not enter into the distinction as a part or a member of the Trinity, nevertheless the persons are not without it, or outside it; because the Father, unless he were God, could not have been the Father; and the Son could not have been the Son, unless he were God. Therefore we say that deity in an absolute sense exists of itself; whence likewise we confess that the Son since he is God, exists of himself, but not in respect of his Person; indeed, since he is the Son, we say that he exists from the Father. Thus his essence is without beginning; while the beginning of his person is God himself." (*Instit.* 1.13.25) |
| SALVATION AND UNION WITH CHRIST | In modern times, the evangelical doctrine of salvation can seem abstract and detached from the person of Christ. However, this was not so from the beginning when it comes to the Reformation. With Calvin came an emphasis on the centrality of union with Christ in matters related to salvation.<br><br>The redemption that Christ won for sinners through his death and resurrection, Calvin argued, remained alien to them until they were united by faith to him through the work of the Spirit. This legal and spiritual union with Christ results in our experience of salvation in all its distinct benefits. Two specific benefits Calvin focused on are justification and sanctification, which he called a *duplex gratia* (Latin for "double grace").<br><br>Put simply, justification is a once-for-all act of God whereby he declares sinners righteous in Christ by faith alone, and sanctification is God's work *in* believing sinners whereby he makes them righteous personally and progressively over time. Distinct, inseparable, and simultaneously received, these two benefits are each essential components of a biblical doctrine of salvation. Calvin's emphasis on union with Christ is thus significant because he recognized that the benefits of salvation cannot be separated from a living faith in the benefactor who is the Savior. | "We must understand that as long as Christ remains outside of us, and we are separated from him, all that he has suffered and done for the salvation of the human race remains useless and of no value for us. . . . To sum up, the Holy Spirit is the bond by which Christ effectually unites us to himself." (*Instit.* 3.1.1)<br><br>"Now, both repentance and forgiveness of sins—that is, newness of life and free reconciliation—are conferred on us by Christ, and both are attained by us through faith. . . . For when this topic is rightly understood it will better appear how man is justified by faith alone, and simple pardon; nevertheless actual holiness of life, so to speak, is not separated from free imputation of righteousness. Now it ought to be a fact beyond controversy that repentance not only constantly follows faith, but is also born of faith." (*Instit.* 3.3.1)<br><br>"Christ was given to us by God's generosity, to be grasped and possessed by us in faith. By partaking of him, we principally receive a double grace [Latin, *duplex gratia*]: namely, that being reconciled to God through Christ's blamelessness, we may have in heaven instead of a Judge a gracious Father; and secondly, that sanctified by Christ's spirit we may cultivate blamelessness and purity of life." (*Instit.* 3.11.1) |

## VOICES OF THE CHURCH

*"We must understand that as long as Christ remains outside of us, and we are separated from him, all that he has suffered and done for the salvation of the human race remains useless and of no value for us."*[6]

JOHN CALVIN (1509–1564)

# *Institutes of the Christian Religion:* An Outline

Representing both scholarly vigor and pastoral sensibility, John Calvin's *Institutes of the Christian Religion* became the most thorough systematic treatment of theology coming out of the Reformation movements of the sixteenth century. Notable for its girth as well as its catechetical value, the volume's four parts resemble the structure of the Apostles' Creed. Calvin would produce eight editions of the Institutes (1536, 1539, 1543, 1545, 1550, 1553, 1554, 1559) before finally considering the work complete. The outline below reflects its final form.

## THE KNOWLEDGE OF GOD THE CREATOR

Twofold knowledge of God

Scripture

Trinity

Creation

Providence

## THE KNOWLEDGE OF GOD THE REDEEMER

The fall, human sinfulness

The law

Old and New Testaments

Christ the Mediator:
His Person (Prophet, Priest, King)
and work (atonement)

## THE WAY IN WHICH WE RECEIVE THE GRACE OF CHRIST, ITS BENEFITS, AND EFFECTS

Faith and regeneration

Repentance

Christian life

Justification

Predestination

The final resurrection

## THE EXTERNAL MEANS BY WHICH GOD INVITES INTO THE SOCIETY OF CHRIST

Church

Sacraments
(baptism and Lord's Supper)

Civil government

# The Three Uses of the Law

As followers of Christ, it is imperative that we learn the purpose of the law that Jesus and his apostles continued to hold in high esteem even in view of the new covenant (see *Matt 5:17–20*; *Rom 7:12*). However, what exactly is "the law"? While Scripture employs the term in varied and nuanced ways, we can consider that "the law" generally refers to the collection of commands contained within the books of Moses, namely, as they are recorded and preserved in Exodus, Leviticus, and Deuteronomy.

Despite the law's breadth, complexity, and apparent antiquatedness, the apostle Paul wrote, "We know that the law is good, provided one uses it legitimately" (*1 Tim 1:8*). Toward the goal of using the law legitimately, the Reformers developed what is commonly known as the threefold use of the law, as described below:

## THE MIRROR

As a mirror, God's law exposes what is wrong with us. In revealing God's perfect and righteous character, the law shows us our moral weaknesses, failures, and shortcomings so that "sin might become sinful beyond measure" (*Rom 7:13*). In its first function, the law magnifies our sin so that we more greatly see our need for God's grace that he provided for us in Christ, which we receive by faith (see *Gal 3:21–26*).

## THE ENFORCER

Not only does the law reveal our need for Christ, but it also possesses a restraining effect on the whole of humanity, believer and unbeliever alike. Even those who do not concern themselves with right and wrong will not live as unrighteously as they could because the law's prescribed punishments act as a deterrent to immoral and unjust behavior. Civil authorities, for instance, carry out this function when they rule in a just fashion that accords with the standards of God's law (see *Rom 13:3–4*; *1 Pet 2:13–14*).

## THE GUIDE

Condemnation is not the law's sole purpose because it also holds a morally constructive and formational function for believers—like that of a guide or sage rather than of a taskmaster. Since the law reveals God's character and concerns for human beings, it follows that it coincidingly reveals how we should live and consequently reflect God's love to our neighbors (see *Rom 13:8–10*). While our adherence to the law will not look exactly like it should have for the ancient Israelites living in Canaan, the core of the law nonetheless paints a picture of the holiness, mercy, wisdom, and justice that should define the people of God throughout the ages (see *Deut 4:5–8*; *Mic 6:8*; *Matt 23:23*). This way of discerning and applying the law's timeless wisdom could be labeled a "principled use" of God's law (see *1 Cor 9:8–11*; cf. *Deut 25:4*).

BIOGRAPHY

# Ulrich Zwingli

Ulrich Zwingli, also known as Huldrych Zwingli, was born on January 1, 1484, in what is today the eastern part of modern-day Switzerland. He is considered to be one of, if not the most, important figures in the Swiss Protestant Reformation (1516–1648). Zwingli was the third of eleven children, born to a father who was a local magistrate and a mother who had a brother in the abbot of Fischingen. Zwingli's uncle Bartholomäus Zwingli, priest of Wildhaus, and would later become dean of Wesen.

When Zwingli was ten, he was sent to Basel to learn Latin and, after three years, was sent to Bern to study. Although the Dominicans tried to persuade Zwingli to join their order, he was promptly removed and enrolled in the University of Vienna and then transferred to the University of Basel where he received both his bachelor's (1504) and master's (1506) degrees.

Zwingli was then ordained to the priesthood and conducted his first Mass in his hometown. In 1506 he went to Glarus and spent time studying, preaching, and teaching but was significantly devoted to independent studying. He would teach himself Greek, the Church fathers, and Hebrew. From 1506 to 1518 Zwingli served two stints as a chaplain to Swiss mercenary soldiers during a tumultuous time for the country, and eventually he would become involved in politics for a brief time. He also corresponded with the humanist scholar, Erasmus, and the publishment of Erasmus's Greek New Testament was pivotal for Zwingli as he read the book voraciously. These factors proved hostile in Glarus at the time, and he moved in 1516 to Einsiedeln where he preached widely to large crowds.

By 1519 Zwingli's theology was becoming more prominent, and by 1520 he was expounding the Scriptures. In 1523 he wrote his *Sixty-seven Articles*, rejecting ideas such as purgatory, fasting from meat during Lent, clerical celibacy, and the Mass. He also began to question the use of images within the church and was able to have them removed in churches. He married Anna Reinhard in 1524, and in 1525 the Mass was officially removed from the Protestant worship services within Zurich.

Conflict occurred with the Anabaptists, but perhaps the more famous is with Martin Luther. There is evidence that Zwingli began these changes without ever hearing of Martin Luther, the contemporary German monk who began the Protestant Reformation in Germany. But they would disagree sharply on the Lord's Supper at the Marburg Colloquy in 1529, with Luther teaching that Christ's body and blood were present within the sacrament while Zwingli held that it was a symbolic remembrance.

Zwingli would die on the battlefield in 1531 when Lucerne, Uri, Schwyz, Unterwalden, and Zug (the Five States) declared war on Zurich. He was forty-seven. His statue is displayed at the Water Church (*Wasserkirche*) in Zurich.

*"Almighty, eternal and merciful God, whose Word is a lamp unto our feet and a light unto our path, open and illuminate our minds, that we may purely and perfectly understand thy Word and that our lives may be conformed to what we have rightly understood, that in nothing we may be displeasing unto thy majesty, through Jesus Christ our Lord. Amen."*[7]

ULRICH ZWINGLI (1484–1531)

# Four Views of the Lord's Supper

| TERM | DEFINITION |
|---|---|
| **TRANSUBSTANTIATION (ROMAN CATHOLIC)** | This view, primarily held by Roman Catholics, teaches that in the celebration of the Mass/Lord's Supper the elements become the body (bread) and blood (wine/juice) of Jesus Christ. "Trans-" means, "to change," and "substantiation" means "substance." Thus, when people partake of the Lord's Supper, they are taking into themselves the actual body and blood of Jesus Christ and, thereby, receive God's grace. To abstain from the Supper is to have one's soul in danger. |
| **CONSUBSTANTIATION (LUTHERAN)** | This view understands that the substance of the bread and wine exist with the body and blood of Christ. Martin Luther, from whom this view originated and is held by Lutherans today, taught that Christ is present "in, with, and under" the bread and wine when the Lord's Supper is celebrated. |
| **MEMORIAL (MAINLY BAPTISTS AND OTHER LOW-CHURCH EVANGELICALS)** | Derived from Ulrich Zwingli's teaching, the memorial view believes the Lord's Supper is to be held "in memory" of Jesus Christ. When Jesus commanded that the Supper be held "in remembrance of me" (*Luke 22:19*), he meant the bread and wine were merely symbols that should remind his people of his sacrifice; that is, his body and blood were given for them. |
| **SPIRITUAL/REAL PRESENCE (REFORMED)** | Originating with John Calvin who was a contemporary with Luther and Zwingli. Calvin disagreed with both transubstantiation and consubstantiation but believed that the Lord's Supper was *more* than just a memorial. Calvin believed the elements are symbols, but they actually bring the presence of Jesus Christ to his people during the Lord's Supper. Thus, for the Spiritual Presence or Real Presence View, the Holy Spirit presents Christ in a unique way for his people and, by faith, enables the recipient to be nourished spiritually by the body and blood of Christ. |

BIOGRAPHY

# Menno Simons

Menno Simons was born in 1496 in Witmarsum, Friesland, known today as the Netherlands, to a family in a poor peasant environment. Simons was trained to become a priest. Learning Latin allowed him to read the Latin Church fathers, and he also maintained some Greek. Interestingly, he never read the Bible during his training. He was ordained to as a priest in either 1515 or 1516 and appointed as chaplain in 1524.

Shortly after his appointment, Simons began to question the teaching of transubstantiation, the belief that the bread and wine of the Lord's Supper become the actual body and blood of Christ. Furthermore, he began to have serious concerns with the practice of infant baptism, noting that it was not practiced anywhere in the Bible. During this time, he was transferred to Witmarsum where he met Christians who participated in the Anabaptist movement. On January 12, 1536 Simons separated himself from the Roman Catholic Church and embraced Anabaptism, which promoted adult baptism, rejected infant baptism, and embraced the separation of church and state. Simons traveled extensively throughout the Netherlands and parts of northern Germany, teaching and helping organize Anabaptist congregations. He rose quickly as an influential leader, and in 1544 the term *Mennonite* was first used to describe the Dutch Anabaptists.

Simons was also an influential and prolific writer. His writings include doctrinal works and letters that influenced the shaping of Anabaptist beliefs and practices. His writings were generally intended to clarify the Anabaptist faith against that of both Catholic and other Protestant attacks on it, while also seeking to quell distortions of it by radicals within the Anabaptist movement itself. While some branch of Anabaptists in Amsterdam and Münster sought reform through violence, Simons advocated for peace. It was certainly this calm sense of leadership that helped the Anabaptist movement gain traction.

Simons was married to Gertrude with whom he had three children. He died on January 31, 1561 in Wüstenfeld, Holstein, and was buried in his garden.

# 3 Views on Baptism

## BAPTISMAL REGENERATION

The ritual of baptism is viewed as a necessary means of salvation; that is, unless one is baptized, one is not saved. Both Roman Catholics and Lutherans hold this position but with differing emphases. *The Catechism of the Catholic Church* states that baptism is a "sacrament" that "brings about the birth of water and the Spirit without which no one 'can enter the Kingdom of God.'" For Lutherans, baptism "saves" in the sense that it confirms the grace of God given to the person who has already come to salvation by faith, and baptism strengthens their faith. Both Roman Catholics and Lutherans practice infant baptism (pedobaptism). While Roman Catholics believe the infant is cleansed from original sin at the moment of their baptism, Lutherans do not; rather, they believe baptism creates faith within the infant that is to be nurtured by the power of the Holy Spirit through God's Word.

## COVENANTAL INFANT BAPTISM

This view is mainly held by Presbyterian and Reformed denominations. Those who hold to this view connect baptism in the NT to circumcision in the OT. Thus, the covenant sign of baptism is administered to infants of believing parents just as circumcision was given to infant males in the OT beginning with Abraham's family. When someone who was not born in a Christian household comes to faith in Christ, they too are to receive baptism as a covenant sign. Although the sign of baptism provides the entrance into the covenant community of the church, it does not initiate salvation but instead objectively affirms God's covenant promises. Whether baptized as infants or believing adults, individuals still must express faith in Christ and true repentance from sin to be saved.

## BELIEVER'S BAPTISM

Traditions like the Anabaptists and Baptists that came into existence during the Reformation and afterwards claim that a return to the NT practice of baptism requires administering baptism to believers alone. Seen as a symbol of a repentant sinner's union with Christ in his death, burial, and resurrection, baptism is also seen as a sign that marks one's entrance into the new-covenant community (the church). According to the Baptist view, only believers belong to the new covenant, and therefore only those who have made a credible profession of faith in Christ should be baptized. Believer's baptism is thus a conscious decision that is made by the individual voluntarily and freely, following the example of those in the book of Acts who expressed their newfound faith and repentance through being baptized.

*"The precious blood of the perfect Passover Lamb Jesus Christ is sprinkled on our conscience, protecting us from the coming judgment of this blind world."*[8]

DIRK PHILIPS (1504–1568)

BIOGRAPHY

# William Tyndale

William Tyndale (ca. 1490s–1536) was a pioneering English scholar and translator whose enduring legacy lies in his crucial role in translating the Bible into English during the tumultuous years of the early sixteenth century. Born in Gloucestershire, England, Tyndale's intellectual curiosity and linguistic prowess set him on a path that would ultimately shape the course of the English Reformation.

At age 12, Tyndale entered Magdalen School just outside Magdalen College at Oxford. He would enter this school only two years later, learning a vast number of subjects. He thrived in the learning of languages, earning a bachelor's degree (1512) and a master's degree (1515).

Tyndale mastered several languages, including Latin, Greek, and Hebrew, which equipped him with the skills necessary for biblical scholarship. Prior to leaving Oxford, he was ordained to the priesthood and went to study at Cambridge University where he began to read some of Martin Luther's works. He left academia to study the Greek New Testament, taking a job in Gloucestershire with the wealthy family of Sir John Walsh. During this time he became convinced of the need for the Bible to be translated into the common language.

His determination to make the Scriptures accessible to the common people clashed with church hierarchy who opposed translating the Bible into the common language. Frustrated by the lack of support in England, he journeyed to the continent, where he began his ambitious translation work. Tyndale completed translating the New Testament in 1525 in Cologne and began smuggling the translation in 1526 into England.

Although he faced strong opposition, Tyndale continued his translation work. He produced an English version of the Pentateuch and parts of the Old Testament in 1530. Tyndale's commitment to translating the Bible was a deeply theological and pastoral endeavor. He believed in the transformative power of Scripture and the idea that every individual should have the opportunity to engage directly with the Word of God.

Tragically, Tyndale's uncompromising dedication to his cause led to his downfall. Betrayed by an associate who was in debt from gambling, Tyndale was arrested in 1535 and imprisoned in Vilvoorde, Belgium. On October 6, 1536, he was executed for heresy, becoming a martyr for the cause of translating the Bible into the common language. His famous last words were: "Lord, open the king of England's eyes."

Despite his death, Tyndale's legacy endured. His translations heavily influenced subsequent English translations, most notably the King James Version, and his martyrdom continued to spur on the Protestant Reformation.

## VOICES OF THE CHURCH

*"I defy the pope, and all his laws . . . and if God spare my life, ere many years I will cause a boy that driveth the plough shall know more of the Scripture than thou dost."* [9]

WILLIAM TYNDALE (CA. 1494–1536)

BIOGRAPHY

# Thomas Cranmer

Thomas Cranmer was born on July 2, 1489 in Nottinghamshire, England. Cranmer's father, Thomas Cranmer, was well established, and the family name dons from the manor of Cranmer in Lincolnshire. Although the early education of Cranmer is lesser known, his family most likely sent him to a grammar school in the village where they lived. When Cranmer was 12, his father died, and at 14 he enrolled in Jesus College, Cambridge, completing the bachelor of arts degree eight years later. He completed his master of arts degree in 1515, choosing to study the writings of Jacques Lefèvre d'Étaples and Erasmus. Cranmer began to study theology and was ordained in 1520, later earning his doctor of divinity in 1526.

In 1532 Thomas Cranmer was appointed as the resident ambassador for Charles V and would see the effects of the Protestant Reformation firsthand as he traveled throughout Charles's realm. Shortly thereafter he was appointed the archbishop of Canterbury on October 1 by Henry VIII, who sought an annulment of his marriage. Cranmer would ultimately declare the marriage of Henry VIII and Catherine of Aragorn invalid. Also during this time Cranmer vocalized support for the Church of England's split from Rome and endorsed having the monarch as the head of the church. Cranmer would prove himself to be a longtime ally and advocate for Henry VIII. As archbishop, Cranmer advocated for Protestant doctrine for the Church of England. Through a series of turbulent events, Cranmer continued to reform the church. In 1549 he published *The Book of Common Prayer* which used English in the church rather than the traditional Latin.

However, when Henry VIII died, his son King Edward VI attempted to promote Lady Jane Grey, a Protestant, as queen. Instead, the Privy Council proclaimed Mary, the daughter of Henry VIII and Catherine of Aragon, as queen. Mary was a staunch Catholic and intended to restore Catholicism in England. She imprisoned Cranmer and sought to make an example of him by sentencing him to death for heresy despite that he already recanted his Protestant views under stress. Yet he would recant his recantations during the process of his execution, renouncing his own hand which signed the recantations. He famously put "this unworthy right hand" into the fire first.

Cranmer was burned at the stake on March 21, 1556, yet his legacy is still seen to this day. The contribution of *The Book of Common Prayer* and the formation of the Church of England still play a pivotal role in the lives of many Christians today.

BIOGRAPHY

# Teresa of Avila

Those who think of a Christian mystic may imagine a person deep in prayer or meditation, completely cut off from the physical world, ignoring the daily pressures of family, neighbors, or chores that sustain life. Teresa of Avila lived a life that argued one could be spiritually invested in the contemplative life and yet not ignore the physical pressures of life.

Teresa de Cepeda y Ahumada was born to an upper-class merchant family in 1515, just one year before the Christian historian and biographer John Foxe was born. Her father was one of the richest men in Avila, even though he had to overcome the prejudice of having a Jewish father. Her mother died when she was 11, and her father sent her to a convent for an education. In 1535 she joined a local Carmelite convent, in spite of her father's disapproval. This convent was known to be lax, giving preferential treatments to those who brought money and possessions into the convent. During the following years, Teresa struggled with the spiritual life and later described her disappointments and failings, which led to a period of ill health that historians believe may have been caused by epilepsy.

She used this time when she was unwell to read spiritual texts, including the first Spanish translation of Augustine's *Confessions*. Reading this open and, at times, painfully honest autobiography likely gave inspiration for her own work, *Life*, which she would write later. Sometime in 1555, Teresa states that she had a second conversion experience. When looking at an artistic depiction of Jesus suffering on the cross, Teresa suddenly realized this as evidence of his love for her. In this and her other book, *Way of Perfection*, she discussed her own mystical visions and moments of ecstasy when meditating on the love of Christ.

By 1560 Teresa became tired of the many visitors to her convent, which would often seek social and political connections. She exited her own convent and founded another, seeking to reform the Carmelite order. The priest John of the Cross would also help in her reforms. They both preached poverty and the renunciation of possessions as a way to follow Christ's example. She would go on to form 14 other monasteries before she died.

Her third work, *The Interior Castle*, is likely her most insightful. In it she imagines a journey through concentric circular rooms until the soul reaches the center where it can commune with God. The exterior rooms are traveled through by doing good works, like giving to others and meditating on Christ. The inner rooms, though, are progressed through by prayer until finally the center room is likened to a marital union with God. Throughout the text, Teresa emphasizes the way the believer should imitate and follow Christ. She argues that Christ's coming in human form, with all of the sensations and pains inherent to the physical realm, encourages the believer to follow the contemplative life and to be present in this life.

BIOGRAPHY

# John Foxe

Jesus's promise to Peter in Matt 16:18 is often explained in light of the founding of the Church or in reference to its ecclesiastical structure. However, in the opening of his book *Actes and Monuments of Christian Martyrs* (commonly called *Foxe's Book of Martyrs*), John Foxe examines it from a different angle. He argues that this passage proves three things about Christ's promises for the Church. First, there *will* be a Church. Second, it will be challenged and attacked by worldly systems and devilish powers. And third, the Church will continue on into the future regardless of these troubles. Foxe then offers his several thousand word text as proof that Jesus Christ has done precisely those three things up to that moment and encourages the reader that he will continue to preserve the Church into the future.

John Foxe was born in Boston, England, which is north of London, around 1516 or 1517. Little is known about his early years until he started attending Oxford in 1534. In the same year, Henry VIII would declare his country's independence from the Roman Catholic Church, setting England on a tumultuous religious trajectory. At some point, Foxe met and became friends with Miles Coverdale as well. Coverdale would eventually compile the first complete English translation of the Bible, which was then published and referred to as The Great Bible, due to its large size. In 1539, the same year Henry VIII authorized the printing of The Great Bible and ordered that one be placed in every church for the availability of parishioners, John Foxe would join the faculty of Magdalen College, Oxford.

Mary I ascended to the English throne in 1553. Early in her reign, she rescinded the Protestant reforms Henry and her brother, Edward VI, had instituted. Any personal copies of the English Bible or anti-papal writings were now outlawed. If a person was found with these documents, it could lead to punishments and fines. John Foxe, his wife, and six children began to be concerned for their safety, so they left for the Continent, where they ended up in Basel, Switzerland. By the winter of 1555, Mary's government would begin burning people at the stake for preaching or distributing documents that ran contrary to Catholic theology and ideas. John Rogers, a friend of John Foxe's, would be one of the first ones burnt at the stake in the public meat market called Smithfield.

Prior to Mary's reign, Foxe had argued against capital punishment. Hearing of those who were being put to death in England, Foxe became firmer in his resolve and began assembling his *Actes and Monuments*. He gathered many different documents including eyewitness accounts, letters, poems, and biographies. By including early church martyrs as well, Foxe would connect these contemporary deaths to the eternal line of the Church foretold in Matthew. Eventually the book would go through four editions during his lifetime, with more than 100 illustrations of the deaths. The text would influence many throughout the Western world, becoming one of the most well-known books aside from the Bible.

BIOGRAPHY

# John Knox

John Knox, the great Scottish Reformer, was born between 1505 and 1515 in Haddington, East Lothian, Scotland. His father, William, was a merchant, and his mother died when he was a child. He was most likely educated at the University of St. Andrews and ordained as a Catholic priest in Edinburgh in 1536. His introduction to the teachings of the reformers led him to embrace the Protestant faith, preaching earnestly for reform within Scotland. These teachings, of course, placed him at odds with the Roman Catholic Church.

Knox evaded arrest for over a year but was imprisoned in the French galleys for 19 months, finally being released in 1549. He journeyed to England where he took refuge and was licensed to work in the Church of England and continued to preach Protestant doctrine. He met his future wife Margery Bowes (d. 1560) during this time, though their marriage date is not recorded.

In 1554 Knox would journey to Geneva where he would meet with John Calvin, and several other Genevan reformers, to sharpen his theological understanding of the Scriptures. It was here, too, that Knox would publish a pamphlet that attacked Mary Tudor. Knox would leave Geneva to minister to a congregation in Frankfurt, return to Geneva again, and would leave Geneva for Dundee in 1559 where Protestant sympathizers were living. Knox would be deemed an outlaw by Mary, queen of Scotland, due to his stalwart commitment to the Protestant cause.

Yet, Knox would continue to preach and reform the church within Scotland. Not only was his influence felt from the pulpit, but it extended beyond the pulpit as well. Knox would play an integral role in shaping the Scottish church by serving as minister of the kirk and drafted the Scots Confession and the Book of Discipline. His commitment to the Protestant faith, his role in establishing the Presbyterian church in Scotland, and his fervent belief in religious freedom solidify him as one of the most influential people in both Scottish and Reformation history. Knox died on November 24, 1572.

BIOGRAPHY

# Blaise Pascal

Blaise Pascal was a French mathematician, scientist, and philosopher who lived a mere 39 years from 1623 to 1662. Pascal was a contemporary to Rene Descartes who famously coined the phrase "I think, therefore I am." During this period there was a strong emphasis on the individual person and the inner man rather than the objective authority of God or his Word, a shift that continues to impact postmodern thought.

Pascal spent much of his life in the world of math and natural science. Inspired by his father's work as a tax supervisor, Pascal developed an early form of the calculator. Though it was heavy and expensive to make, the Pascaline calculator led the way for later innovations. Pascal also developed a detailed system for determining probabilities. Though Pascal intended his work for applications in gambling, God would use it for a very different purpose later in his life.

Pascal grew up Catholic, but it was not until he was 31 years old that Pascal had a life-altering encounter with God, which resulted in a quest for truth in Scripture. Augustine's writings were a major influence on Pascal as he sought to understand and interpret the Bible. This quest eventually resulted in the work called *Pensées*, translated as *Thoughts*, the compilation of disparate notes containing his famous, but often misunderstood, "Pascal's Wager." Pascal sought to prove from his work in probabilities that faith in God is reasonable. He argues that there is little to lose by believing in the God of the Bible but everything to lose by not believing.

Pascal did not intend to argue people into faith. Pascal held to an Augustinian understanding of faith that it is brought into being by the work of God in the one who believes. His goal was not to produce faith in his readers but to legitimize faith as a reasonable risk in light of what is at stake. Pascal did not view math and science as opposed to faith in an infinite God; rather, he believed that God's natural order provides a certain amount of predictability. At the same time, Pascal resisted the current of rationalism he saw taking root in theology. Scripture was Pascal's ultimate authority, not reason. Pascal argued that human passions tinge human reason beyond reliability. It is only by trusting the Word of God as the ultimate source of truth that people may find the order God has worked into the universe he created.

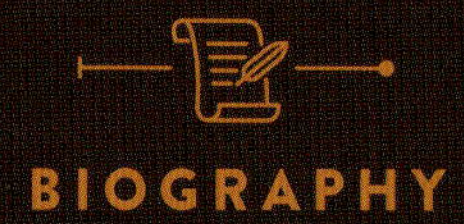

BIOGRAPHY

# John Bunyan

John Bunyan was a tinker, a traveling repairer of pots and pans, in seventeenth-century Bedfordshire, England. He was among the recruits for the Parliamentary Army from Bedford and fought in the first years of the English Civil War. After leaving the army in 1647, Bunyan married and resumed his trade as a tinker.

One day in Bedford, Bunyan overheard a group of women talking about their meetings at the Bedford Free Church and was so impressed with their conversation, he began attending their meetings. There Bunyan heard John Gifford preach the Scriptures with evangelical character, doctrinal clarity, and experimental application. Bunyan was converted and became an avid student of the Scriptures. He was also enriched by a study of Martin Luther's *Commentary on the Epistle of Paul to the Galatians*. After Mr. Gifford's death, Bunyan became the congregation's preacher.

Bunyan's wife died in 1658, leaving him four children, the oldest a blind daughter, Mary. Bunyan remarried the following year, but in 1660 he was imprisoned for preaching without a license. With the restoration of the monarchy in 1660, it had again become illegal to meet for religious gatherings outside of the parish church. Bunyan could have been released at any time if he agreed not to preach, but Bunyan believed preaching was his calling. He refused to cease preaching and remained in prison for 12 years. Bunyan's blind daughter Mary was very close to her father and learned the way from her home to the Bedford prison, often bringing her father a jug of soup for his supper.

Bunyan had his Bible and John Foxe's *Book of Martyrs* with him in prison, and he spent his time studying, writing, and even occasionally preaching. In prison he wrote *Grace Abounding to the Chief of Sinners* and *The Pilgrim's Progress*, an imaginative allegory of the Christian life that is rich with biblical imagery. In the margins of *The Pilgrim's Progress*, Bunyan included Scripture references further exploring the biblical truths taught in the story, and the book became an instant bestseller and remains so today.

Charles Spurgeon repeatedly read *The Pilgrim's Progress* throughout his life. Spurgeon wrote that reading Bunyan was almost like reading the Bible itself, for he believed Bunyan's soul was saturated with Scripture. "Why, this man is a living Bible! Prick him anywhere his blood is Bibline, the very essence of the Bible flows from him. He cannot speak without quoting a text, for his very soul is full of the Word of God."

# 3 Forms of Church Government

| FORM OF GOVERNMENT | INSTITUTIONS | WHERE AUTHORITY LIES | SCRIPTURAL BASIS |
|---|---|---|---|
| **EPISCOPAL** | Episcopal<br>Lutheran<br>Methodist<br>Orthodox<br>Roman Catholic | Authority lies within the bishops (Gk. *episkopos*, "overseer") and the structure of the church. Although each institution differs from who is the "head" of the church, the leadership structure is similar for each congregation. The bishop/elder/pastor oversees the congregation but is subject to the rulings of a diocese. | *Matt 16:18–19; Acts 6:6; 14:23; Gal 1:19; 2:9* |
| **PRESBYTERIAN** | Presbyterian<br>Reformed | Authority resides with an elder (Gk. *presbuteros,* "elder") or group of elders who may possibly *lead* or *rule* a congregation. For elder-led congregations, the congregation will have the final say on decisions that are presented to them by the church elders. Congregations which are elder ruled rely on the church elders to make the decisions and may or may not have input. | *Acts 14:23; 20:17; 1 Tim 5:17; Titus 1:5; 1 Pet 5:1–2* |
| **CONGREGATIONAL** | Baptist<br>Congregationalist<br>Evangelical Free<br>Independent<br>Mennonite | The church's authority is found within the congregation which emphasizes the priesthood of the believer. The local church is autonomous, and no outside authority has control over the church's function. Each church is free to cooperate with a larger group or network of churches. The members of the local congregation make the decisions that govern the church. | *Acts 15:12,22–25; Col 1:18; 1 Pet 2:9* |

# Fourfold State of Man

| PRE-FALL MAN (INNOCENCE) | POST-FALL MAN (SIN AND MISERY) | REBORN MAN (GRACE) | GLORIFIED MAN (GLORY) |
|---|---|---|---|
| Able to sin | Able to sin | Able to sin | Able to not sin |
| Able to not sin | Unable to not sin | Able to not sin | Unable to sin |

Those responsible for framing the historic Protestant confessions of faith coming out of the Reformation saw the movement's understanding of humanity, the fall, and free will as standing in continuity with the teaching of Augustine (see "Augustine, Pelagianism, and Semi-Pelagianism" on page 65). Reflected in the confessional theology that came out of the sixteenth and seventeenth centuries is the notion of the "**fourfold state of man.**" In particularly, this framing of the fall's effect on the inclination of the human will is seen in chapter 9 of the Westminster Confession of Faith (1646), arguably the most comprehensive statement of Protestant doctrine in confessional form ever produced.

The chapter begins with a basic statement about the faculty of the human will: "God hath endued the will of man with that natural liberty, that is neither forced, nor by any absolute necessity of nature determined, to good or evil" (IX.1). Following this description of free will in principle, the confession goes on to present the state and capability of the human will within the context of salvation history.

- **SCRIPTURE CITATIONS:** *Jas 1:13–14; Deut 30:19; Isa 7:11–23; Matt 17:12; John 5:40; Jas 4:17*

Prior to the fall, this chapter of the confession refers to man in "his state of **innocency**" when he possessed the freedom and power "to will and to do that which was good and pleasing to God" (WCF IX.2). The human will, for this brief period, was **able to sin** and **able not to sin.**

- **SCRIPTURE CITATIONS:** *Eccl 7:28; Gen 1:26,31; Col 3:10; Gen 2:16–17; 3:6,17*

However, because of humanity's mutability, it was possible for him to fall, and that he did: "Man, by his fall into a **state of sin**, hath wholly lost all ability of will to any spiritual good accompanying salvation" (IX.3). Indeed, he is "not able, by his own strength, to convert himself." Now being "averse to good," the human will, left to itself, is **able to sin** and **unable not to sin.**

- **SCRIPTURE CITATIONS:** *Rom 8:7–8; John 6:44,65; 15:5; Rom 5:5; 3:9–10,12,23; Eph 2:1,5; Col 2:13; John 3:3,5–6; 1 Cor 2:14; Titus 3:3–5*

In the fourth paragraph, the confession states that "when God converts a sinner, and translates him into the **state of grace**," he frees him from the bondage to sin, and through grace, "enables him freely to will and to do that which is spiritually good" (IX.4). Even in his newfound state of grace, humanity still possess a "remaining corruption" that keeps him from perfectly desiring to do only good and in fact does "also will that which is evil." Thus, similarly to the prefall state, in grace, converted humanity is **able to sin** and **able not to sin**.

- SCRIPTURE CITATIONS: *Col 1:13; John 8:34,36; Rom 6:6–7; Phil 2:13; Rom 6:14,17–19,22; Gal 5:17; Rom 7:14–25; 1 John 1:8,10*

Not until the final phase of salvation, most commonly known as glorification, is humanity's will entirely spared of the presence and effects of sin entirely: "The will of man is made perfectly and immutably free to good alone, in the **state of glory** only." This everlasting state of glory is experienced by the soul during the intermediate state in heaven after death and then in both body and soul during the resurrection age in the new heaven and new earth after Christ's return. Permanently and ceaselessly, redeemed humanity will—to quote from a well-known hymn—"be saved to sin no more," meaning they will be both **able to not sin** and **unable to sin**.

- SCRIPTURE CITATIONS: *Heb 12:23; 1 John 3:2; Jude 24; Rev 21:27*

BIOGRAPHY

# John Owen

John Owen was born in 1616 in Stadhampton, Oxfordshire, to a Puritan household. He attended school at Queen's College, Oxford, earning his bachelor of arts in 1632 and his master of arts in 1635. After earning these degrees, he continued to study and was eventually ordained into the Church of England. He served as chaplain to Oliver Cromwell during the English Civil War, citing his Puritan beliefs as to why he sided with the Parliamentary cause. Throughout his life he would preach on numerous occasions before parliament and the king.

Owen became a pastor at Coggeshall in Essex, and it was during this time he wrote and published *The Death of Death in the Death of Christ*, which brought about a lengthy debate with another Puritan pastor, Richard Baxter. In 1644 he married Mary Rooke, and the couple had eleven children. Tragically Owen would bury ten of his children and outlive his wife by eight years. Serving as a pastor did not prevent Owen from being involved in politics. Not only did he serve as chaplain to Cromwell, but Owen also served on several important committees to expand religious reform during Cromwell's reign.

Cromwell, the chancellor of Oxford University, appointed Owen to the role of dean of Christ Church Cathedral and made him vice-chancellor of Oxford University in 1652. Owen worked diligently to promote religious tolerance and restore the high academic standards for which Oxford University was known. Though Owen and Cromwell worked closely together, and a friendship ensued, Owen wrote a petition against Cromwell becoming king. Once Cromwell died and his son, Richard Cromwell, succeeded his father, Owen lost his position. When the monarchy was restored and Charles II became king, persecution of dissenters began. When the Restoration took place in England in the later 1660s, Owen would publish pamphlets arguing for the dissenters and their role within the English nation.

Owen was a prolific writer, and it is estimated that he published somewhere around 8 million words. His works include a lengthy commentary on Hebrews, several works on the Holy Spirit, treatises on sin, the atonement, and theological exposition against Arminianism. Some of his unpublished works include books for children and sermon manuscripts.

His later years included his dedication to pastoral care and aiding and nurturing several congregations within London, especially after the Great Fire in 1666. He was offered the presidency of several schools, such as Harvard College, but chose to continue his pastoral responsibilities. From 1680 until his death in 1683, Owen continued to serve in ministry and writing. His emphasis on personal holiness, the sovereignty of God, dependency on the Holy Spirit, and the Christian's life as being marked by knowing God continues to influence Christians and inspire theologians to this day.

## VOICES OF THE CHURCH

*"Always be killing sin or it will be killing you."*[10]

JOHN OWEN (1616–1683)

BIOGRAPHY

# Anne Bradstreet

In 1630, 18-year-old Anne Bradstreet, along with her parents and husband Simon, came to America from England as part of the group of Puritans led by John Winthrop. Anne Dudley had married Simon Bradstreet, a pastor's son, when she was 16. When they immigrated to America, the Dudleys and Bradstreets left behind a life of some comfort and wealth for the freedom to worship and serve God. Both Anne's father and husband would serve as governor of the young Massachusetts colony, which made Anne among the leading families of the colony.

Anne's eight children all survived to adulthood, a rarity in those days. In the midst of the many responsibilities for her household, Anne wrote poetry. In 1650, her brother-in-law and father had some of her poems published in London as "The Tenth Muse Lately Sprung up in America." Her brother-in-law wrote that the poems were "The Word of a Woman, honoured, and esteemed where she lives, for her gracious demeanor, her eminent parts, her pious conversation, her courteous disposition, her exact diligence in her place, and discreet, managing of her Family occasions, and more than so, these Poems are but the fruit of some few hours, curtailed from her sleep and other refreshments."

In the epitaph she wrote for Dorothy Dudley, her mother, Anne pictured the ideal of a Christian woman, in many ways reflecting the woman in Proverbs 31.

> A worthy Matron of unspotted life, A loving Mother and obedient wife, A friendly Neighbor pitiful to poor, Whom oft she fed and clothed with her store, To Servants wisely aweful but yet kind, And as they did so they reward did find; A true Instructer of her Family, The which she ordered with dexterity. The publick meetings ever did frequent, And in her Closet constant hours she spent; Religious in all her words and wayes Preparing still for death till end of dayes; Of all her Children, Children lived to see, Then dying, left a blessed memory.

Though Anne Bradstreet is remembered today as the first English poet in America, when she wrote her autobiography for her children, she did not mention her poetry. Shortly before her death, she wrote in her journal, "Upon the Rock Christ Jesus will I build by faith, and if I perish, I perish. But I know all the powers of Hell shall never prevail against it, I know whom I have trusted, and whom I believe, and that he is able to keep what I have committed to his charge."

## VOICES OF THE CHURCH

*"Christ is never sweet until sin is felt to be bitter."*[11]

THOMAS WATSON (1620–1686)

BIOGRAPHY

# Isaac Watts

Isaac Watts was an English minister and writer, best known for his extensive work in adapting psalms for New Testament believers and popularizing original hymns for corporate worship. Watts was born into a devoted family of nonconformist Christians in 1674. Although it was illegal to worship in churches that were not authorized by the Church of England, Watts's parents made the sacrifices required to worship according to their consciences. As a result of his refusal to submit to the state church, Watts's father was imprisoned twice and further forced to live separately from his family for two years.[12] Isaac Watts learned the value of Scripture from an early age, and his parents' willingness to suffer rather than compromise biblical teaching cemented Isaac's commitment to the Word of God.

Although Watts was not allowed to earn a college degree from Oxford or Cambridge because of his refusal to conform to the state church, he was an exceptional student and had a keen mind for verse and rhyme. Christianity during this time was heavily influenced by the Enlightenment, and Christians tended to be more focused on clear reason than emotion or passion. Though Watts was an expert in logic, he was deeply concerned with engaging the heart as well as the mind in worship. Watts deeply loved the Psalms, and he worked diligently to understand and apply them from a Christ-centered perspective. He believed that the psalms of David were uniquely adaptable for interpretation in light of the Messiah Jesus.[13] Though his work was often interrupted by long bouts of illness, Watts persevered, eventually publishing *Psalms of David: Imitated in the Language of the New Testament* in 1719.

Though this collection contains many hymns sung today, including "Joy to the World," Watts's reinterpretations were poorly received at the time.[14] Even nonconforming churches primarily sang directly from the Psalms with only minor changes to make them singable in English. Watts's goal was not to paraphrase the psalms but to reinterpret them in light of Jesus as the Son of God and the descendant of David who will reign forever. Watts felt that he best honored David by making David's psalms useful for worship in the Christian church.[15]

Watts honored his parents' legacy of faith through his dedication to the Word of God and his willingness to persevere through suffering to worship him. He mirrored their refusal to conform under pressure as well as their passionate devotion to Jesus Christ. Watts recognized and loved Jesus through Old Testament Scripture through the lens of the New Testament.

## VOICES OF THE CHURCH

*" 'What are these false apostles doing?' Paul cries. 'They are turning Law into grace, and grace into Law. They are changing Moses into Christ, and Christ into Moses. By teaching that besides Christ and His righteousness the performance of the Law is necessary unto salvation, they put the Law in the place of Christ, they attribute to the Law the power to save, a power that belongs to Christ only.' "*[16]

MARTIN LUTHER (1483–1546)

# Modern Period

ca. AD 1700–PRESENT

# HISTORICAL OVERVIEW

**SUMMARY** Christianity from the 1700s to the present era has undergone significant change across its landscape. From the establishment of new denominations, the rise of theological debates within those denominations, the missionary efforts taken upon by several noteworthy people, social and cultural reforms, and the spread of Christianity throughout the known world, the transformation has been notable to say the least.

**KEY EVENTS** In the eighteenth century, the movement known as the Enlightenment saw a rise against the basic teachings of Christianity through individuals who challenged these beliefs through science and reason. Despite this challenge, the Great Awakening began to spread within England and the New England colonies of North America. The nineteenth century saw the missionary movement take the gospel message to Asia, Africa, and the Pacific regions. While the missionaries evangelized and integrated themselves within their newfound communities, many German Liberal-Protestant theologians began to question the veracity of the Bible. The twentieth century saw the advent of several wars, notably the World Wars, the Cold War, and the Vietnam War. During these times, there was significant social upheaval with the arrival of the sexual revolution, campus protests over war, and the Civil Rights movement. Furthermore, the Pentecostal and charismatic movements also took root during this time, emphasizing personal experience and supernatural gifts in their expression of the Christian faith. In the twentieth-first century, Christianity continued to spread and become more diverse through the invention of the Internet and the push toward globalization. Thanks to digital technology, Christians now had an opportunity to "meet" with one another across the globe to provide encouragement and prayer. Yet the social upheaval continued as the sexual revolution morphed into the LGBTQ+ phenomena that continues to be a point of debate and contention internally and externally for the Christian church.

**KEY FIGURES** Voltaire and Jean-Jacques Rousseau advocated for secularism and an overall societal break with the Church during the Enlightenment. Preachers like John Wesley, George Whitefield, and Jonathan Edwards accordingly fanned the flames through their proclamation of the gospel message in the Great Awakening. People such as Adoniram Judson, David Livingstone, Hudson Taylor, William Carey, and many others spread Christianity abroad and encouraged newfound believers in the faith. Martin Luther King Jr., along with many others, led protests and marches to bring about social change for the African American community.

**KEY IDEAS** With the introduction of the higher-critical method in the nineteenth-century, men like Julius Wellhausen, F. C. Baur, and Rudolf Bultmann argued against foundational tenets of a Christian doctrine of Scripture. Yet, coming to the defense of biblical inspiration and authority, theologians such as B. B. Warfield and Charles Hodge continued to affirm the truthfulness of the Bible.

**KEY WORKS**

- *On the Origin of Species,* Charles Darwin. The pioneering work on evolutionary biology.
- *Sinners in the Hands of an Angry God,* Jonathan Edwards. This sermon preached by Edwards urges a call of repentance and implores listeners to turn to God for forgiveness of sins before it is too late.
- *The Inspiration and Authority of the Bible,* B. B. Warfield. A collection of articles and essays on the doctrine of inspiration.

# Timeline:
## (ca. AD 1700–CURRENT)

**1703–1791**
John Wesley

**1703–1758**
Jonathan Edwards

**1707–1788**
Charles Wesley

**1714–1770**
George Whitefield

**1730s–1740s**
First Great Awakening

**1725–1807**
John Newton

**1759–1833**
William Wilberforce

**1760–1831**
Richard Allen

**1761–1834**
William Carey

**1753–1833**
Lemuel Haynes

**1796**
London Missionary Society sends first missionaries

**1795–1835**
Second Great Awakening

**1813–1855**
Søren Kierkegaard

**1821–1822**
Friedrich Schleiermacher, the "Father of Liberal Theology," publishes *The Christian Faith*

**1834–1892**
Charles Spurgeon

**1859**
Charles Darwin's *Origin of Species* is published

**1861–1865**
American Civil War

**1867–1951**
Amy Carmichael

**1886–1968**
Karl Barth

**1892–1983**
Corrie ten Boom

**1898–1963**
C. S. Lewis

**1906–1945**
Dietrich Bonhoeffer

**1906**
Azusa Street Revival begins

**1913–2003**
Carl F. H. Henry

**1914–1916**
War World I

**1921–2011**
John Stott

**1925**
The Scopes Trial held in Dayton, TN

**1926–2020**
J. I. Packer

**1933–1945**
The Holocaust

**1939–1945**
War World II

**1947–1991**
The Cold War

**1947**
First manuscripts of the Dead Sea Scrolls discovered

**1949**
Billy Graham leads citywide Crusade in Los Angeles

**1950–1953**
The Korean War

**1950**
The Civil Rights Movement begins

**1954–1975**
Vietnam War

**1956**
Missionaries Jim Elliot and others killed

**1962–1965**
Second Vatican Council

**1974**
First Lausanne Conference held in Switzerland

**1979**
Moral Majority established by Jerry Falwell

**2001**
Terrorists attack World Trade Center and Pentagon in U.S.

# Events of the First and Second Great Awakenings

1 John Wesley arrives and serves as a pastor in Savannah, Georgia, for two years (1735-1737).

2 Jonathan Edwards preaches "Sinners in the Hands of an Angry God" in Northampton, Massachusetts (1741).

3 George Whitefield begins his first American preaching tour in Pennsylvania (1739).

4 Barton Stone holds camp meetings in Cane Ridge, Kentucky (1801).

5 Revivals arrives in New England through the preaching of men such as Timothy Dwight and Lyman Beecher (1810–1825).

6 Charles Finney begins months-long revival in Rochester, New York (1830).

# HISTORIC CHRISTIAN DOCTRINES

## Creation Out of Nothing

*(Gen 1:1)*

The Bible teaches that God created the universe—everything both visible and invisible—out of nothing (sometimes expressed in the Latin phrase, *creation ex nihilo*). This means that before God created anything, nothing else existed except God himself. God alone is eternal; every created thing has a beginning. Therefore, the eternal God rules over all of his creation, and he alone is worthy of worship. Denial of this doctrine has implications for God's sovereignty over, and providence in, creation. Because God created out of nothing, creation has meaning and purpose and points us to the Creator.

## Clarity of Scripture

*(Ps 119:105)*

Because God gave us his Word as authoritative in all matters related to life and faith, we believe his Word was written in a way that can be understood with the help of the Holy Spirit. Believing the Scriptures are clear does not mean that every part is equally easy to interpret; neither does it mean we will never make mistakes in our interpretation. It does mean that, with God's help, people are capable of understanding the biblical text for themselves as they employ correct methods of interpretation.

## Inerrancy of Scripture

*(Matt 5:18)*

Inerrancy refers to the belief that the Scripture is completely truthful, without any mixture of error, in all its teachings, no matter what subject it addresses. Believing the Scriptures to be inerrant does not preclude the biblical authors' inclusion of observations from a human observer, the use of round numbers, unusual grammatical constructions, or varying perspectives on a particular event. It does mean, however, that Scripture is an infallible guide to salvation and that it is truthful in all that it affirms (Matt 5:18; John 10:35; Titus 1:2; Heb 6:18).

## Miracles

*(Acts 4:29–31)*

A miracle is an event in which God makes an exception to the natural order of things, or supersedes the natural laws, for the purpose of demonstrating his glory and/or validating his message. Miracles are recorded throughout Scripture; miraculous signs and wonders were oftentimes evident when a prophet or an apostle was speaking God's message to the people. Because we believe God to be all-powerful and personally involved in this world, we believe he can and does perform miracles.

## The Problem of Evil

*(Rom 8:28)*

Many atheists have argued that if God is all-powerful, all loving, and knows everything, evil would not exist in the world as humans know it today. But because evil exists in the world, God must not exist (or if he does exist, then he is not good or all-powerful). Despite its powerful rhetoric, appealing to evil as an argument against God fails: first, because outrage over bad things in this world presupposes a "good" moral standard that does not exist apart from God, and second, because God could have a good reason (though unknown to us) for allowing evil and suffering to continue for a season. Given what we know about God's character and purposes, Christians can rest assured that, even in the midst of evil, God is working all things for our good.

# The Great Awakenings

| | KEY LOCATIONS | KEY INDIVIDUALS |
|---|---|---|
| **FIRST** ca. 1730–1755 | England, New England Colonies and the English colonies of Novia Scotia, New Brunswick, and Prince Edward Island | Solomon Stoddard, Jonathan Edwards, George Whitfield, Henry Alline |
| **SECOND** ca. 1790–1840 | Western New York State; the American Frontier; Logan County, KY; Dickson, TN | Richard Allen, Henry Ward Beecher, Lyman Beecher, Alexander Campbell, Charles Grandison Finney, Luther Rice |
| **THIRD** ca. 1855–1930 | America and Korea, East Tennessee, Azuza Street (Los Angeles, CA) | Charles Spurgeon, Dwight L. Moody, Hudson Taylor, William Booth, Ira Sankey, Mary Baker Eddy, Charles Taze Russell |
| **FOURTH** ca. 1960–1980 | Primarily in the United States following World War II | Billy Graham, Martin Luther King Jr., Pope John Paul II |

BIOGRAPHY

# John Wesley

John Wesley was born on June 17, 1703, to Samuel and Susanna Wesley in Epworth, Lincolnshire, England. He was the fifteenth child born to the devout Anglican couple, and he would prove to be an important figure in the Protestant movement.

John was educated at both Charterhouse (1714) and Christ Church, Oxford, and was elected a fellow of Lincoln College, Oxford, in 1726. He joined the "Holy Club," a group formed by his younger brother Charles, which studied the Bible, prayed, and examined how to live holy lives. In 1728 he was ordained to serve an Anglican priest and traveled to the Georgia Colony in British America where he first experienced Moravian settlers on his journey over. He arrived in Georgia in 1736 and served as minister for almost two years before returning to England.

In 1738 he, along with his brother Charles, underwent a religious experience at Aldersgate Street where he heard the reading of Martin Luther's preface to his commentary on Romans. Coupled with a Moravian meeting, Wesley trusted in Christ and became a Christian.

After his conversion, Wesley began to preach with Charles and their friend, the evangelist George Whitefield. Being excluded from churches, the three began "open-air preaching," and their preaching was met with great numbers of listeners as well as hostility. Although he agreed that open-air preaching met people who would likely not enter a church building, he also believed that the Anglican liturgy offered much.

Wesley began to organize people into what was called "class meetings" that emphasized accountability, spiritual discipline, and support among believers. His early days with the "Holy Club" likely served as a model for these meetings. He would also ride frequently throughout Great Britain, preaching wherever he could to whoever would hear. It is estimated that he rode 250,000 miles and preached more than 40,000 sermons.

Wesley was a prolific writer and penned several sermons, essays, and theological works that played a significant role in helping to form Methodist theology and its practice. Wesley married at age 48 to a widow, Mary Vazeille, in 1751. Unfortunately, Mary would leave John due to his busyness with the Methodist movement. On March 2, 1791, at the age of 87 and surrounded by friends, John Wesle died. His work established a conglomeration of Methodist societies and preaching circuits that were not just contained to England, and the Methodist movement still continues today.

BIOGRAPHY

# Jonathan and Sarah Edwards

Jonathan Edwards (1703–1758) is recognized as one of America's leading theologians. Born in 1703, the only son of 11 children and the son and grandson of pastors, it was expected that Jonathan would be a minister. Edwards conversion occurred at the age of 15, after reading 1 Tim 1:17, "Now to the King eternal, immortal, invisible, the only God, be honor and glory forever and ever. Amen," Edwards wrote that when reading this Scripture he had a "new kind of apprehension and idea of Christ and the work of redemption, and the glorious way of salvation by him."[1]

Edwards completed his studies at Yale, married Sarah Pierpoint in 1727, and succeeded his grandfather as pastor of the church in Northampton, Massachusetts. His sermons were thoroughly based in Scripture as well as rich with practical application, reflecting Edwards's brilliant intellect as well as his pastoral heart. Edwards's preaching is recognized as an important catalyst to the revival known as the Great Awakening, which spread throughout the American colonies in the 1730s and 1740s. His numerous books were well read in his own day, in both England and America, and many, especially *Religious Affections* and *The Freedom of the Will*, continue to be studied today. *The Life of David Brainerd*, the biographical sketch about the missionary to the American natives, has encouraged numerous missionaries in later years, including William Carey, who is considered to be the "Father of Modern Missions."

When the British evangelist George Whitefield visited America and stayed with the Edwards family, he was especially moved by the love between Jonathan and Sarah. "A sweeter couple I have not yet seen. . . . She talked feelingly and solidly of the Things of God and seemed to be such a Help meet for her Husband."[2] The Edwards had 11 children, three sons and eight daughters. Led by Jonathan, the family daily read the Scriptures and prayed together in both the morning and evening. While Jonathan worked in his study most of the day, Sarah managed the household and governed the children. Visitors often commented on the Edwards's well-mannered and courteous children. The love Jonathan and Sarah had for each other encouraged the children's love and respect for their parents. Though she often visited Jonathan in his study throughout the day, daily at four in the afternoon, the couple would go for a walk or horseback ride together, and Jonathan would share his studies with Sarah.

In 1758, Jonathan accepted the position as president of the new college at Princeton, New Jersey. Sarah was in Massachusetts preparing for the move, while Jonathan was in Princeton preparing for his new position. However, Jonathan fell ill from complications of a smallpox vaccination and died on March 2, 1758. His last words were, "Give my kindest love to my dear wife, and tell her that the uncommon union which has so long subsisted between us has been of such a nature as I trust is spiritual and therefore will continue forever." When Sarah was told of her husband's death, she said, "The Lord has done it: He has made me adore his goodness that we had him so long. But my God lives and he has my heart."[3]

BIOGRAPHY

# Charles Wesley

Charles Wesley was born on December 18, 1707, in Epworth, Lincolnshire, the eighteenth of 19 children. His father, Samuel Wesley, was an Anglican cleric in the town, and his mother, Susanna, was the daughter of a Dissenter from the Church of England. Charles received his education at home, first, from his mother, and then attended Westminster School at eight years of age. He later matriculated to Christ Church, Oxford. In 1727 Charles began a prayer group with classmates, and in 1729, his brother John, as well as George Whitefield, joined the group, which became known as the "Holy Club." They primarily focused on Bible study and living a holy life. Charles graduated in 1732 with a master's degree in classical languages and was ordained as a priest in the Anglican order.

In 1735, Charles began a chaplaincy in the Georgia Colony in British America but left shortly thereafter to return to England. In 1738 both Charles and John had a religious experience and a profound conversion in Aldersgate Street that was marked by a personal encounter with Christ. From this point, Charles began to preach and write hymns. In 1739 he was appointed as curate in St. Mary's Church, Islington, but was forced to resign when he faced opposition by church leaders to his evangelical preaching. Finding no welcome within the church, Charles, along with his brother John and Whitefield, began "open-air preaching" and were met with great a number of listeners. Together, they are the most significant figures in the creation of Methodism. Charles traveled around Great Britain for a number of years but refrained from long journeys in 1756 after being sick for some time.

In 1749 Charles married Sarah Gwynne (1726–1822), and she would travel with Charles throughout Britain until 1753. Together they had eight children, with only three surviving past infancy.

Charles was a prolific writer, composing poetry and doctrinal works. Yet he is perhaps best known for his hymns. It is estimated that Wesley penned over 6,500 hymns throughout his life, and his hymns became an integral part of the Methodist movement, so much so that he became known as the "Bard of Methodism." Some of his hymns, which are still sung today, include: "Hark! The Herald Angels Sing," "And Can It Be That I Should Gain," "Come, Thou Long Expected Jesus," "Jesus, Lover of My Soul," "O for a Thousand Tongues to Sing," and "Christ the Lord Is Risen Today." He died on March 29, 1788, at the age of 80, and a memorial stone still stands today in the gardens in Marylebone High Street.

BIOGRAPHY

# George Whitefield

George Whitefield was an eighteenth-century English preacher who preached 18,000 sermons in 34 years of itinerant ministry. Whitefield helped establish Methodism, though he would later hand the work over to John Wesley. In addition to being a passionate preacher, an ordained priest in the Church of England, and one of the founders of Methodism, Whitefield conceived and built a home for orphans in Georgia.

Whitefield and John and Charles Wesley were friends during their time at the University of Oxford, forming a spiritual brotherhood known as the "Holy Club." Although Whitefield and the Wesleys were committed to living out the teachings of Scripture, the men did not understand communion with God as the basis of a holy life. It was Henry Scougal's *The Life of God in the Soul of Man* that God used to reorder Whitefield's understanding of the relationship between behavior and spiritual change. Whitefield came to understand that God's presence in an individual's life births obedience rather than obedience earning God's presence. John Wesley would later learn the same truth through his own conversion experience in 1738.

Whitefield understood that the Holy Spirit alone could bring the lost to salvation, but he also took his own responsibility as God's ambassador very seriously. Whitefield preached in the open air, sometimes preaching to more than 30,000 people at a time from a portable pulpit. Whitefield's preaching, along with that of Jonathan Edwards, helped fan the Great Awakening into flame in the American colonies. Whitefield developed the concept of revival meetings in Britain and in the United States, where the Holy Spirit empowered his preaching to bring many souls into saving relationship with the Father.

For his many accomplishments, Whitefield did have a terrible blind spot regarding slavery. Whitefield agreed with Jonathan Edwards that slavery was an acceptable practice according to the Bible, so long as masters treated their slaves with kindness and were willing to teach their slaves the gospel. Whitefield argued that masters were robbing themselves by withholding the gospel from slaves, since Christian slaves would be more obedient. Whitefield went so far as to argue for the legalization of slavery, and slaves largely maintained Whitefield's property in Georgia where the home for orphans was located.

On the one hand, Whitefield's commitment to evangelism and passionate preaching serve as a glorious example of the power Scripture can have on the life of an individual who loves the God its pages describe. On the other, Whitefield's blindness to the evil of slavery serves as a stern warning that even the spiritually mature must read God's Word attentive to their own hearts, asking the Holy Spirit to reveal blind spots through its pages. Whitefield's life is a powerful testimony to the sinfulness of man and the sovereignty of the God who can use imperfect people to accomplish his perfect purposes.

BIOGRAPHY

# Susannah Wesley

Born on January 20, 1669, Susannah Annesley was the youngest of 25 children of Samuel Annesley, a prominent London minister. When she was 20, Susannah married Samuel Wesley, also a Church of England minister. Considering himself a scholar and poet, Susannah's husband had great ambitions and sought to promote himself into a prominent position in the church. He was often imperious and demanding with Susannah. The couple had 19 children, with nine surviving to adulthood. John Wesley was the fifteenth and Charles Wesley the eighteenth child.

With a large household to manage, Susannah methodically arranged her days and week. She always spent an hour a day in private devotions. Six days a week, six hours a day, she spent in the education of her children at home, sometimes even writing their textbooks. Each school day began and ended with the reading of the Scripture and the singing of a psalm. At least once a week Susannah met individually with each of the children, reviewing their studies and encouraging them in their spiritual walk. To be an "instrument of doing good" to her children was her greatest desire.

In 1709 a disastrous fire destroyed the rectory in Epworth, endangering the lives of the entire Wesley family. Toddler Charles was among the first rescued from the blazing home, while six-year-old John Wesley was the last to be saved from the fire. John always considered himself a "burning stick snatched from the fire" (Zech 3:2). Twenty-nine years later, John and his brother Charles experienced another rescue when they came to saving faith in Jesus Christ. John wrote, "I felt my heart strangely warmed. I felt I did trust in Christ, Christ alone for salvation: and an assurance was given to me that he had taken away *my* sins, even *mine,* and save *me* from the law of sin and death."[4]

The brothers became evangelists, preachers, and leaders of the Great Awakening, which truly transformed England and beyond. John Wesley organized Methodist societies to provide pastoral care for the newly converted. Charles Wesley aided especially in writing hymns which became cherished by the Christian church—hymns such as "Jesu, Lover of My Soul," "Love Divine, All Loves Excelling," "Hark the Herald Angels Sing," and "Christ the Lord Is Risen Today." Both brothers were building on the methodical instruction they had received from their mother Susannah.

Susannah died at the age of 73, surrounded by her children. The epitaph Charles wrote began:

> In sure and steadfast hope to rise
> And claim her mansion in the skies,
> A Christian here her flesh laid down,
> The cross exchanging for a crown.[5]

# Views on the Days of Creation

**THEISTIC EVOLUTION (SOMETIMES CALLED "PROGRESSIVE CREATION")**

A view that attempts to harmonize a biblical creation of the world with scientific claims on evolution. God is the ultimate source and sustainer of life who created the world, but some would believe that Adam came about by the process of natural evolution that was guided by God. This view allows for scientific claims to be introduced for evolution while providing the individual with maintaining a belief in God.

**GAP THEORY**

The belief that a "gap" in time exists between Gen 1:1 and Gen 1:2. In verse 1, God created everything in perfection, but in verse 2 the creation is called "formless and empty" with "darkness" existing due to a cataclysmic event, possibly the fall of Satan. Genesis 1:3–2:3 details the restoring of the original earth. This view allows for a scientific understanding of the earth's age and geological history to be reconciled to the biblical account of creation.

**DAY-AGE THEORY**

A theological interpretation of Gen 1 which understands the "day" (Hb. *yom*) to mean an undefined, long period of time rather than a literal 24-hour day. Each day represents a certain era of Earth's history, which allows harmonizing the biblical account with scientific claims regarding the age of the Earth and the universe.

**24-HOUR INTERPRETATION**

Understands the Hebrew word for "day" (*yom*) to mean a literal 24-hour day rather than a long period of time. All of creation took place within six, 24-hour days of creation. This position is held by "young Earth" proponents who believe the Earth is a few thousand years old. This view is a traditional understanding of Genesis 1.

**ANALOGICAL-DAY INTERPRETATION**

This approach suggests that the six days are not identical to a human workweek in their quantity of hours but rather describe God's creative work in analogical terms (e.g., Exod 20:9–11).

**FRAMEWORK INTERPRETATION**

Focusing on the structure of the passage, this approach argues that the days of Genesis 1 do not refer to a linear sequence of 24-hour periods but instead are a literary construction that represents God's creative work in a topical manner where days 1–3 are parallel to days 4–6.

**REVELATORY-DAY INTERPRETATION**

According to this view, the days refer to 24-hour periods, but creation did not occur during these days. Rather, God spent the course of the six days revealing to the writer how he made the heavens and the earth.

**RELIGIOUS POLEMIC VIEW**

The account reflects the ancient, prescientific cosmology of the ancient Near East, and thus it does not speak to science or history but only makes theological claims since it is primarily meant to dispute rival creation accounts and their respective deities.

BIOGRAPHY

# John Newton

John Newton (1725–1807) is most known as the author of "Amazing Grace." The hymn's haunting lyrics become more so when we understand just what a wretch Newton was before God rescued him and how much that grace echoed throughout this life and ministry.

While he was a young man, Newton's rebellious behavior stood out even in life at sea, which was brutal and rough. Whether during his time as a captive impressed into service by the British navy, or while serving freely, Newton gained the ire of every captain. One handed Newton over to his African mistress who kept Newton as a slave for a time. But even this horrific experience did not stop Newton from becoming a slave trader himself and, eventually, a slave ship captain.

In 1748, a terrible storm at sea caused Newton to turn to God, begging him to spare his life. Newton would later call this momentous event his "great turning day." That day was, however, only the start of what would prove to be a long, slow conversion.

The journals Newton kept during his slave ship voyages over the next few years show his deep depravity, so deep that he sometimes joined his shipmates in raping female slaves, a routine practice that was seen simply as a benefit for men engaged in the trade. Only after marrying, did Newton's conscience compel him to refrain from these vile acts, and he eventually began to treat the enslaved people on his ships more humanely.

Not until he left sea life did Newton's eyes begin to open to the evil of all he had done. Nor could he shake the sense of God's continual intervention in his life. Increasingly, he sensed a call into the ministry. Although he had no affiliation with any denomination and was significantly influenced by the evangelical revivalists John Wesley and George Whitefield, Newton eventually aimed for ordination in the Church of England. Because of his connections to evangelicals (who were considered controversial by institutional authorities), the process took several years, various refusals, and, ultimately, the patronage of an influential earl before a bishop would agree to ordain Newton in 1764.

Newton immediately took an appointment at Olney church. There he collaborated with his friend, the poet William Cowper, in writing and publishing *Olney Hymns,* the volume in which "Amazing Grace" first appeared.

After becoming rector of St. Mary Woolnoth in London in 1780, Newton became a mentor to a young member of Parliament named William Wilberforce, who was recently converted to the Christian faith. Newton counseled Wilberforce to serve God by remaining in Parliament, advice that changed the course of history because of the role Wilberforce played in the abolition of the slave trade. Wilberforce's efforts were greatly assisted by Newton's published accounts of what he had witnessed all those years in the slave business.

Even so, it was perhaps in his role as a pastor and a preacher Newton most profoundly changed the world. The Church of England in which Newton served long resisted the spirit of revival spreading outside its walls. But Newton brought that spirit inside. The churches where Newton ministered were forced to build out the walls in order to accommodate the crowds that came hear him teach about the amazing grace that made a man once blind see.

BIOGRAPHY

# William Cowper

The words of William Cowper (1731–1800) are better known than the name of the one who penned them. These words include verses from some of the church's most enduring hymns, such as:

> There is a fountain fill'd with blood
> Drawn from Emmanuel's veins;
> And sinners, plung'd beneath that flood,
> Lose all their guilty stains.
>
> God moves in a mysterious way,
> His wonders to perform;
> He plants his footsteps in the sea,
> And rides upon the storm.
>
> Sometimes a light surprises
> The Christian when he sings;
> It is the Lord who rises
> With healing in his wings.

Cowper (pronounced "Cooper") was born into a well-connected family in Hertfordshire, England, and, as was expected by his family, pursued the law profession. The final step before taking an appointment as a clerk, however, required a public examination, which the sensitive and melancholy Cowper found difficult to face. The pressure precipitated a mental health crisis and suicide attempt; as a result, Cowper was placed in an asylum where he found improved health and embraced evangelical Christianity.

In 1767, John Newton invited Cowper to reside with him on the grounds of Olney church where Newton offered him emotional and spiritual comfort and support along with the opportunity for Cowper to serve in lay ministry in the parish. The two men developed a highly creative collaboration that resulted in the writing and publication of the *Olney Hymns* (pronounced "Owney"), which included the hymns quoted above as well as Newton's own "Amazing Grace."

Following another crisis and suicide attempt in 1773, however, Cowper became convinced, despite Newton's counsel otherwise, that his attempt to take his own life and ongoing mental torments put him outside of God's will, making him unsuitable to continue the work of lay ministry or hymnody.

Cowper did continue to write poetry, however. And while the church knows Cowper through his hymns, the literary world knows him for his highly praised poetry, most notably *The Task* (1785) and "The Castaway" (1803). His poetry blended classical aesthetics with modern sensibility, often seeing within the natural world reflections of the state of the individual soul.

Cowper's poetry also reflected the ideals of evangelical Christianity, including its spirit of reform based on the virtues of kindness and benevolence. This spirit is exemplified in his abolitionist poem, "The Negro's Complaint" (1788), which presents the sorrow and suffering of slavery from the perspective of an enslaved man. Likewise, the compassion toward animals seen frequently in Cowper's poetry supported the evangelical movement's pioneering efforts in animal welfare. His poetry's deep emotional and spiritual themes led Hannah More to call Cowper a poet she could read on Sunday.

Cowper was one of the most beloved and respected poets during his lifetime and beyond, helping to usher in the Romantic period of English literature and giving voice to the evangelical faith that helped save his life.

BIOGRAPHY

# Lemuel Haynes

Lemuel Haynes was born to a white indentured servant and an unknown black man in Connecticut in 1753. At a young age, he was indentured to Deacon David Rose. Through Rose and his wife, Haynes learned about Christianity and came to faith at a young age. Haynes was able to attend a local school where he learned to read, and this reading was often applied to the Bible, sermons, and the psalter.

In 1774, when Lemuel's indentured servitude ended, he joined the militia. The Revolutionary War was brewing, and Lemuel fought as a patriot, fully invested in the message of equality for which so many Americans were fighting.

After the war, Lemuel settled down and became a farmer. He spent his spare time studying theology and reading sermons. Every Sunday, Deacon Rose—now a blind man—would ask Lemuel to read a sermon to him aloud. One Sunday, Lemuel read his own sermon. Shocked by the passion of Lemuel's reading, Rose asked the young man if he had read from Davies, Watts, or Whitfield. Lemuel replied, "It's Lemuel's."

Many took notice of Lemuel's intellect, and he was eventually recruited to come and learn at Dartmouth, a position he turned down to study Greek and Latin under an individual scholar. Lemuel became the first black man in America to be ordained to preach and spent the rest of his life serving in and around New England.

Lemuel was not always met with friendliness. In addition to his theological prowess, he was also actively involved in the cause for abolition, preaching boldly against the slave trade. Despite the kindness of so many white parishioners, going so far as to honor his marriage to white schoolteacher, Elizabeth Babbitt, Lemuel was also often met with vitriol.

Lemuel died in 1833, leaving behind his wife, his 10 children, and a legacy of Christian service.

BIOGRAPHY

# William Wilberforce

When William Wilberforce (1759–1833) won his first parliamentary seat in 1780 at the age of 21, he was neither a believer nor an abolitionist. But in 1784, Wilberforce read *The Rise and Progress of Religion in the Soul* by Philip Doddridge, an influential Dissenting minister of the early eighteenth century. This began a process of conviction and wrestling that eventually led Wilberforce to request a secret, nighttime meeting with John Newton, the ex-slave ship captain turned minister. Wilberforce thought his only option if he chose to become a serious Christian was to enter the ministry. Newton, however, encouraged Wilberforce that he could serve God in Parliament. By God's providence and that sage advice, that is what Wilberforce did.

On April 14, 1786, Good Friday, Wilberforce took Communion for the first time. Soon, his long-held views against slavery became a conviction. On Sunday, October 28, 1787, Wilberforce wrote in his journal these now famous words: "God Almighty has set before me two great objects, the suppression of the slave trade and the reformation of manners."

The following year, he met England's leading abolitionists: Thomas Clarkson, Granville Sharp, Charles Middleton, and Hannah More. They soon convinced him to join their efforts to abolish the slave trade. These abolitionists took an incrementalist approach, developing bills and strategies that would chip away at the industry and improve conditions for slaves until the practice could be outlawed. They knew, too, that the way to change laws was to change hearts and minds first. Thus, on the day Wilberforce was prepared to present a bill before Parliament requiring improved conditions on slave ships, Hannah More released her poem, "Slavery," which would appeal to the public while Wilberforce appealed to lawmakers. Eventually, this multipronged strategy worked. It took decades, but, led by Wilberforce, Parliament passed the Slave Trade Act of 1807, ending the slave trade throughout the British Empire.

Wilberforce wrote in his journal of two great objects, however. In 1797, Wilberforce published a popular and influential theological work, *A Practical View of the Prevailing Religious System*, a work that aimed to persuade the many who held to nominal Christianity to exchange it for genuine, personal faith. The evidence of surface-level faith was all around in this callous society. The cruelties Wilberforce and his evangelical friends witnessed—whether in the form of slavery, child labor, capital punishment, or animal cruelty—had, they believed, a coarsening effect on everyone. This is why in 1824 Wilberforce helped establish the first Society for the Prevention of Cruelty to Animals and worked with Christian clergymen to publish sermons and tracts promoting the humane treatment of animals. The early evangelicals believed that benevolence—goodwill—rightly extended to all of God's creation.

These evangelical reform efforts have been described as an attempt to "make goodness fashionable." Their success is proven by the unprecedented social reforms that came to define the Victorian age that followed. The most significant victory was the Slavery Abolition Act which liberated most enslaved persons throughout the British Empire. It was passed in 1833, one month after Wilberforce's death.

BIOGRAPHY

# William Carey

Born in England on August 17, 1761, William Carey was inspired from boyhood by stories of his uncle's travels in Canada and James Cook's travelogues detailing his discovery of Pacific islands, with these stories instilling in him a desire to see the world. Carey was apprenticed to a shoemaker when he was 14, and while the occupation did not stick, the faith he gained as a result did. Having lied to his master about money, Carey prayed, promising he would never do it again if God would keep him from being caught. However, his master did find out, as did the entire village. The guilt Carey felt as a result led him to see his deep need for a Savior, and he sought forgiveness from God and began following Christ.

Reaching manhood during the time in which William Wilberforce was fighting in British Parliament to abolish the slave trade, Carey protested the trade by abstaining from purchasing and using sugar. He grew in his love for Scripture and began preaching in local churches, but his early interest in uncharted lands inspired his compassion toward those who had never heard the gospel. He wanted to take the message of Christ to the places Captain Cook had explored.

At the time, this idea of foreign missions was unfamiliar. There were no sending agencies, and most British churches were not interested in sending out workers when there was so much to be done in their own country. He wrote a pamphlet calling for people to end their love for money and comfort and instead to obey the command of Jesus in Matt 28:19–20. In 1792, he preached to a Baptist association, sharing a sermon from Isa 54 on "spreading the tent" and sharing the gospel with those around the world who had not yet heard it. This sermon included his famous words: "Expect great things from God. Attempt great things for God." Carey continued to push to be sent out to spread the gospel, an effort that finally paid off in 1793 as he sailed to India with his family as the first missionary sent by the newly formed Baptist Missionary Society.

William Carey lived in India for the next 40 years until his death on June 9, 1834. He eventually settled in Calcutta, where he worked with other missionaries to build schools. The heart of Carey's work was in translating the entire Bible into six Indian languages and the New Testament into more than 20, a feat made all the more remarkable when a fire destroyed much of the translation work at one point. Carey suffered through government persecution and ongoing conflict between older and younger missionaries, finding respite in his large garden, where he spent hours working the land and enjoying God's creation.

Carey was adamant that he not be lauded with praise after his death, writing to a friend that nothing like "the faithful servant of God" should be said about him. He continued, "All such expressions would convey a falsehood. To me belong shame and confusion of face. I can only say, 'Hangs my helpless soul on Thee,'" quoting a line from a hymn written by Charles Wesley.

Upon his death, there were 14 British missionary societies and similar groups in America and other countries. Carey's efforts established sending models still used around the world today.

BIOGRAPHY

# Richard Allen

Richard Allen was born into slavery in Philadelphia but spent most of his formative years in Delaware. He was converted at the age of 17 and showed such a talent for preaching that his master allowed him to hold small church services in his house. Nat Turner's slave rebellion in 1831 would eventually lead to a tightening of the reigns around black religious freedom for fear of future uprisings, but Allen was able to operate in the years before the rebellion with relative ease, being welcomed into homes and churches to teach both enslaved and free.

Allen's master became so convicted by the 17-year-old's preaching that he himself was converted and convicted of slavery's immorality. He allowed Allen and his brother to purchase themselves. For the next several years, Allen preached wherever he could, traveling surrounding states and only stopping to work to earn money when his clothing became bare.

In 1786, Allen wound up in Philadelphia and became a member at St. George's Methodist Church. There, Allen led prayer meetings that inspired even more participation from black congregants—sometimes to the chagrin of their white fellow members.

The Methodist church took a liberal stance on slavery when compared to other Protestant denominations of its day, but their worship services were still routinely segregated. Black parishioners made up 10 percent of Methodists but were still often forced to sit in separate seating during worship services. When this trend came to St. George's, Allen and some of his fellow black congregants were asked to vacate the white seating section of a service in the middle of prayer.

This small action became the catalyst for Allen to begin a new black congregation with colaborer Absalom Jones. In 1816, the African Methodist Episcopal Church (AME) was born, and Allen served as the first bishop.

In addition to his work in uniting five black denominations under the AME banner and founding the oldest and largest formal black institution in the country, Allen and his wife were also active in aiding refugees on the Underground Railroad. He died in 1831.

# How Do We Know God Exists?

With the transition from the premodern to the modern world, new questions about the universe emerged, especially questions about God's existence and his relevance to human life. While modern thinkers were not the first to raise these questions, the new forms of these questions gave raise also to new formulations of arguments for God's existence and appeals for why the existence of the triune God of Christian theism matters.

## ARGUMENTS FOR GOD'S EXISTENCE

| QUESTION | CORRELATING ARGUMENT | DESCRIPTION |
|---|---|---|
| **Why is there something rather than nothing?** | **COSMOLOGICAL ARGUMENT** | The basic premise of this argument is that every effect has a cause. Since the universe appears to be made up of contingent and temporal parts and thus caused, there must be a self-sufficient uncaused cause to explain the existence of the universe. |
| **Why does morality always seem to matter?** | **MORAL ARGUMENT** | Beyond cultural conventions and social norms, human beings conceive of certain moral obligations as being right or wrong on an objective level. For objective morality to truly exist and have meaning, ultimate justice must be established at some point. Ultimate justice is not obtainable apart from an omniscient, omnipotent, and morally perfect judge. |
| **Why do things seem to have order and purpose?** | **TELEOLOGICAL ARGUMENT** | Though impersonal, the universe appears to possess intention and cohesion (e.g., design). Since impersonal entities cannot account for intention and cohesion, the universe must be the product of personal intent that exists beyond it. |

| QUESTION | CORRELATING ARGUMENT | DESCRIPTION |
|---|---|---|
| **Why does beauty exist?** | **AESTHETIC ARGUMENT** | This argument looks to the apparent unassailability of beauty as a reality that humans universally recognize in the world. When understood not merely in accordance with preference and taste, beauty suggests there must be more to life than physical survival and the subjective experiences of sentient creatures. |
| **How do we account for transcendent and immaterial realities like logic, truth, language, math, the relationship between universals and particulars, the laws of nature, the obligation of intellectual honesty, etc.?** | **TRANSCENDENTAL ARGUMENT** | Transcendental preconditions are necessary to make sense of the universe and of human experience, and these preconditions cannot be found in nature itself. To engage in any kind of thought at all presupposes the reality of logic (laws of thought), the capacities of human language, the coherence of universals and particulars, and the moral imperatives that truth entails. Only the personal triune God who is transcendent, self-sufficient, immutable, and sovereign can account for these transcendental preconditions. |

BIOGRAPHY

# Jane Austen

"May the sick and afflicted, be now, and ever in Thy care; and heartily do we pray for the safety of all that travel by land or by sea, for the comfort and protection of the orphan and the widow and that Thy pity may be shown upon all captives and prisoners." These words are from one of three extant prayers written by Jane Austen (1775–1817). The petitions made in these lines echo biblical passages such as Matt 25:36; Luke 4:18; Jas 1:27; and Heb 13:13.

Austen is well known to most by her novels (or their popular film adaptations). Less known is Austen's quiet, steady, lifelong devotion to the Christian faith and to the Church.

The biblical worldview that underlies Austen's social world is not immediately obvious in her works. Yet this daughter of one Anglican clergyman and sister to two others knew Christian doctrine deeply, lived a life steeped in the worship and liturgy of the Church of England, and wrote frequently in her personal correspondence about her faith. All these qualities underlie every one of her novels.

Austen lived during the height of the evangelical movement that was sweeping across the Transatlantic region. While she was a young woman sharing drafts of her stories within her family circle, evangelicals such as William Wilberforce and Hannah More were in their public prime, advocating for social reform and the abolition of the slave trade. Austen's more reserved Anglicanism eschewed the activism of evangelicalism. "I do not like the evangelicals," she once confessed. Yet, a few years later, she admitted, "I am by no means convinced that we ought not all to be Evangelicals, and am at least persuaded that they who are so from reason and feeling, must be happiest and safest." Austen's thoughts reflect those of many in her time, during a period of division and controversy in the church (and, by extension, society) as the nation's church confronted many challenges from within and without, doctrinal, political, and social.

Austen's works address these questions only obliquely. Her stories extol the Christian virtues such as kindness, love, joy, humility, patience, forbearance, and charity and gently mock the absence of these through her many foolish characters. In this way, her novels transcend the debates of her time.

Her novels, as well as her life, show that Austen understood marriage to be a Christian calling, that being well-matched was a matter of temporal and eternal significance. She broke off her own engagement after just one day, apparently recognizing before it was too late an ill foundation for this marriage. She, like a surprising number of her literary sisters, never did marry. Yet family remained important to her as she was surrounded throughout her too short life by the love of her parents, brothers, nieces, nephews, and her beloved sister. In fact, it was with the help of one of her brothers that her first novel, *Sense and Sensibility*, was published in 1811. Several more novels followed in the ensuing years, with the last two of her completed works being published posthumously, the year following her death in 1817, probably of Addison's disease.

BIOGRAPHY

# Adoniram and Ann Judson

The love of Christ motivated Ann and Adoniram to endure a lifetime of suffering while serving God in Burma. Adoniram, referencing the apostle Paul's words in Eph 3:17–19, said, "If I had not felt certain that every additional trial was ordered by infinite love and mercy, I could not have survived my accumulated sufferings."[1]

Adoniram and Ann were among the first missionaries to set sail from the United States. But the two did not initially make such a bold declaration for Christ. Adoniram grew up in Massachusetts, the son of a pastor and his wife. Extremely intelligent, he renounced his faith at age 20. But the death of his unsaved friend shook him to the core, and he recommitted his life to Christ. Ann Hasseltine, just one year younger, had a different struggle. She was captivated by a life of parties and fashion. But at age 16, Ann got serious about her faith and dedicated her life to serving Jesus.

The couple met at a family dinner and just one month later were engaged. Adoniram declared his intent not only to marry Ann but to take her "to a heathen land."[2] Ann's parents knew they would most likely never see their daughter again. Ann said, "[God] has my heart in his hands, and when I am called to face danger, to pass through scenes of terror and distress, he can inspire me with fortitude."[3]

The Judsons sailed for India in 1812. Three years later, most spent in language training, they celebrated their first convert. During that same season, they grieved the death of two children. Six years into their service, they had established a church of 10 members but faced increasing persecution by the Burmese government. Despite these ongoing trials, the couple translated most of the Bible into Burmese, baptized converts, discipled new Christians, planted churches, and started a school. Ann became the first person to translate any part of the Bible into Siamese (Thai), when she finished the Gospel of Matthew in 1819.

Burma, located between India and China, was ruled by a feared monarch known for torture and mass executions. In 1824, as England and Burma engaged in war, Adoniram was accused of being a spy and taken to prison where he endured severe torture. Every day Ann would walk two miles each way, hoping to bring Adoniram food. Finally, she set up camp with her baby outside the prison walls and gave birth to their third child while her husband was still in prison.

After Adoniram was released, Ann became very ill and died of cerebral meningitis at age 37, followed soon after by her infant daughter. Adoniram was left to continue their mission, but Ann's legacy would not be forgotten. Her memoir, printed after her death, was republished again and again, inspiring future missionaries. And her work on behalf of women's education and church planting would impact generations for Christ. Adoniram served in Burma for the remainder of his life, remarrying twice, and reaching many with the gospel.

BIOGRAPHY

# Fanny Crosby

Frances "Fanny" Crosby was born on March 24, 1820 in Brewster, New York. At six weeks old, a cold caused her eyes to swell, and an unfortunate medical treatment apparently ruined Crosby's sense of sight, leaving her permanently blind.

From a young age, Crosby developed a love for poetry and music. She loved to hear church music coming through the hills, and by the time she was eight, she was writing her own poems. Her Christian grandmother instilled in her a love for Scripture, and she memorized whole books of the Bible. Just before she turned 15, she left home to live and study at the New York Institute for the Blind in New York City.

Her love for writing poetry continued, although her blindness presented challenges. Unable to sit and write one line at a time, crossing out words and replacing them as needed, she instead had to form entire poems in her head, working until they were perfect before asking a friend to write them down for her.

After she finished her time as a student, Crosby stayed on at the institute as a teacher. She continued writing and had several books of poetry published. At age 23 she was the first woman to speak in the United States Senate when she recited a poem before joint houses of Congress on a trip in which she joined lobbyists arguing for education for the blind. While she was not a political figure, her experiences led her to build relationships with three U.S. presidents: John Tyler, James K. Polk, and Grover Cleveland, whom she knew when he was 17 and working at her school, often transcribing her poems.

A cholera outbreak in New York City when she was 29 led to the deaths of several residents of the institute. As a friend lay dying, he asked if he would see Crosby in heaven, which caused her to question her faith. Later, singing the line, "Here Lord, I give myself away," in a church service, she said, "For the first time I realized that I had been trying to hold the world in one hand and the Lord in the other." She gave her life to Christ.

After her conversion, she used her gift for poetry to begin writing hymns. Having musical talent, she played the guitar, piano, harp, and organ. This was a natural progression, and her early memorization of Scripture came out in her writing. By the time of her death, she had written more than 8,000 hymns. Some of the most well-known are "Blessed Assurance," "To God Be the Glory," and "Praise Him, Praise Him."

In 1858, she married a fellow musician who was also blind and had taught at the institute with her. A year later, Crosby gave birth to a daughter, Frances, who died in her sleep shortly after she was born. Her marriage had ups and downs, and she never earned much from her writing. Having lived near many slums and rescue missions, she felt great compassion toward the poor and was known for giving away most of what she earned,

Fanny Crosby died on February 12, 1915, at the age of 94. She once told a pastor she was thankful she was blind, "Because when I get to heaven, the first face that shall ever gladden my sight will be that of my Savior."

## VOICES OF THE CHURCH

*"Every friend of Jesus is a friend of missions. Where there is a healthy spiritual life, there is a love for the missionary cause."*[6]

—ANDREW MURRAY (1828–1917)

BIOGRAPHY

# Charles and Susannah Spurgeon

Susannah Thompson was born in London, England, on January 15, 1832, and her future husband, Charles Haddon Spurgeon, was born in Kelvedon, England, on June 19, 1834. Charles would one day be known as the "Prince of Preachers," but when he and Susie met in 1853, he was a country preacher who traveled to London to give a sermon at New Park Street Chapel, a Baptist church that was without a pastor. Susie came to hear him preach in the Sunday evening service, and they struck up a friendship in which Charles cared for her soul, giving her a copy of his favorite book, John Bunyan's *The Pilgrim's Progress*. Susie's faith was strengthened, and Charles was asked to take on the role of pastor of New Park Street Chapel, moving into the world of Victorian ideals and Dickensian poverty. Shortly thereafter, the two were married and began a lifetime of ministry together.

Charles had become a Christian at the age of 15 when a snowstorm caused him to walk through the doors of a Methodist chapel and hear a message telling him to "look unto me" (Isa 45:22, KJV). He went on to pastor the church in London (later named the Metropolitan Tabernacle) for 33 years and started The Pastors' College, which sent out hundreds of pastors to plant churches. Susie worked to have his sermons translated and started a book fund that gave almost 200,000 books to pastors. They opened orphanages, an aid society for pastors, a maternal society to help impoverished mothers and their children, and supported multiple mission efforts around the world.

An event early in Spurgeon's ministry left him dealing with periodic depression for the rest of his life. He was preaching to an enormous crowd at the Surrey Gardens Music Hall while throngs outside the hall pressed to enter when someone yelled "fire," leading to a stampede that left seven people dead and 28 others injured. The memory of this event would revisit him, leading to bouts of terrible depression. He also struggled through theological disagreements and received threatening letters due to his antislavery stance. Susie suffered under a gynecological illness for years, unable to travel with Charles but determined to continue serving however she could.

Commenting on Matt 20:27–29, Charles Spurgeon wrote, "Let us be willing to be door-mats at our Master's entrance-hall. . . . In our Lord's Church, let the poor, the feeble, the distressed have the place of honor, and let us who are strong bear their infirmities. He is highest who makes himself lowest; he is greatest who makes himself less than the least." The Spurgeons lived to be poured out, with Charles perhaps at times taking on too much and being run down physically. Their lifelong love for each other was exceeded only by their love for Christ, and Susie mourned greatly upon Charles's death at the age of 57 on January 31, 1892. She served for 11 more years until she died on October 22, 1903.

## VOICES OF THE CHURCH

*"Thy greatest refuge, O child of God! in all thy trials, is in a man: not in Moses, but in Jesus; not in the servant, but in the master.... He has not a rod, but a cross... which can open the Red sea and drown thy sins in the very midst. He will not leave thee."*[7]

CHARLES SPURGEON (1834–1892)

BIOGRAPHY

# Amy Carmichael

"If I refuse to allow one who is dear to me to suffer for the sake of Christ, if I do not see such suffering as the greatest honor that can be offered to any follower of the Crucified, then I know nothing of Calvary love."[8]

Inspired by 1 Corinthians 13, Amy Carmichael penned these lines in 1938 after a lifetime of learning their significance. Eventually published in a book simply titled, *If,* they capture Amy's calling to work among India's most vulnerable, suffering with them in order to share "Calvary love."

Amy was born in 1867 in Ireland, the oldest of seven children, but it wasn't until she was a teenager at boarding school that she confessed personal faith in Jesus: "'My mother had often talked to me about the Lord Jesus. . . . I had felt the love of the Lord Jesus and nestled in his love just as I had nestled in her arms. But I had not understood that there was something more to do, something that may be called coming to him."[9]

In 1892, at age 25, Amy set sail for Japan to serve with a foreign missionary organization, but because suffering from neuralgia, a chronic condition that caused intense nerve pain, she soon returned to England. Still determined, she set out for South India in 1895, where she devoted herself to learning the Tamil language, wore Indian clothes, and lived among the people. When Amy met a seven-year-old young girl named Preena, who had escaped from a Hindu temple, she discovered that young children were being subjected to a form of prostitution by Brahmin temple priests. It became her life's mission to rescue them, and Amy founded the Dohnavur Fellowship, which included baby nurseries, homes, cottage homes, hospitals, and schools. By 1913, they had rescued and housed 130 young girls. Amy faced heated opposition to this rescue work but said, "When I consider the cross of Christ, how can anything that I do be called sacrifice?"[10]

In 1931, a serious fall left Amy an invalid, but still she did not leave India. She poured her energy into her missionary work and writing poetry and books (37 in all) about her relationship with God.[11]

Amy died in India at age 83, having served God faithfully for more than 55 years and never taking a furlough. Her grave marker says simply "Amma" the Tamil word for "mother." In 1948, three years after she died, temple prostitution was outlawed in India. The Dohnavur Fellowship still serves children in India today.

BIOGRAPHY

# Dora Yu

For Dora Yu, Chinese evangelist and missionary to Korea, the promise of Ps 27:1 held great comfort. She said, "Ever since I can remember, I prayed every day to God, rarely forgetting. For me, Christ was a really personal God. My sister was often afraid of the dark at night, but I said to myself, 'Since Jesus is with me, why be afraid?'"[12]

Born in China, Dora's paternal grandfather was a devout disciple of Confucius and Mencius. Her father turned to Christianity through the influence of Presbyterian missionaries, so Dora grew up on a mission compound and in a Christian household.

At age 15, Dora left home to attend medical school. During this time both of her parents died, plunging her into a spiritual depression. One night, after repenting and rededicating her life to Christ, she felt this burden lift and became overwhelmed by the love of God. The next day she wrote, "It seems that the face of the whole world has changed; even the sun shines more brightly."[13]

Briefly engaged at age 19, she called it off due to her devotion to ministry and determined to remain single. Four years later, she became one of the first females to graduate from the school of medicine and traveled to Korea as one of China's first cross-cultural ministries. As a missionary, she was involved in education, preaching, and medicine. She helped another woman found a girl's school and established a local chapel.

But after five years, Dora sensed that God was leading her back to China. Korea, she felt, had been her idea and not God's. The Chinese church was experiencing a time of great revival, so Dora decided to focus her energy solely on evangelism. She also made a public decision to cut all funding and depend on God for her every need. This time was spiritually intense for Dora and produced great fruit in evangelism.

For Dora, being in communion with God meant living constantly in his presence. She maintained a devout prayer life, giving her every thought and word to the Lord. She urged people not merely to believe in God for salvation but to develop a daily relationship with him. In 1920, she led a revival at Fuzhou for two months, one attended by a woman named Lin Heping, who was born again. The woman had a 17-year-old son, Ni Tuosheng (Watchman Nee), who gave his life to Christ. She did not realize then that this young man would start the house movement in China and later become a martyr for the faith.

In 1927, Dora was invited to be the main speaker at the Keswick Convention in England. Her speech, urging the church to beware of liberal theology, was widely published. By 1931, her health began to suffer. That spring, she passed the torch to the next generation of missionaries and returned to her permanent place of rest in Shanghai.

BIOGRAPHY

# Corrie and Betsie Ten Boom

Betsie Ten Boom was born on August 19, 1885, followed by her younger sister Corrie on April 15, 1892. Two of four siblings, they grew up in Haarlem, Holland, as the children of a watchmaker and his wife, both of whom were faithful Christians. Corrie followed in her father's footsteps, becoming the first woman licensed as a watchmaker in Holland. After their mother's death, Betsie worked to keep the house and take care of the many family members and friends who came and went. The Ten Booms were known for their compassion and care, taking in foster children, serving the poor in Haarlem, and sharing the truth of God's Word with anyone who entered their home.

Corrie and Betsie's brother, Willem, became a pastor. He led the Dutch Reformed Church's ministry to displaced Jews coming from Germany due to Nazi oppression. While Holland's prime minister assured the people there would be no war due to their neutrality, the country fell quickly to German occupation. Soon, the Ten Booms noticed their Jewish neighbors disappearing. They were forced into action when German troops threw their neighbor out on the street, joining Willem as part of the Dutch Underground operation hiding Jews from Nazis.

The Ten Booms built a secret hiding place within the wall of Corrie's bedroom. Corrie was 50 and Betsie 57 when this work began. Along with their father, they provided a safe place for an estimated 800 Jews and other refugees over the course of a year and a half before they were betrayed to the Gestapo in 1944. The women bid a quick goodbye to their father before being taken to prison. Corrie was given a Bible by a generous nurse, and she and Betsie were able to use it to encourage many desperate women in the dark days to come.

The sisters spent time in different prisons, eventually ending up in Ravensbruck, a German extermination camp. As they entered their new barracks, they quickly realized the beds were infested with fleas. Corrie cried out to her sister, "Betsie, how can we live in such a place?" Earlier that day, the sisters had read 1 Thess 5:16–18, and Betsie told her sister they should give thanks to God for everything, including the fleas in their bunks. Corrie responded, "Betsie, there's no way even God can make me grateful for a flea."

Yet in the coming days, the sisters learned that because their barracks were flea infested, the guards refused to enter. This left the women free to hold Bible studies every night, the words of Scripture being translated around the room to the many languages represented.

Already in poor health, Betsie became sick and weak under the harsh work conditions, eventually dying in the camp hospital. Before she died, she told Corrie about her vision to provide a place of healing for those who had suffered during the war—not just prisoners but also the guards. She believed the gospel was good news for oppressed and oppressor alike.

Three days after Betsie's death, Corrie was released. Years later, she discovered her release had been the result of a clerical error. One week after she was freed, all women her age at the camp were killed.

Corrie lived out the rest of her days speaking about the light of Christ she experienced in the darkness of the camps. Quick to admit her own fear and weakness, she pointed to the forgiveness and grace of God. Corrie's book, *The Hiding Place*, became an international bestseller, sharing hope and love with millions of readers around the world. She died in California on her ninety-first birthday, April 15, 1983.

BIOGRAPHY

# Dorothy Sayers

Dorothy Sayers was born in Oxford, England, on June 13, 1893. Her father was a chaplain and headmaster of the Christ Church Choir. She was an only child and developed an early love for entertaining family and friends through elaborate theatrical productions. She played violin and read voraciously. Her imagination and talent for writing were obvious from an early age, and her education led her to Oxford where she studied modern languages and medieval literature, becoming one of the first women to receive a degree from the university.

After her time at Oxford, Sayers worked for a marketing agency, writing popular ad campaigns. But her lifelong love for stories led her to begin writing mystery novels built around a detective she named Lord Peter Wimsey. These novels thrust Sayers into some degree of fame, but while her professional life was thriving, her personal life was not.

A series of events and broken relationships left Sayers unexpectedly pregnant and unmarried. Secretly giving birth to a son, she told none of her family members other than a cousin who agreed to take in the baby and raise him. Sayers sent money and made visits, but her son, John Anthony ("Tony"), did not know Sayers was his mother until he was much older. She eventually married "Mac" Fleming, a divorced father of two. Their marriage started out happily, but Fleming's PTSD from the first world war eventually plunged him into physical pain and depression, which in turn put a strain on the marriage.

After establishing herself as a gifted detective writer, Sayers was given opportunities to write on faith and apologetics. She had a burden that people might understand theology, especially when it came to seeing Jesus as God incarnate—fully God and fully man—something that many even in the church did not seem to grasp or teach. This desire led her to write radio dramas for children and religious plays for the church, followed by essays and books on the Christian faith. One such book is *The Mind of the Maker* in which she uses her experience of the creative process to illuminate the doctrine of the Trinity. Sayers is also known for her highly regarded translation of Dante's *The Divine Comedy.* After World War II, Sayers wrote and spoke on the value of work as a vocation and calling, basing her convictions on a desire to "seek first the kingdom" (Matt 6:33) and to offer oneself fully to God.

Over the years, Sayers developed a friendship with C. S. Lewis, and the two corresponded and critiqued each other's writing. Lewis cheered her on in her apologetic work, and she encouraged him in his. They also sharpened each another, with Sayers helping Lewis to better understand women. She wrote on this topic in her book, *Are Women Human? Penetrating, Sensible, and Witty Essays on the Role of Women in Society*, drawing attention to the way Jesus never mocked or joked about women and, instead, took their questions seriously. She wrote, "Perhaps it is no wonder that the women were first at the Cradle and last at the Cross. They had never known a man like this Man—there never has been such another."

Sayers died suddenly from a coronary thrombosis on December 17, 1957. She was 64 years old.

# How Should We Defend the Hope Within Us?

## A SURVEY OF CHRISTIAN APOLOGETIC METHODS[14]

| APOLOGETIC METHOD | DESCRIPTION | ADHERENTS |
|---|---|---|
| **Classical** | This approach begins with arguments for God's existence based on reason (e.g., natural theology and the traditional theistic proofs). Once theism has been established, specific claims about Christianity are presented, usually pertaining to Christ's deity, the historical reliability of the Bible, evidence for Jesus's resurrection, etc. | William Lane Craig, R. C. Sproul, Norman Geisler, Peter Kreeft, C. S. Lewis, B. B. Warfield |
| **Evidential** | Rather than begin with philosophical arguments, this approach appeals to specific historical evidences usually by making a case for Jesus's bodily resurrection. The resurrection then is used to validate Jesus's claims about his deity and his teaching about the authority of Scripture. | Gary Habermas, Michael Licona, Josh McDowell, Lee Strobel, John Warwick Montgomery, Joseph Butler |
| **Presuppositional** | Emphatic about the necessity, authority, and efficacy of God's revelation in nature and Scripture, this approach denounces any appeal to humanity's sense of autonomy. Instead, the apologist should point out that unless we presuppose the existence of the biblical God, we cannot account for the possibility of human knowledge. | Cornelius Van Til, Greg Bahnsen, John Frame, K. Scott Oliphint, William Edgar, James N. Anderson |

| APOLOGETIC METHOD | DESCRIPTION | ADHERENTS |
| --- | --- | --- |
| **Eclectic/Integrationist**<br><br>**(sometimes called "Cumulative Case")** | Rather than pursuing a strict formula or "one-size-fits-all" method, this approach seeks to glean insights and arguments from all the standard approaches and integrate them collectively in building a compelling case for Christianity to a given person. | Edward J. Carnell, C. Stephen Evans, Paul Feinberg, Francis Schaeffer, Kenneth Boa, Robert Bowman Jr. |
| **Fideism** | Having its name derived from the Latin word *fide* (meaning "faith"), the fideist approach insists that the truths of the Christian faith are beyond rational argument. Instead of looking to authenticate Christianity through appeals to reason and evidence, fideism emphasizes the need for a personal encounter with God as revealed in Christ. | Blaise Pascal, Søren Kierkegaard, Karl Barth, Donald Bloesch |

BIOGRAPHY

# C. S. Lewis

C. S. Lewis, or "Jack," as he was called by those who knew him, was born in Belfast, Ireland, on November 29, 1898. The younger of two sons, Lewis faced the sorrow of his mother's death a few months shy of his tenth birthday. With her death came a loss of his sense of security, which was exacerbated as he spent many of the following years in different boarding schools.

He spent time in church as a child, but in his late teens he told a friend he believed in no religion, classifying Christianity as "one mythology among many." He was drawn to the stories of classical mythology as a child and went on to study medieval and Renaissance literature at Oxford University. During his first year at Oxford, Lewis joined the British Army to fight in World War I. He was wounded in the Battle of Arras on April 15, 1918, and was discharged from the Army later that year.

After finishing his studies at Oxford, Lewis was appointed English fellow of Magdalen College, Oxford, where he tutored English language and literature and gave public lectures. He formed a friendship with Catholic writer and Oxford professor J. R. R. Tolkien, who frequently joined Lewis and other writers and thinkers, called "The Inklings," for weekly meetings to read and critique one another's work and enjoy robust discussion. It was Tolkien and another friend who spoke with Lewis at length one night in 1931 about the truth of Christ's incarnation and sacrificial death, a conversation that led him to believe in Christ as the Son of God days later.

Beginning in 1933, Lewis entered a prolific season of teaching and writing. His Christian faith motivated and infused his writing as he wrote everything from allegory to science fiction to literary critique. In 1942 he began giving radio talks on the BBC, and these apologetic lectures were eventually published as the classic book *Mere Christianity*. At Oxford he spoke at and presided over a new forum for discussing the intellectual difficulties connected with Christianity, the Socratic Club, of which his friend Dorothy L. Sayers was a fellow member. But it was *The Screwtape Letters*, a collection of fictional letters between a prominent devil and his nephew, that launched Lewis to international renown.

Lewis wrote more than 30 books and perhaps is now best known for the seven books in his children's series, The Chronicles of Narnia. He continued to write as he took on the role of professor of medieval and Renaissance English literature at Cambridge University. In his personal life, he married Joy Davidman Gresham in 1956. After Joy's death in 1960, Lewis wrote *A Grief Observed*, a partly autobiographical work about faith in the midst of loss.

In 1961 Lewis was diagnosed with kidney inflammation, a condition that limited his mobility and gave him pain. He died on November 22, 1963, and his body was buried in the cemetery of his local parish church, Holy Trinity. In his own words in the final installment of the Narnia series, *The Last Battle*, Lewis at last was "beginning Chapter One of the Great Story which no one on earth has read: which goes on forever: in which every chapter is better than the one before."

## VOICES OF THE CHURCH

*"We can ignore even pleasure. But pain insists upon being attended to. God whispers to us in our pleasures, speaks in our conscience, but shouts in our pains: it is His megaphone to rouse a deaf world."*[15]

C. S. LEWIS (1898–1963)

BIOGRAPHY

# Dietrich Bonhoeffer

Dietrich Bonhoeffer was born on February 4, 1906, in Breslau, Germany (now Poland). From a young age, Bonhoeffer wanted to be a pastor and study theology. His older brother Walter was killed in the First World War, and his family suffered the loss and the difficult years in the war's aftermath.

As Hitler rose to power, Bonhoeffer witnessed other pastors and church leaders seeking greater influence and power by embracing Hitler's leadership. Bonhoeffer saw a lack of true faith in men who would compromise for power. He knew it was possible to preach and study the Word without having true faith because he had done so. He wrote to a friend about his own discovery of the Bible after he had preached many times, saying, "I had not yet become a Christian. . . . Also I had never prayed, or prayed only very little. . . . It became clear to me that the life of a servant of Jesus Christ must belong to the Church, and step by step it became plainer to me how far that must go."

Bonhoeffer's faith was put to the test repeatedly. He preached against the growing practice of hanging Nazi flags in churches and disfellowshipped pastor friends who persecuted Jews. He taught his pastoral students to rely on God in the midst of persecution and trials. Yet Bonhoeffer did not always choose the path of least resistance. When asked to preach the funeral message for his brother-in-law's Jewish father, he listened to church leaders who instructed him not to do so. He later regretted his decision, writing to his brother-in-law to seek forgiveness for his weakness.

After that, Bonhoeffer stood against church leaders who swore oaths of loyalty to Hitler and those who would not allow Jewish Christians in leadership. He eventually lost his pastoral position, so in 1939 he left for America where he was free to preach and write without threat. Yet he recognized that he had left his home country during a time in which he might be needed. He believed it was his duty to live through this period with other Christians in Germany.

Returning to Berlin, Bonhoeffer joined a resistance movement as Hitler advanced his military and genocidal mission. The resistance formed plans to overthrow Hitler, and Bonhoeffer became a double agent, taking a government position so he could pass information necessary for helping Jews escape Germany. Eventually, the resistance movement realized it would be impossible to remove Hitler without killing him. Bonhoeffer joined the assassination plot and waited in expectation as two assassination attempts failed.

On April 5, 1943, Bonhoeffer was arrested and charged with "subversion of the armed forces." He spent 18 months in a Berlin prison before being shuffled around and eventually transferred to Flossenbürg concentration camp, where he preached the Sunday after Easter for the other prisoners in his cell. He read 1 Pet 1:3, talking about their captivity and how healing comes through Christ. Shortly after his sermon, the door opened, and he was told to come with the guards. He told a fellow prisoner, "This is the end—for me the beginning of life." He was executed on April 9, 1945. Two weeks later, Flossenbürg was freed by Allied forces.

## VOICES OF THE CHURCH

*"As we embark upon discipleship we surrender ourselves to Christ in union with his death—we give over our lives to death. . . . When Christ calls a man, he bids him come and die."*[16]

DIETRICH BONHOEFFER (1906–1945)

BIOGRAPHY

# Esther Ahn Kim

Ahn Ei Sook (later known by her married, American name, Esther Ahn Kim), was born in Korea on June 24, 1908. In 1910, after years of war, the empire of Japan annexed Korea, making it part of Japan for the next 35 years. Koreans were forced to conform to Japanese culture and religion, even giving up their Korean names. Ei Sook, due in large part to the faith of her mother, was a Christian. Having studied in Japan, she came home to Korea to teach music at a Christian school.

One day Japanese soldiers took everyone from Ei Sook's school and many others from the community to the local Shinto shrine, where they were forced to bow to a Japanese god. As she walked to the shrine, Ei Sook remembered how Shadrach, Meshach, and Abednego refused to bow to the statue of Nebuchadnezzar, knowing that God had the power to deliver them but also that, even if he did not, they would still not bow. "Today on the mountain, before the large crowd," she silently prayed, "I will proclaim that there is no other God beside You. This is what I will do for Your holy name." As the order came to bow to the sun goddess, the crowd obeyed—all except Ei Sook.

Running from authorities seeking to arrest her, she ended up in Pyongyang, where she met with other Christians, some of whom had been imprisoned for their faith. One day, a stranger named Elder Park came to her house and told her God had commanded him to come to Pyongyang to see her. Because she knew the Japanese language and culture due to her time studying there, he believed the two of them must travel to Japan to warn the people of God's coming judgment. Ei Sook looked for excuses to avoid going, but after fasting, praying, and reading her Bible for three days, she knew God was calling her to go, and she believed nothing could be worse than disobeying him.

Ei Sook and Elder Park went to the Imperial Diet, a gathering of the highest Japanese officials. Many of these leaders had no knowledge of the harsh treatment Koreans, and Christians in particular, received at the hands of Japanese soldiers. They told these leaders they had a message from God: Japan would suffer his judgment by fire falling from the sky if they did not turn from their sin against him and his people. They were immediately arrested for disturbing the assembly.

From 1939 to 1945, Ei Sook lived in a Japanese prison in Pyongyang. Her time was spent ministering to her fellow female prisoners, many of whom had lived through devastating experiences. She prayed, "I am a weakling. Unless I live each day holding Your hand, I'll become too frightened. Lord, hold my hand firmly so I won't part from You."

After her release from prison, Ei Sook moved to the United States to attend seminary, where she met and married a pastor, Don Kim. Don pastored a church in Los Angeles for almost 40 years. Ei Sook, known in America as Esther Kim, wrote her story in a book called *If I Perish,* which quickly became a bestseller in Korea and Japan. She died in 1997 after battling Alzheimer's.

## VOICES OF THE CHURCH

*"He is not silent. The reason we have the answer is because the infinite-personal God, the full trinitarian God, has not been silent. He has told us who he is. Couch your concept of inspiration and revelation in these terms, and you will see how it cuts down into the warp and woof of modern thinking. He is not silent. That is the reason we know. It is because he has spoken."*[17]

FRANCIS SCHAEFFER (1912–1984)

# Development of Cults and Sects (1700s–Modern Period)[18]

| CULT | YEAR & LOCATION | HEAD-QUARTERS | FOUNDER | KEY TEXTS AND PRIMARY BELIEFS |
|---|---|---|---|---|
| Mormonism (Latter-day Saints) | 1830 near Rochester, New York | Salt Lake City, Utah | Joseph Smith (1805–1844) | *The Book of Mormon, Doctrine and Covenants, Pearl of Great Price,* and the Bible (KJV or Joseph Smith's "Inspired Version"). "Heavenly Father" was once a man but became God, retaining a physical body with his wife (Heavenly Mother). The Father, Son, and Holy Spirit/Ghost are three separate gods, and worthy members of the *LDS* will be exalted to godhood, just as Heavenly Father. Jesus is a created spirit child and the oldest of all people and spiritual beings, including Lucifer. His death does not provide full atonement for sin but only a resurrection for everyone. People are saved by works (faithfulness to the church/church leaders, Mormon baptism, tithing, ordination, etc.), and no one receives eternal life (i.e., godhood) apart from Mormon membership. |
| Jehovah's Witnesses (Watchtower Society) | 1879 in Pennsylvania | Brooklyn, New York | Charles Taze Russell (1852–1916) | Any Watchtower publication, the *New World Translation* of the Bible, *Reasoning from the Scriptures, What Does the Bible Really Teach?,* and the magazines *Watchtower* and *Awake!* There is only one person in the Godhead, that being Jehovah, and there is no Trinity. Jesus is the first creation of Jehovah. He is not God, and prior to living upon the earth he was Michael the archangel. Jehovah made creation through him. Jesus died on a stake and was resurrected as a spirit while his body was destroyed. He returned in spirit (i.e., invisibly) in 1914. To obtain salvation, people must be baptized as Jehovah's Witnesses and perform door-to-door evangelism, though salvation is limited only to 144,000 which has already been reached. The 144,000 will live as spirits in heaven while a "great crowd" will live on earth to obey God perfectly for 1,000 years or risk annihilation. |
| Christian Science | 1875 in Massachusetts | Boston, Massachusetts | Mary Baker Eddy (1821–1910) | *Science and Health, With Key to the Scriptures, Miscellaneous Writings, Manual of the Mother Church,* the Bible (not a reliable document), *Christian Science Journal,* and *Christian Science Sentinel.* God is all that exists and is the impersonal principle of life, truth, and love, and everything else (all matter) is an allusion. Jesus was not the Christ but one who expressed the Christ idea, for in Christian Science "Christ" means perfection and is not a person. Jesus was not God nor did God become man. He did not die or suffer for sins and, therefore, was not resurrected and will not return in a physical form. The Holy Spirit is an impersonal power. All of humanity is saved, and sin, evil, sickness, and death are not real. Heaven and hell are both sates of mind, and the only way to reach a heavenly state of mind is to attain harmony—that is, oneness with God. Christian Science serves as the foundation for most Prosperity Gospel teachings as well as the New Apostolic Reformation Movement. |

| CULT | YEAR & LOCATION | HEAD-QUARTERS | FOUNDER | KEY TEXTS AND PRIMARY BELIEFS |
|---|---|---|---|---|
| **Scientology** | **1954 in California** | **Major facilities in California and Florida** | **Ron L. Hubbard (1911–1986)** | *Dianetics: The Modern Science of Mental Health, The Way to Happiness*, and other writings by Hubbard. Rejects the biblical description of God as the supreme being and teaches that everyone is an immortal spirit (*thetan*) and have an unlimited amount of powers over its own universe. Jesus is not mentioned frequently in their teachings, nor is the Holy Spirit part of their belief system. There is no sin that needs repentance, and salvation is obtained through freedom in reincarnation. There is no hell and heaven is viewed as a "false dream." |
| **New Age** | **Became popular in the 1980s and 1990s.** | **No specific location** | **No founder. Foundation is from Hinduism, Eastern mysticism, and paganism** | There is no direct holy book, but proponents use selected passages from the Bible, *I Ching*, various Hindu, Buddhist, and Taoist writings, as well as many Native American beliefs, astrology, mysticism, and magic. Everyone and everything is God, which is an impersonal force and not a person. Peole have unlimited power dwelling with them and need to discover this hidden power. Jesus is only a spiritual model, serving now as an "ascended master." He, too, was a practician of the New Age and believed that divine power, which he obtained, is available to everyone. He did not die but rose to a higher spiritual realm. The Holy Spirit is a psychic force. Bad karma must be offset with good karma, and supernatural power is obtained through meditation and self-awareness ("reborn"). Reincarnation occurs only when a person obtains oneness with God, and a resurrected eternal life does not exist, neither does a literal heaven or hell. |
| **Wicca** | **Rise in popularity in the 1930s–1950s** | **No specific headquarters** | **No specific founder. Popularized by Margaret Murray (1862–1963) and Gerald Gardner (1884–1964)** | No specific holy book. Several groups use *The Book of Shadows, A Witches' Bible*, and *The Spiral Dance*. The Supreme being within this system is known as the Goddess, which can take a variety of names. It is either a symbol of an impersonal force or a personal being. Sometimes Jesus is either viewed as a spiritual teacher or is rejected altogether. Humanity is not sinful and, therefore, does not need saving. Nature is equated with the Goddess, so the preservation of nature is important. At death, some believe in reincarnation or life after death (Summerland), but there is not an official teaching on the afterlife. Many Wiccans practice divination and spellcasting. |
| **Bahá'í** | **1844 in Iran** | **Haifa, Israel** | **Mirza Husayn Ali Nuri (Bahá'u'lláh; 1817–1892), the Báb (1819–1850), and 'Abdu'l-Bahá (1844–1921)** | The writings of Bahá'u'lláh and 'Abdu'l-Bahá, *Kitáb-i-Aqdas, Kitáb-i-Íqán*, and *Hidden Words*. God is an unknowable being, but he revelaed himself through nine prophets ("manifestations"), which include Jesus, Muhammad, Krishna, Buddha, and Bahá'u'lláh. Thus, Jesus is one of many manifestations of God upon the earth, though the former manifestation supersedes its predecessor. Jesus is not God, did not rise from the dead, and is not the only way to God, though the "Christ spirit" returned and indwelt Bahá'u'lláh, who is greater than Jesus. The Holy Spirit is a divine energy from God, and salvation is obtained in faith in the manifestation of God as taught by Bahá'u'lláh. Eternal life is based on good works, and those faithful are rewarded. Neither heaven nor hell exist but are "allegories for nearness and remoteness from God." |

BIOGRAPHY

# Carl F. H. Henry

Carl Ferdinand Howard Henry was born in Long Island, New York, in 1913. Born to Karl F. Heinrich and Johanna Waethroeder, German immigrants and nominally Methodist, he was confirmed in the Episcopal church at age 12, though he would temporarily reject the faith. After graduating from high school in 1929, Henry began working at *The Islip Press* as a journalist and rose quickly through the ranks. At 19 he became an editor for *The Smithtown Times*, but an encounter with Mildred Christy would forever change the trajectory of his life. Christy would often quip to Henry that she was praying for him. Unbeknown to him at the time, Christy lost a son in a motorcycle accident in California who Henry resembled. Christy prayed that God would give her a son in the ministry, and she believed Henry was the answer to her prayers. Christy often asked Henry to church, and finally Henry agreed to go listen to a guest speaker. On June 10, 1933, Carl Henry professed faith in the Lord Jesus Christ and became a Christian.

Shortly thereafter, Henry enrolled in Wheaton College where he met his wife, Helga. He continued to work in journalism while a student at Wheaton. He and Helga married in 1940 while Henry completed two degrees from Wheaton. He later earned a doctor of theology from Northern Baptist Theological Seminary and was ordained as a Baptist in 1942. While teaching at Fuller Theological Seminary in Pasadena, California, he completed the PhD from Boston University in 1949. He would remain at Fuller as a professor until he left to create *Christianity Today*, a magazine intended to compete with the more theologically liberal magazine *Christian Century*. Henry would serve in this role until 1968.

Henry served at various teaching positions in his career, both in the United States and around the world. He was also instrumental in helping create the Evangelical Theological Society, an annual meeting of evangelical scholars committed to serious academic discussions within the disciplines of biblical studies, church history, and theological studies. Henry's magisterial six-volume *God, Revelation, and Authority* (1976–1983) discusses the development of this theme within church history and how God uniquely reveals himself to his people. Another significant book Henry wrote is *The Uneasy Conscience of Modern Fundamentalism* where Henry critiques the social gospel liberalism and rejects hard-line fundamentalism.

Carl Henry was a premier evangelical scholar of his time, but he was also a Baptist by conviction. He served the Southern Baptist Convention during the contentious times as the convention moved to solidify their conservative identity. Henry died on December 7, 2003, at 90 years old.

BIOGRAPHY

# Billy Graham

William "Billy" Franklin Graham was born on November 7, 1918, at his family's home near Charlotte, North Carolina, and spent his childhood on a dairy farm. Spending some of his formative years in the Depression, Graham was raised with a strong work ethic and a love for reading. While he grew up in church, he became a Christian in 1934 when he attended a revival meeting held by a traveling evangelist.

After studying at Bob Jones University and Florida Bible Institute, Graham finished his studies at Wheaton College with a degree in anthropology. Having been ordained as a minister while still in Florida, he preached frequently while at Wheaton and began pastoring a church while still in school. At Wheaton he met his future wife, Ruth Bell, whose parents were medical missionaries in China. He and Ruth had five children.

The years after Wheaton found Graham serving in a variety of roles, eventually becoming the first full-time staff member of Youth for Christ. In this position he traveled around America and Europe preaching the gospel in the postwar era. In 1949, he erected tents in a Los Angeles parking lot for a preaching crusade. Originally scheduled to last three weeks, popular demand extended the meeting to eight weeks. Media attention launched Graham to become a household name, and similar crusades in London and New York in the following years cemented his legacy as an evangelist.

Graham would go on to lead crusades on six continents, holding the final ones in New York in 2005 and New Orleans in 2006, months after the city was ravaged by Hurricane Katrina. It is estimated that he preached to live audiences of 210 million people in 185 countries during his ministry. He also developed radio and television ministries, wrote more than 30 books, and in 1956 cofounded *Christianity Today* magazine. He had a personal audience with 12 consecutive American presidents and was at times criticized for his political involvement.

Speaking on the power of Scripture from Heb 4:12, Graham wrote about his preaching, "The people were not coming to hear great oratory, nor were they interested merely in my ideas. I found they were desperately hungry to hear what God had to say through His Holy Word."

Graham died of natural causes at home in Montreat, North Carolina, on February 21, 2018. He was 99 years old. He was the fourth private American citizen to lie in honor at the United States Capitol rotunda, and the first religious leader to receive the honor.

## VOICES OF THE CHURCH

*"Courage is contagious. When a brave man takes a stand, the spines of others are often stiffened."*[19]

BILLY GRAHAM (1918–2018)

BIOGRAPHY

# John Stott

John Stott was born in London on April 27, 1921. His father was a doctor who went on to become the royal family's physician, and John was educated at Rugby School, where his father studied before him. While at Rugby, a friend invited Stott to a Christian meeting, and he continued to attend. A few weeks before he turned 17, Stott heard a guest speaker, E. J. H. Nash, who asked the young men the question posed by Pilate in Matt 27:22, "What should I do then with Jesus, who is called Christ?" Nash spent time with Stott, answering his questions. Stott became a Christian that evening, and he and Nash carried on a weekly correspondence for more than seven years.

In 1940, Stott began his studies at Cambridge University, where he spent time with a Christian student organization and helped Nash run Christian camps in the summer and on holidays. While he started his time at Cambridge studying modern languages, he later switched to theology. He struggled with the liberal theology prominent at the time and wrestled through challenges to the authority of Scripture, finding encouragement in the writing of nineteenth-century pastor Charles Simeon. After university, he was invited to become curate, or assistant pastor, of All Souls, the church his family had attended in London. He was ordained a few months after the end of the Second World War, and Stott quickly went to work getting to know the people within his parish and became rector of the church five years later. He developed multiple outreach and discipleship ministries out of the church, even establishing a children's church service. His innovative ministry in his city established a framework now used around the world.

Stott had a passion for student ministry, no doubt inspired by his own conversion as a student. He went on missions to universities around England and in Canada and the United States. Many of the messages he preached on these trips became his book *Basic Christianity*, which has sold over 2.5 million copies and been translated into more than 50 languages. Stott chose to donate all the income from his books and his speaking honoraria, launching a ministry called Langham Partnership to develop and supply resources to biblical leaders around the world. He had a global vision, spending time with students and pastors in Latin America, Africa, Asia, and the Middle East.

Stott served in many leadership roles in the church in England and was honorary chaplain to Queen Elizabeth II for more than 30 years. He was burdened that Christians bring not just emotions but also intellect to their faith, leading him to establish The London Institute for Contemporary Christianity, which offers courses to lay Christians to assist them in relating their faith to life and mission. When a TV reporter asked him what his ambition was after he had accomplished so much, he responded, "To be more like Jesus."

Stott died at the age of 90 on July 27, 2011. His tombstone was engraved with the following, echoing the words of 1 Cor 2:2: "Who resolved both as the grounds of his salvation and as the subject of his ministry to know nothing except Jesus Christ and him crucified."

## VOICES OF THE CHURCH

*"Our greatest claim to nobility is our created capacity to know God, to be in personal relationship with him, to love him and to worship him. Indeed, we are most truly human when we are on our knees before our Creator."*[20]

JOHN STOTT (1921–2011)

BIOGRAPHY

# J. I. Packer

James Innell Packer was born outside of Gloucester, England, on July 22, 1926. A childhood head injury left him unable to participate in sports, sparking a love for reading and writing. He studied the classics and won a scholarship to Oxford University, where he was involved in the Oxford Inter-Collegiate Christian Union and became a Christian during one of the organization's meetings. He attended lectures by C. S. Lewis and was introduced to Puritan writing in his time at Oxford, both of which greatly influenced his life. He stayed on at Oxford and obtained his doctorate in 1954 and was ordained a priest in the Church of England.

After serving as a parish minister for a few years, Packer went on to teach at theological colleges in England and worked as the director of Latimer House in Oxford, an evangelical think tank he started with John Stott. Along with Stott and Martyn Lloyd-Jones, Packer became one of the most prominent evangelical leaders in England. In 1979, he accepted a post to teach systematic theology at Regent College in Vancouver, where he moved with his wife and three children.

His book *Knowing God*, published in the United States in 1973, became an international bestseller and sold over 1.5 million copies. In 2006, *Christianity Today* magazine conducted a survey to discover the top 50 books that have shaped evangelicals, and *Knowing God* was fifth on the list. Packer's writing and editing led to opportunities to write and serve as executive editor of *Christianity Today*. He also served as general editor of the English Standard Version of the Bible, a project near to his heart that reflected a lifelong commitment to the inerrancy and reliability of Scripture.

Whether in teaching systematic theology, writing books and editorials, or preaching, Packer was passionate about helping people know God truly, not just to know about him. Writing in *Knowing God* on the idea of God as Father, as Jesus spoke of him in passages like Matt 6 and John 5, Packer stated:

> You sum up the whole of New Testament religion if you describe it as the knowledge of God as one's holy Father. If you want to judge how well a person understands Christianity, find out how much he makes of the thought of being God's child, and having God as his Father. If this is not the thought that prompts and controls his worship and prayers and his whole outlook on life, it means that he does not understand Christianity very well at all.

Packer died in Vancouver, British Columbia, on Friday, July 17, 2020, on his sixty-sixth wedding anniversary. He was 93 years old.

# Building on the Core:

## IDENTIFYING ESSENTIAL, DISTINCTIVE, AND PERIPHERAL DOCTRINES

Although we must stand on the absolute authority and sufficient clarity of Scripture, we must come to terms that not all theological issues are of equal importance. Some doctrines are in fact more foundational than others. While Christians are committed to absolute truth, not all absolutes are equals. Neither are all doctrinal truth made as prominent or clear throughout the Bible. Therefore, we must exercise discernment when it comes to prioritizing certain doctrines. Which truths must we divide over? Which teachings might affect how we determine which church we join? And which perspectives can we truly agree to disagree about while still belonging to the same fellowship? The visual on the facing page is designed to help with the endeavor of identifying essential, secondary, and tertiary doctrines.

The concentric circles in this visual represent the varying degrees of doctrinal importance, the middle circle standing for the core truths of Christianity and the wider circles conveying where we should categorize secondary and tertiary doctrines.

- **Core Doctrines (Essentials):** These are the foundational truths of Christianity. Some might label the core doctrines as "catholic" (universal) or "orthodox" (standard). These are considered essential because without them, a belief system cannot be considered authentically Christian.

- **Secondary but Significant Doctrines (Distinctives):** This category refers to teachings where differences do not entail a denial of any essential truths but might affect the mission and health of the church. For this reason, convictions in this area might result in where you choose to become a church member.

- **Tertiary Doctrines (Peripheral Issues and Questions):** While certain issues in this area can sometimes be controversial, one's position or stance should not affect the core doctrines or where one might worship. This is an area where Christians should grant much levity with one another and be willing to hold differences of opinion.

## CORE DOCTRINES (ESSENTIALS)

- Incarnation
- The Trinity
- Biblical Authority
- Salvation by Grace Alone in Christ Alone

## SECONDARY BUT SIGNIFICANT DOCTRINES (DISTINCTIVES)

- Ecclesiology (church government, structure, and membership)
- Corporate Worship (regulative vs. normative)
- Meaning and Mode of Baptism (infant vs. believers alone; immersion, sprinkling, or pouring)
- Nature of the Lord's Supper (real presence, memorialist, or consubstantiation)
- Ordination (church leadership and gender relations)
- Gifts of the Spirit (cessationist, charismatic, or Pentecostal)

## TERTIARY DOCTRINES (PERIPHERAL ISSUES AND QUESTIONS)

- Millennial Views (amillennialism, premillennialism, postmillennialism)
- Specifics about the Age of the Earth
- Certain Issues in Ethics and Politics
- Certain Questions about Eschatology (future of ethnic Israel, the identity of antichrist, sequence of end-times events)

# Complementarianism vs. Egalitarianism

| | COMPLEMENTARIANISM | EGALITARIANISM |
|---|---|---|
| DEFINITION | God restricts women from serving in certain roles within the local church but, rather, encourages women to | There are no biblically based prohibitions for women to serve in any capacity in the local church. |

BIOGRAPHY

# Elizabeth Elliot

In January 1956, Elisabeth Elliot was a tall, blonde, 28-year-old missionary in Ecuador, married to the man she had loved since college, and mother to a 10-month-old daughter. She waited and prayed as her husband Jim and four of his missionary colleagues attempted to bring the gospel to the Waodani, a remote, unreached people group who lived in isolation deep in the Amazon jungle. Though initially friendly, the tribal warriors turned on the missionaries and speared all five of them to death.

The story made international headlines. Incredibly, even as she mourned, Elisabeth reasoned that if Jim loved the Waodani enough to die trying to reach them, she loved them too and would endeavor to do the same. Eventually, prayerfully, she took her little daughter, her snakebite kit, Bible, and journal and lived in the jungle with the Stone-Age people who killed her husband. Compelled by her friendship and forgiveness, many came to faith in Jesus.

This courageous, no-nonsense Christian went on to write dozens of books, host a long-running radio show, and speak at conferences all over the world. She was one of the few prominent female voices in the Christian subculture in the second half of the twentieth century. She was a pillar of coherent, committed faith who also knew well that God's mysterious will cannot be diagrammed or codified. She was a beloved and sometimes controversial icon who was not primarily concerned with being "liked" but with obeying the Word of God. She was a strong but, like all of us, flawed and vulnerable woman whose life losses compelled her to become utterly submitted to doing God's will, no matter the cost. For Elisabeth, the central question was not, "How does this make me feel?" but, simply, "Is this true?" If so, then the next question was, "What do I need to do about it to obey God?"

If Elisabeth drew her direction from Scripture, it was also the source of her comfort. After Jim's terrible death, and after other aching losses in her life, she returned time and again to the reassurance she found in Isa 43. And when she died in 2015, an excerpt from that Scripture was chiseled onto her gravestone. It is a testament to the great Rock on which we can all build our faith: "When thou passest through the waters, I will be with thee."

# Contention over the Covenants: A Survey of Competing Systems

When it comes to making sense of God's plan of redemption and the relationships between the biblical covenants, several primary and competing theological systems have developed among Protestant-Evangelical Christians over the last several centuries. Presented in the table below is a survey of the four most prominent views:

- **Traditional Covenant Theology** (as taught in accordance with the Westminster Confession of Faith)
- **1689 Federalism** (a form of Baptist covenant theology taught in accordance with the Second London Confession)
- **Progressive Dispensationalism** (a contemporary modification of a system that existed in a classic and traditional forms)
- **Progressive Covenantalism** (a newer system that emphasizes the unity of God's plan progressively revealed through a plurality of covenants; sometimes identified with New Covenant Theology)

| | TRADITIONAL COVENANT THEOLOGY (WCF) | 1689 FEDERALISM (2LC) | PROGRESSIVE DISPENSATIONALISM | PROGRESSIVE COVENANTALISM |
|---|---|---|---|---|
| **Covenant of Redemption (*Pactum Salutis*)** | A term used to refer to the archetypal covenant, or pact, among the persons of the Trinity to redeem sinners through the work of God the Son | Same understanding as WCF but sees a different relationship among the covenant of redemption, covenant of grace, and new covenant | Neither a point of emphasis nor contention for dispensationalism; not concerned with an archetypal foundation for the administrations (or dispensations) of God's rule on earth | Like WCF and 2LC, though not as emphasized; affirms the unity of the triune God's covenantal plan to redeem a people for himself wherein each of the three persons act inseparably but carry out a specific role in accomplishing and applying redemption |
| **Covenant of Works** | Sometimes called the "covenant of life," refers to the conditions placed on Adam and Eve in the garden where they were offered life for obedience and death for disobedience (Gen 2:16–17) | Same understanding as WCF | Does not affirm the existence of a historical covenant until Noah and thus does not recognize a covenant existing from creation; earlier forms of this system referred to this era in the garden as "innocence" | Affirms the concept but prefers the term "creation covenant" to avoid giving the impression that Adam before the fall needed to earn or merit God's favor |
| **One or Many Covenants?** | There is one covenant in substance called "the covenant of grace," which is expressed and administered across the multiple historical covenants (Noahic, Abrahamic, Mosaic, Davidic, and new) | In contrast to WCF, sees the covenant of grace exclusively identified with the new covenant established by Christ while the OT covenants are typological of and subservient to the new covenant, not the same in substance | Acknowledges multiple historical covenants but places more emphasis on the different ways God related to and governed humanity across history, these eras roughly falling between the covenants; primarily emphasizes the differences between ethnic-national Israel and the church | Similar to 2LC in emphasizing the progressive nature of the multiple OT covenants, prefers to speak of the unity of God's one redemptive plan rather than a singular covenant in respecting the distinctions and expressions among the historical covenants |
| **Significance of Abrahamic Covenant** | God's promises to Abraham belong to believers and their physical offspring, keeping God's purposes attached to both physical and spiritual realities, as reflected in the covenant sign of circumcision that signifies the ongoing nature of God's promise and the inclusion of children in the covenant community | Though anticipatory of new-covenant realities, God's promises to Abraham are multi-faceted, both physical and spiritual and to be understood in context; thus, God's promises to Abraham are partly fulfilled in Israel's occupation of Canaan but spiritually fulfilled in Christ and the church | Though this covenant fits within God's larger plan to bless all nations, the promises to Abraham regarding offspring and land will be fulfilled ultimately in a physical sense with a great multitude of Abraham's biological descendants inheriting the promised land forever; Gentile believers nonetheless benefit spiritually from these promises | Similar to 2LC, the Abrahamic covenant has multiple facets, some aspects being fulfilled in Israel's occupation of the promised land and some aspects being typological of the blessings that would come to all nations through Christ, the true offspring of Abraham, in whom believers, both Jew and Gentile, become the offspring of Abraham by faith rather than biological lineage |

| | TRADITIONAL COVENANT THEOLOGY (WCF) | 1689 FEDERALISM (2LC) | PROGRESSIVE DISPENSATIONALISM | PROGRESSIVE COVENANTALISM |
|---|---|---|---|---|
| **Relationship between Israel and Church** | Since there is only one covenant substantively, there is only one people of God throughout redemptive history; the church as the new-covenant people is the expanded and restored true Israel that includes both Jew and Gentile | Similar to WCF but places an emphasis on Christ as the true Israel who succeeded where the nation failed; the church is not seen as a direct replacement of Israel but exists in Christ as the new Israel, consisting of Jew and Gentile | Though both entities are part of God's redemptive plan, there remains a hard distinction between the covenant people of ethnic-national Israel and the new-covenant entity that is the church because of different sets of promises being made to each respectively; the church eventually will dissipate with non-Jewish believers coming to exist as part of God's multinational worldwide kingdom | Similar to 2LC, with an emphasis on Christ as the typological fulfillment of Israel; indirectly, the church is the true Israel in Christ, a new entity consisting of Jew and Gentile but distinct from ethnic-national Israel |
| **Membership of New Covenant** | Though the new covenant being the most fully realized administration of the covenant of grace, both believers and their children remain as covenant members since this has been the standard going back to the Abrahamic covenant | The new covenant being exclusively identical with the covenant of grace, only believers, those who are truly regenerate, belong to the covenant community since they alone are united to Christ, the covenant head and mediator | Sees two different kinds of features in the new covenant promises, some physical/national and some spiritual, the former not yet belonging to the Jewish people and the future kingdom and the latter existing already in the church; only believers in Christ are members of the church as the spiritual new-covenant community | Same as 2LC |
| **Baptism** | A sign and seal of the new covenant and is to be received by believers and their children, marking their membership in the new covenant (e.g., infant baptism and believer's baptism) | An ordinance of the new covenant to be received by believers alone since only those in Christ are members of the new covenant (e.g., believer's baptism) | An ordinance for the church as a spiritual entity representing the new covenant; to be received only by believers in Christ (e.g., believer's baptism) | Same as 2LC (e.g., believer's baptism) |
| **The Sabbath Day** | A creation ordinance perpetuated in the Mosaic covenant on the seventh day; transferred to the Lord's Day (first day of the week) in the new covenant because of Christ's resurrection | Same as WCF | A commandment given to Israel that is not a binding ordinance for the church as a separate spiritual entity; recognizes the Lord's Day in view of Christ's resurrection | Seen typologically as pointing forward to ultimate rest in Christ consummated in the new heaven and new earth; recognizes the Lord's Day in view of Christ's resurrection |
| **Understanding of the Mosaic Law** | The law given to Moses and Israel consists of three categories: moral (eternal); civil (national); and ceremonial (fulfilled in Christ); only the moral law remains binding on the church as the new-covenant people of God | Same as WCF | Though there is spiritual truth that the church can appropriate in principle from the Mosaic law, the commands are not binding on the church because they belong to a different era of God's kingdom rule | Sees the Mosaic covenant as a holistic unit to be understood according to God's purposes for Israel while in the land, and so the law's commands and ordinances cannot be neatly separated as moral, civil, and ceremonial; instead, Christ fulfilled the entirety of the law as a covenant and established a "new and better" covenant |
| **Millennial Views** | Primarily amillennialism and some postmillennialism (with a minority holding to historic premillennialism) | Same as WCF | Dispensational premillennialism, maintaining that in Christ's reign over a thousand-year kingdom the land promises to Israel will be entirely fulfilled | Primarily amillennialism and historic premillennialism |

# Sources

## THE EARLY CHURCH

[1] Robert Louis Wilken, *The First Thousand Years: A Global History of Christianity* (New Haven: Yale University Press, 2012).

[2] "The Epistle of Ignatius to the Smyrnæans," in *The Apostolic Fathers with Justin Martyr and Irenaeus*, ed. Alexander Roberts, James Donaldson, and A. Cleveland Coxe, vol. 1 in *The Ante-Nicene Fathers* (Buffalo, NY: Christian Literature Company, 1885), 87. [Logos].

[3] Justin Martyr, "Dialogue with Trypho," *Exodus, Leviticus, Numbers, Deuteronomy*, ed. Joseph T. Lienhard, *Ancient Christian Commentary on Scripture: Old Testament*, vol. III (Downers Grove: IVP, 2001), 242.

[4] Clement of Alexandria, "Adumbrations," *James, 1-2 Peter, 1-2 John, Jude*, ed. Gerald Bray, vol. XI in *Ancient Christian Commentary on Scripture: New Testament* (Downers Grove: IVP, 2000), 87.

[5] Irenaeus of Lyons, "Irenæus against Heresies," in *The Apostolic Fathers with Justin Martyr and Irenaeus*, ed. Alexander Roberts, James Donaldson, and A. Cleveland Coxe, vol. 1 in *The Ante-Nicene Fathers* (Buffalo, NY: Christian Literature Company, 1885), 428. [Logos].

[6] This reference is to the church universal. The creed existed before the word catholic was applied to the Roman Church.

[7] *Epistle to Diognetus* 9.2–5, in *The Apostolic Fathers in English*, ed. Rick Brannan (Bellingham, WA: Lexham Press, 2012). [Logos].

[8] The information about the writings provided in this feature is derived from Rick Brannan's "Introduction" in *The Apostolic Fathers in English* (Bellingham, WA: Logos Bible Software, 2012).

## THE PATRISTIC CHURCH

[1] Kruger, Michael. "The Complete Series: Ten Basic Facts about the NT Canon That Every Christian Should Memorize." Canon Fodder, June 4, 2024. https://michaeljkruger.com/the-complete-series-ten-basic-facts-about-the-nt-canon-that-every-christian-should-memorize/.

[2] Athanasius of Alexandria, *On the Incarnation of the Word, in A Select Library of the Nicene and Post-Nicene Fathers of the Christian Church, Second Series*, vol. 4, ed. Philip Schaff and Henry Wace (New York: Christian Literature Company, 1892), 40–41. [Logos].

[3] Ephrem the Syrian, "Commentary on Genesis 20:3," Fathers of the Church: A New Translation (Washington, DC: Catholic University of America Press, 1947), 91:169.

[4] Gregory Nazianzen, *Orations* 28.4, in *A Select Library of the Nicene and Post-Nicene Fathers of the Christian Church, Second Series*, vol. 7, ed. Philip Schaff and Henry Wace (New York: Christian Literature Company, 1894), 289–290. [Logos].

[5] Ambrose, "Letter 55(8).8," Exodus, Leviticus, Numbers, Deuteronomy, ed. Joseph T. Lienhard, Ancient Christian Commentary on Scripture: Old Testament, vol. III (Downers Grove: IVP, 2001), 21.

[6] John Chrysostom, "On the Epistle to the Hebrews," Psalms 51–150, ed. Quentin F. Wesselschmidt, Ancient Christian Commentary on Scripture: Old Testament, vol. VIII, 2.

[7] Augustine, "Confessions, 10:29," Augustine of Hippo: Selected Writings, by Mary T. Clark (Mahwah, NJ: Paulist Press, 1984), 145.

[8] Cyril of Alexandria, Festal Letter, 10:4, in Sources Chrétiennes, eds. H. deLubac, J. Daniélou, et al. (Paris: Editions du Cerf, 1941-), 392:230, quoted in Galatians, Ephesians, Philippians, ed. Edwards, 238.

[9] Portions of these lists were derived from the appendix of Stephen J. Nichols, *For Us and For Our Salvation: The Doctrine of Christ in the Early Church* (Wheaton, IL: Crossway, 2007), 157.

[10] These three axioms are derived from James R. White, *The Forgotten Trinity: Recovering the Heart of Christian Belief* (Bloomington, MN: Bethany House Publishers, 1998), 26–28.

## THE MIDDLE AGES

[1] The excerpt of the Rule provided above was taken from "#201: Benedict's Rule," Christian History Institute, 2024, https://christianhistoryinstitute.org/study/module/benedicts-rule. Biblical quotations were changed to match the CSB translation.

[2] Gregory the Great, quoted in *The Gospel According to John*, by Johann Peter Lange, in *A Commentary on the Holy Scriptures: Critical, Doctrinal, and Homiletical* (New York: Charles Scribner's Sons, 1900), 624.

[3] Bede, "On 1 John," Patrologia Latina, ed. J.P. Migne (Paris: Migne, 1844-1864), 93:102, quoted in James, 1–2 Peter, 1–3 John, Jude, ed. Gerald Bray, Ancient Christian Commentary on Scripture: New Testament vol. XI (Downers Grove: IVP, 2000), 201.

[4] John of Damascus, "Orthodox Faith," Fathers of the Church: A New Translation, ed. R. J. Deferrari, vol. 37 (Washington, DC: Catholic University of America Press, 1947), 342-43.

[5] Joseph Early Jr., A History of Christianity: An Introductory Survey (Nashville, TN: B&H, 2015), 174–80; Justo L. Gonzalez, *The Story of Christianity*, vol. 1: *The Early Church to the Dawn of the Reformation* (New York: HarperCollins, 1984), 311–19,362–65.

[6] "Theology and Doxology, Ligonier Ministries, May 15, 2009, https://www.ligonier.org/learn/devotionals/theology-and-doxology.

[7] *The "Summa Theologica" of St. Thomas Aquinas*, trans. Fathers of the English Dominican Province (London: Burns Oates & Washbourne, n.d.); Mitchell L. Chase, "Senses and Sensibility: The Words of Aquinas on the Word of God," *Credo Magazine*, June 27, 2022, https://credomag.com/article/senses-and-sensibility.

[8] *The "Summa Theologica" of St. Thomas Aquinas*, trans. Fathers of the English Dominican Province (London: Burns Oates & Washbourne, n.d.); Timothy Pawl, "The Five Ways," in *The Oxford Handbook of Aquinas*, ed. Brian Davies and Eleonore Stump (New York: Oxford University Press, 2012): 115–31.

[9] Nancy Pearcey, *Total Truth: Liberating Christianity from Its Cultural Captivity* (Wheaton, IL: Crossway, 2005), 78–83.

[10] John Huss, "To the believers in Prague," Letters of John Huss, by Émile de Bonnechose, trans. Campbell Mackenzie (Edinburgh: William Whyte & Co., 1846), 33.

[11] Vatican I, Chapter 4: "On the Infallible Teaching Authority of the Roman Pontiff, 1869–70"; emphasis added.

## THE REFORMATION CHURCH

[1] Martin Luther, "Lectures on Galatians 1525," Luther's Works, 26:88.

2 Martin Luther, *The Bondage of the Will*, trans. J.I. Packer and O.R. Johnston (Grand Rapids, MI: Revell, 1957; *Concordia: The Lutheran Confessions*, Second Edition, gen. ed. Paul Timothy McCain (St. Louis: Concordia, 2006), 340; Iain Boyd, "Martin Luther's Personal Presence of Christ in the Lord's Supper, March 17, 2011, https://trinitypastor.wordpress.com/2011/03/17/martin-luthers-personal-presence-of-christ-in-the-lords-supper; Some elements of style and formatting have been adapted.

[3] Nancy Pearcey, *Total Truth: Liberating Christianity from Its Cultural Captivity* (Wheaton, IL: Crossway, 2005), 80–82.

[4] Ibid.

[5] John Calvin, *Institutes of the Christian Religion*, 2nd ed. John T. McNeill, trans. Ford Lewis Battles, The Library of Christian Classics (Louisville, KY: Westminster John Knox Press, 2011).

[6] John Calvin, *Institutes of the Christian Religion*, vol. 1, ed. John T. McNeill (Louisville, KY: Westminster John Knox Press, 2006), 537.

[7] Huldrych Zwingli, quoted in *Theology of the Reformers*, rev. ed, by Timothy George (Nashville, TN: B&H, 2013), 133.

[8] Dirk Philips, "Concerning Spiritual Restitution", Early Anabaptist Spirituality: Selected Writings, 237.

[9] William Tyndale, quoted in *The Unquenchable Flame: Discovering the Heart of the Reformation*, by Michael Reeves (Nashville, TN: B&H, 2010), 123.

[10] John Owen, The Mortification of Sin, abridged by Richard Rushing (Carlisle, PA: The Banner of Truth Trust, 2004), 5.

[11] Thomas Watson, Puritan Gems (Louisville: GLH Publishing, 2013), 10.

[12] Graham Beynon, *Isaac Watts: His Life and Thought* (Ross-shire, Scotland: Christian Focus Publications, Ltd, 2013).

[13] Graham Beynon, "The Helpfulness of the Lesser Known Work: Isaac Watts on the Passions" in *Themelios*, 42 no 3 Dec 2017, p 479-493

[14] David W. Music, "The Early Reception of Isaac Watts's Psalms of David Imitated" in *The Hymn*, 69 no 4 Fall 2018, p 14-19

[15] Thomas Wright, The Life of Isaac Watts (London: C.J. Farncombe & Sons, Ltd, 1914).

[16] Martin Luther, Galatians, Crossway Classic Commentaries (Wheaton: Crossway Books, 1998), 37.

## THE MODERN CHURCH

[1] *Works of Jonathan Edwards, Letters and Personal Writings* (*WJE* Online, Vol. 16), ed. George S. Claghorn. New Haven: Yale University Press, 793-794.

[2] George Whitefield. *A Continuation of the Reverend Mr. Whitefield's journal from Savannah, June 25.1740 to his arrival at Rhode Island, his travels in the other Governments of New-England, to his departure from Stanford for New York.* Boston: D. Fowle for S. Kneeland and T. Green, 1741, 83.

[3] George Marsden. *Jonathan Edwards.* New Haven and London: Yale University Press, 2003, 494-495.

[4] *The Journal of John Wesley*, ed. Percy Livingstone Parker. Chicago: Moody Press, 1951. https://ccel.org/ccel/wesley/journal/journal.vi.ii.xvi.html.

[5] Eliza Clarke. *Susanna* Wesley. London: W.H. Allen & Co., 1886, 210.

[6] Andrew Murray, The Believer's New Life (eBook: Lulu.com, 2007), 129.

[7] Charles Spurgeon, "Israel at the Red Sea," www.spurgeon.org.

[8] Carmichael, Amy. *If*. Christian Literature Crusade, 1992.

[9] Pena, Madeline. "Amy Carmichael: Mother to India." Bethany Global University (2021): https://bethanygu.edu/blog/stories/amy-carmichael/.

[10] Ibid.

[11] Carmichael, Amy. *If*. Christian Literature Crusade, 1992.

[12] Li Yading, "Yu, Dora (Yu Cidu) (1873-1931) Chinese Evangelist and Missionary to Korea. Boston University School of Theology History of Missiology, Taken with permission from the Biographical Dictionary of Chinese Christianity. 2014; https://www.bu.edu/missiology/2020/03/02/yu-dora-yu-cidu-1873-1931/

[13] Ibid.

[14] Kenneth D. Boa and Robert M. Bowman Jr., *Faith Has Its Reasons: An Integrative Approach to Defending Christianity*, 2nd ed. (Waynesboro, GA: Paternoster, 2006); Steven B. Cowan, gen. ed., *Five Views on Apologetics* (Grand Rapids, MI: Zondervan, 2000).

[15] C. S. Lewis, The Problem of Pain (New York: Touchstone, 1996), 83.

[16] Dietrich Bonhoeffer, The Cost of Discipleship (New York: Simon & Schuster, 1959), 89.

[17] Francis A. Schaeffer, *He Is There and He Is Not Silent* (Wheaton: Tyndale House Publishers, 1972), 18.

[18] Adapted from *Christianity, Cults, and Religions* (Torrance, CA: Rose Publishing, 2010).

[19] Billy Graham, "A Time for Moral Courage,"Reader's Digest (July, 1964).

[20] John Stott, The Contemporary Christian (Downers Grove: IVP, 1992), 39.